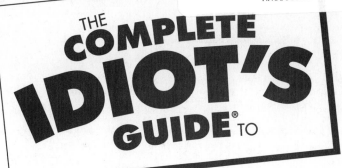

Barter and Trade Exchanges

by Jerry Howell
with Tom Chmielewski

ALPHA

A member of Penguin Group (USA) Inc.

ALPHA BOOKS

Published by the Penguin Group

Penguin Group (USA) Inc., 375 Hudson Street, New York, New York 10014, USA

Penguin Group (Canada), 90 Eglinton Avenue East, Suite 700, Toronto, Ontario M4P 2Y3, Canada (a division of Pearson Penguin Canada Inc.)

Penguin Books Ltd., 80 Strand, London WC2R 0RL, England

Penguin Ireland, 25 St. Stephen's Green, Dublin 2, Ireland (a division of Penguin Books Ltd.)

Penguin Group (Australia), 250 Camberwell Road, Camberwell, Victoria 3124, Australia (a division of Pearson Australia Group Pty. Ltd.)

Penguin Books India Pvt. Ltd., 11 Community Centre, Panchsheel Park, New Delhi—110 017, India

Penguin Group (NZ), 67 Apollo Drive, Rosedale, North Shore, Auckland 1311, New Zealand (a division of Pearson New Zealand Ltd.)

Penguin Books (South Africa) (Pty.) Ltd., 24 Sturdee Avenue, Rosebank, Johannesburg 2196, South Africa

Penguin Books Ltd., Registered Offices: 80 Strand, London WC2R 0RL, England

Copyright © 2009 by Jerry Howell

International Standard Book Number: 978-1-59257-931-0
Library of Congress Catalog Card Number: 2009928396

11 10 09   8 7 6 5 4 3 2 1

Interpretation of the printing code: The rightmost number of the first series of numbers is the year of the book's printing; the rightmost number of the second series of numbers is the number of the book's printing. For example, a printing code of 09-1 shows that the first printing occurred in 2009.

Printed in the United States of America

Publisher: *Marie Butler-Knight*
Editorial Director: *Mike Sanders*
Senior Managing Editor: *Billy Fields*
Senior Acquisitions Editor: *Paul Dinas*
Development Editor: *Michael Thomas*
Senior Production Editor: *Janette Lynn*
Copy Editor: *Cate Schwenk*

Cartoonist: *Steve Barr*
Cover Designer: *Bill Thomas*
Book Designer: *Trina Wurst*
Indexer: *Tonya Heard*
Layout: *Chad Dressler*
Proofreader: *Jennifer Connolly, John Etchison*

Contents at a Glance

Contents

Introduction

There is a $10 billion per year barter industry in North America, according to reports from the U.S. Commerce Department and trade association officials. Industry sources estimate there are nearly 500,000 members of trade exchanges in the country, and perhaps 30 percent of the world's total business is conducted through barter. Other estimates suggest one third of all small businesses in the United States use some form of barter.

Then there's the growth of "community dollar" groups across the country, taking shared trade to the personal level.

Barter is an ancient form of transaction that never got old, and continually adapts to the times. In this book, we go over how to use barter to your advantage, particularly for businesses looking to improve their cash flow and increase profits. Much of the book focuses on business-to-business transactions conducted through commercial trade exchanges.

How to Use This Book

We review the forms of barter, including direct trades, community dollars, and trade exchanges. All barter transactions involve an alternative form of currency. That alternative can give specific advantages to both the buyer and the seller, and unique opportunities to realize profit.

The book is organized into five parts:

Part 1, "Barter—an Alternative Currency," takes a quick look at barter's history and how it naturally transformed into currency. Yet barter is not obsolete, evolving instead to various forms of community-based and business-to-business barter economies that supplement the broader cash-based economy.

Part 2, "Trade Exchanges," covers the companies that run local and regional business-to-business barter activity. Businesses become members of an exchange so that instead of depending on "direct trade" for their barter activity, they broaden their reach through the use of "trade dollars."

Part 3, "Barter Strategies," advises you on how best to use barter and even when not to use it.

Part 4, "Advanced Trade Techniques," points out ways you can use barter to leverage highly profitable deals. But be warned: these techniques require creativity, hard work, and careful monitoring to make the deals pay off.

Part 5, "Start Your Own Trade Exchange," is for those readers who want to go deeply into bartering and run their own trade exchange. As the owner of a trade exchange, you need to run your own barter economy, balancing the amount of trade dollars in circulation, growing and servicing membership, and brokering deals. There's no one way to run a trade exchange, but there are some common questions you need to answer.

Extras

Within each chapter are notes to help guide the reader through the ins and outs of barter.

def•i•ni•tion

These boxes contain terms and phrases that have specific meanings for trade exchanges and direct barter.

Barter Bits

These sidebars include tips, insights, and trivia to make barter work for you.

Balance of Trade

Here you find advice and cautions to prevent your trades from undermining your cash flow.

Trade Tales

These boxes contain anecdotes that show how people, businesses, and organizations have used barter to their advantage.

Acknowledgments

I'd like to acknowledge some people, who, without their assistance, friendship, and support, this book would have been impossible.

When I first started Midwest Business Exchange, there were some members who not only supported me, but I learned from *them*. I'd like to thank Butch Shearer and Ted Klinger from Pappy's, John Brown from Park Lane Florists, and from Portage Printing, Bob and Sue Nicol, and Craig Vestal. I'd also like to thank Art Pearce and Bruce Woerner from Battle Creek Area Habitat for Humanity.

I'd also like to thank some special friends in the barter industry, including Tom McDowell, Jack Schacht, Fran Crumpton, and Alan Zimmelman. Their assistance and input into the book were invaluable. Special gratitude goes to my team of Omar Towghi, Lance Dorsey, Dave Forster, and Jim Coash, who also contributed.

I would particularly like to thank Tom Chmielewski for his time, talent, and expertise.

Finally, I'd like to thank my family—my dear wife Liz and our two daughters Shantal and Amanda—as they not only encouraged me to write the book, but also supported me throughout the process.

—Jerry Howell

Trademarks

All terms mentioned in this book that are known to be or are suspected of being trademarks or service marks have been appropriately capitalized. Alpha Books and Penguin Group (USA) Inc. cannot attest to the accuracy of this information. Use of a term in this book should not be regarded as affecting the validity of any trademark or service mark.

Part 1

Barter—an Alternative Currency

Cash has value only because we believe it has value. After all, a $1 bill has no inherent worth beyond the paper it's printed on. But it represents the value of the goods it can buy.

People and businesses don't always have cash on hand, but they do have services they can provide, or goods in stock. People can use those goods and services to back their own form of currency in a barter economy, and they've been doing it for thousands of years. In this part, you'll learn how primitive barter developed into complex economies and how barter continues today in many forms.

A History of Barter: I Have Water, You Have a Cow

In This Chapter

♦ Barter's beginnings: filling basic needs

♦ Barter evolves into currency but never disappears

♦ When a cash economy falters, people turn to barter

♦ Trade exchanges bring in a new business model

♦ Countertrade enters a global economy

We have all bartered. We remember times when as a school kid, we were bored with the lunch our moms packed for us, but salivated over the lunch the geeky kid across the table had. But he was just as bored with his mom's culinary choices. So, we traded.

No one had to teach us how to do trade. It just came naturally to us. In fact, it came naturally to all of humanity. At a time when humanity was just becoming, well, human, the idea of trading occurred to someone who thought it might be easier to get something he needed by trading rather than beating someone over the head with a club and just taking it.

The idea of trade and barter never left us, even as we developed a more complex, money-based economic system over the millennia. Indeed, trade and barter is the basis of our economic system and still offers an alternative to cash.

Economy on the Hoof

When academics and historians trace the concept of barter and money, they go back to around 9000 B.C.E. and the first domestication of cattle. In this case, cattle can mean anything, from cows, to sheep, to camels. Cattle could assure a family's subsistence.

But even if the cattle were kept where they could graze, they needed water. And if the local watering hole was held by some guy with a spear, the cattle man could either make his own spear and try to take the water by force, or trade a couple of extra cows for water for the rest of his herd. The spear thrower could keep one cow for himself, but trade the other cow for, say, a shield. And thus, an economy was born. The primitive cow herders evolved into today's agribusiness, and the spear throwers into warlords and, later, investment bankers.

The guy with the spear may have thought he had power, but it was the man with the cattle who had wealth. And as long as he had extra cattle, he could "spend" his cattle on other needs, such as vegetables, pottery, and even a spear and shield for himself. It was a system that depended on direct trade and the trading partners needing what each other had. But in a primitive society the needs are basic, and urgent.

As the society became more complex, people began trading for cattle not because they needed the meat, but because they could in turn trade the cow for something else they needed. Cattle became a rather inconvenient yet effective form of money as a means to make indirect trades.

Equating cattle with wealth has never really gone out of style. We've all seen the Hollywood version of that wealth portrayed in the American West. A truer version of how cattle are used as barter in a primitive society can be found in today's Africa. An article in the *Zimbabwe Standard* in 2008 told of a woman in the village of Dongamuzi who made a "deal she knows is unfair, but she also knows she has little choice but to barter one of her few remaining cows for six buckets of maize to feed her family."

Trade Tales

In the Sudan, the trade of cattle can turn deadly. The *Sudan Tribune* reported in May of 2008 that a failed barter exchange between cattle holders resulted in a gunfight and a reported loss of 36 lives. The gunfire erupted when a proposed trade of a bull for a heifer fell apart. One of the traders demanded exchanging his heifer for a colored bull, a sign of riches and of great reputation in cattle-keeping communities. The bull owner said no deal, and was shot dead.

The woman told the newspaper that one bucket of maize was equal to four live chickens or a goat, while five buckets of maize were where negotiations started for a cow. The villagers used to be able to get cash for their livestock, but the people selling maize stopped taking the Zimbabwe dollar because of a rapid drop of value in the currency.

The rate of exchange for a cow may increase or decrease, depending on the market. But it never loses its base value of being able to feed people. For this reason, cattle continue to be a valuable instrument of barter.

Shell Game: The Beginning of Currency

A cow may have inherent value, but it can be tough to carry around on a shopping trip. As economies became more complex, and the goods available for trade more varied, the old barter system of direct trade began to break down. Even if you had highly prized cattle, if the person you wanted to trade with didn't need meat, your cattle became worthless in that exchange. What you needed was some way to represent the value of the trades you had made in a form that was easy to exchange for other goods—and easy to carry in your purse.

The answer for people living in China around 1200 B.C.E. was right under their feet, if they were prone to walking along the seashore. What they found there were cowrie shells, brightly colored, high-gloss sea shells.

Because of their unique beauty, cowrie shells had long been used as decorations and jewelry. They were found in the tombs of Egyptian pharaohs and depicted on cave walls.

When the trade in cowrie shells reached China, the Chinese began to use it as a form of currency to such an extent that the shape of the shell was used in their pictograph for money. Basically, the shells were used to keep track of the value of trades and allowed for an easy exchange of commodities.

But unlike the dollar bill of today, which really is worth more than the paper it's printed on, a cowrie shell had intrinsic value for its beauty, and in some circles, for the magic it was believed to hold. Arab merchants practiced a major trade in cowrie shells, centered on the Maldive Islands in the Indian Ocean, before the Chinese began to use them as actual currency.

Metal Trades

While the Chinese paid for goods with sea shells, parts of the Middle East began engaging in metal exchange. It was more practical as a primitive form of currency. Metal was small enough to carry around. You didn't have to keep it healthy like cattle, and it was durable. Egyptians began using copper rings to purchase goods around 2500 B.C.E.

Metal had an additional value of being able to be cast or fashioned into its own objects of value.

Babylonia practiced an extensive barter system based on barley and uncoined silver. Barley, a basic commodity in that society, provided the standard value for other products, with silver used for expenses of greater value. Records from that time recorded the value of commodities not in prices, but as an exchange value.

The use of metals during this time, however, presented its own problem. Basically, the metal had to be weighed in each exchange to determine its worth.

Coins of the Realm

The Chinese were so taken by cowrie shells that they began imitating them in base metals to represent money, beginning at the end of the Stone Age, around 1000 B.C.E. They also began to use miniaturized bronze tools as another type of coin.

Egyptians used lumps of gold shaped to resemble small sheep because sheep were the basis for their trading. Around 600 B.C.E., Lydia, a part of what is now Turkey, circulated a bean-shaped coin made of a mix of gold and silver. But the Lydians added a stamped design to their coins, certifying they were of standard weight and value. With that, people no longer had to weigh the lumps of metal to determine worth.

The rulers at the time knew a good thing when they saw it, so to imprint the coins with the authority of ruling factions, they had the coins stamped with images of numerous gods, and, surprise, themselves.

Coins stamped with the images of gods and emperors began showing up first in Lydia, but Greek, Persian, Macedonian, and Roman empires all followed suit. Unlike the Chinese coins made from base metals, these new coins were made from scarce metals such as bronze, gold, and silver. Again, like the cowrie shells, they had intrinsic value. But while coins of precious metal could always be melted down for other uses, they were made specifically for use as currency, making it easier for the aforementioned emperors to collect taxes.

Paper Money: The End of the World as They Knew It

It was the Chinese who made the great leap of turning currency from an object of actual value to a marker of representational worth. That is, they came up with paper money.

Paper money first showed up in China around the ninth century C.E. as local currency, and by 960, the Sung dynasty issued the first general circulation notes to offset a shortage of copper for striking coins. It seemed a good idea at the time, and it was a good idea for a time. The notes had a limited time before they needed to be turned in for an exchange of something of real value, usually coins. But in the later years of the Sung dynasty, the government began printing paper money without limits to fund their rule, bringing on hyper-inflation. The paper money became worthless, and by 1455, the new Ming dynasty ended the use of paper money, a ban that lasted for hundreds of years.

Barter Bits

The first bank note in China wasn't paper. It was leather. Historians say that in 118 B.C.E., China issued bank notes in the form of leather, 1-foot squares of white deerskin, with edges done in vivid colors.

Marco Polo reported on the use of paper money in China in the thirteenth century, but it wasn't until 1661 that the first issue of paper money in Europe began. Stockholm Banco in Sweden introduced the first banknotes, but overextended their circulation to the point that it had to call in government aid. I know, sounds familiar. Nevertheless, other European banks soon followed with their own bank notes.

Trade and Currency in the New World

As Europeans came to the Americas, their complex history of interaction with Native Americans included barter and direct trades. European traders used beads and trinkets to exploit gift exchange with the natives to gain territory and other advantages. Fairly quickly, a belt embedded with shell beads used by Native Americans called *wampum* became a simple form of currency in this trade.

def•i•ni•tion

wampum Contraction for the Algonquian word *wampumpeage* (pronounced *wom pom pe ak*) or "white shell beads."

Native Americans had given strong cultural significance to shell beads long before Europeans arrived on their shore. The beads were made from clam, conch, and other shells. Natives along the East Coast used disc-shaped wampum beads for decoration and barter. Wampum carried strong symbolic importance in religious, social, and political practices. Archaeologists have found similar materials and discerned similar uses farther south and even on the California coast.

The first European reference to wampum may have been Jacque Cartier's report of highly valued, white shell beads used by the St. Lawrence Iroquois in 1535. It was Cartier who compared those beads to the use of gold and silver as money among the Europeans. By the seventeenth century, wampum became a kind of currency between settlers and Native Americans.

The website nativetech.org quoted a contemporary report of the eighteenth century that a "fathom (6 feet of strung beads) of white wampum was worth 10 shillings and double that for purple beads." Because coins were in short supply in the colonies, English settlers used wampum as their own currency, or resorted to musket balls as their own coinage. A musket ball was worth a farthing when spent. But it could also be used to get dinner when employed for its original purpose and shot from a musket.

Barter Endures

When money is scarce, goods of common use, such as wampum or musket balls, become a regular exchange in barter and soon become a substitute for cash. The colonial era in America was primarily a barter economy.

Common goods traded included beaver pelts, corn, nails, tobacco, and deer skins. Indeed, the trading of deer or buckskin gives us our modern slang for dollar, "buck."

After the American Revolution, the United States began to print paper money, as did individual states. Inflation was so bad in the early nineteenth century, however, that people depended on barter again, and on bank promissory notes that could be exchanged for gold. But that promise held true only if all the note holders didn't show up on the bank's doorstep at the same time, demanding their gold.

A more stable federal cash currency evolved after the Civil War, but barter in the United States never completely went away. Whenever the economy in this country dives, barter booms.

The Great Depression

With the Crash of 1929 and the Great Depression that racked the '30s, great numbers of people faced a shortage of cash. But they still had goods. They still had skills. And they were hungry. So they began trading what goods they had and services they could offer for food, lodging, and anything else they needed to keep afloat. If they couldn't afford room and board, they worked for the landlord in exchange. Students from farmlands trying to go to school paid for tuition with produce. If you had special skills that filled basic needs—sewing, baking, carpentry—you found you could do all right on barter.

Barter Bits

"Moonshiners, bless them, exchanged goods with just about everybody."

—Lynn Parramore, recesesionwire.com

But as the ranks of the unemployed grew, they organized themselves to help each other and form their own barter rings. In the summer of 1931, a group of labor activists and left-wing radicals formed the Unemployed Citizens League (UCL) of Seattle. The group was active on several fronts, including seeking relief for its members through financing from the government. But the UCL also created a cooperative barter economy based on self-help.

The idea spread rapidly across the country, and at its peak in the spring of 1933, the UCL had 200,000 members.

Trade Tales

In his book *The New Deal* (Wiley-Blackwell, 2000), author Ronald Edsforth wrote that Southern California's Unemployed Cooperative Relief Association used the slogan "Self Help Beats Charity" to urge families to trade labor for food in the region's fruit and vegetable fields. Economist Ralph Borsodi organized down-and-out suburbanites in New York and other metro areas to exchange clothes, furniture, and even works of art for food in barter markets he organized. "No one will ever know how many Americans survived through private barter ... during the winter of 1932 to 1933. But we do know that various combinations of unemployed workers and middle-class reformers organized impressive barter economies in many urban areas."

The Natural Development Association (NDA) was formed in Salt Lake City for the harvest of 1931 when a real estate salesman figured unemployed workers would be willing to work the fields if they were paid in kind. During the winter of 1932–1933, the NDA spread to six Western states.

Other organizations, including Minneapolis's Organized Unemployed Inc., took the barter concept further, issuing *scrip* redeemable only at its distribution centers. The NDA also began issuing scrip, calling it "vallars."

People who used vallars could buy and sell basic goods, and even get a meal at a "daylight" restaurant. The restaurant was open only in daylight because the power company didn't accept vallars.

def•i•ni•tion

Scrip Substitute money, usually issued by someone other than the government. Most common when regular money is unavailable, scrip represents an IOU, redeemable at one or more participants or businesses.

Barter Resurgence in the 1970s and 1980s

As the economy stabilized after the 1930s, the barter systems that grew in the Depression faded but never went completely away. And as the gas crisis of the 1970s morphed into a recession in the early 1980s, barter made a comeback. But it had a different look.

Barter clubs that arose in the 1980s still had a "self-help" bent to them, but there was also a growing recognition in business that barter was good for more than the individual. For-profit trade exchanges began to arrive on the scene in the 1970s, and even major businesses began to use barter on international deals, all of it with a highly capitalistic bent (in contrast to the barter clubs of the 1930s, which had significant socialist and communist origins).

Rather than deal with individuals, commercial trade exchanges brokered business-to-business deals through indirect barter. Just as the NDA of the '30s issued scrip in the form of vallars, trade exchanges issued trade dollars to facilitate barter among its members. Unlike the barter clubs of the Depression that faded as the country went back to work, however, trade exchanges developed a business model that didn't depend on the rest of the economy going south. The exchanges focused not so much on desperation and dire needs as it did on excess capacity and preserving cash flow. Because of that, trade exchanges flourished beyond general economic downturns.

Since the 1970s, there has also been a rise in international companies and even countries using a form of barter referred to as *countertrade.*

def•i•ni•tion

Countertrade   A transaction that links imports and exports of goods or services in addition to, or instead of, financial payments.

It may seem like a fancy word for barter. But when trade crosses international boundaries and may involve multimillion and even billion-dollar deals, you need a fancy word to help satisfy legal complications and make accountants and lawyers feel more comfortable. Countertrade in its varied forms allows companies to be more flexible and execute deals more quickly in an international market.

Money can be involved in a countertrade deal, either as part of the exchange, or as a promise for one party to buy a commodity from a country later in exchange for selling goods to that country now. Yet, however complex the deal, it generally results in goods and services being transferred in both directions.

One of the more famous countertrades occurred in 1990 between PepsiCo, Inc. and the Soviet Union. PepsiCo agreed to give the Soviets soft-drink syrup for Stolichnaya Russian vodka and 10 commercial ships. *The New York Times* reported the agreement was worth $3 billion, and maybe three times as much when Pepsi sold the vodka retail. The 10-year deal allowed Pepsi to expand its bottling network in the Soviet Union, at the same time allowing the Soviet vodka to expand its market in the United States. As for the 10 ships, PepsiCo added to that deal later on by taking 17 submarines, a cruiser, a frigate, and a destroyer in exchange for Pepsi products. (No, the cola wars weren't heating up. The ragtag fleet was sold for scrap to pay for shipping the Pepsi syrups to the Soviet Union.)

The countertrade business continues to grow at the beginning of the twenty-first century. China is making aggressive use of reciprocal agreements in Africa, building extensive infrastructure in exchange for copper and cobalt supplies.

Trade Tales

While countertrade emerged as a major marketing tool in the late '70s, it was practiced well before then. Dan West, former executive director of the American Countertrade Association and former director of countertrade for Monsanto Corp., wrote in the *Barter News* (barternews. com) that Monsanto performed its first countertrade transaction in 1935. Monsanto sold saccharin to a company in northern China, but the company was unable to pay in currency. What they did have to offer was frozen mackerel. Monsanto took the mackerel for resale later. By the 1990s, the countertrade business for Monsanto had risen to $200 million a year.

Saudi Arabia entered into an agreement with Pakistan, trading oil for food. Like many Gulf states, Saudi Arabia has too little water for a viable agriculture. Pakistan needs energy. Even in a global economy, the basic needs are what drive trade.

Barter in the Twenty-First Century

The recession that began in 2008 has renewed interest in barter, for businesses and for individuals. The biggest problem in direct barter, however, is finding someone who has what you need and needs what you've got. If you just depend on your neighbors, you may find that no one on your street or the block over can help you out.

The Internet, however, allows you to expand your network, from the city, to a region, to anywhere.

Bartering on Craigslist rocketed up in 2008 and 2009 as money became short. A transaction can be as simple as bartering for school clothes in exchange for accounting, home renovations for lodgings, or a used car for a great sound system. In one case, a New York funeral director offered a free funeral for construction work on his patio. That deal didn't go through, though. His landlord turned out to be a competing funeral director. Nevertheless, by the nature of Craigslist, people are utilizing creative trades to get through tough times.

Other Internet sites, some with special interests, also offer ways for individuals to connect with trading partners. One of these with a great name is seedypeople.co.uk. It's a gardening site for people swapping unwanted or surplus seeds with fellow gardeners.

Tomato seeds for cucumbers. Pepsi for vodka and used submarines. Oil for food. The barter economy has been around longer than a cash economy and always seems to rise when cash falters.

The Least You Need to Know

◆ Barter comes naturally to all of us and has been around since the beginning of human society.

◆ As needs expanded, the need for indirect trades gave rise to currency and eventually a cash society.

◆ During economic downturns, direct barter rises to meet basic needs.

◆ Indirect trade has expanded barter to small businesses and big companies alike. Even countries engage in barter.

Chapter 2

Forms of Barter

In This Chapter

- ◆ Direct trade: barter at its simplest, if you're lucky
- ◆ How to use the Internet to broaden your network
- ◆ Community dollars as an alternate currency
- ◆ Time dollars for social good
- ◆ Trade exchanges help improve profits

Barter comes in various forms and complexity, from simple one-to-one casual trades between friends, to involved reciprocal agreements between international corporations and countries that may take a decade to play out. In this chapter, we look at the forms of barter individuals and business owners get involved in regularly.

All forms have their advantages and their limits. But they all allow you to go beyond the cash economy to get what you need or want.

Direct Trade

The one-to-one trade is the simplest form of barter, but it's the hardest to pull off once you go beyond basic needs and wants. Say you just bought a riding mower, but your old mower is still perfectly good. What you really want now is an outdoor gas grill—not a five-star, restaurant-grade grill with chrome finish, side burners, a small refrigerator for beverages, and cup holders. But if you can find someone who just bought one of those, maybe he'll trade you his old grill for your old mower.

Good luck. Your neighbor just bought one of those grills, but he already gave the old one to his kid. Someone down the street has an extra grill, but he doesn't have a lawn. Just trees, flower beds, and mulch. A neighbor on the next block would love to have your mower, but the only thing she has to trade are three buckets of paint—pink paint. You hate pink.

You've just run into this form of barter's key problem. For a direct trade to work, it requires a *coincidence of need*, sometimes called a double coincidence of need by economists who embrace redundancy over simple English.

def•i•ni•tion

Coincidence of need The basic requirement in a direct trade, where one party possesses what a second party needs, while coincidently the second party possesses what the first party needs.

Even if you find someone who has what you need or desire, if the other person isn't interested in anything you have, no deal. Now if the guy who doesn't have a lawn happens to need some pink paint for his baby daughter's bedroom, you can slip into an indirect three-way trade. You trade the mower for the paint and then trade the paint for the grill. You do have a double coincidence of need and everybody's happy.

Three-way trades are fairly common in the limited and arcane world of baseball. Finding them in the world where most of us play and work is harder. Remember that *one* coincidence is, as defined in a dictionary, "a remarkable concurrence of events or circumstances without apparent causal connection." The definition for a *double* coincidence is "get real."

Direct trades are not likely to work except by happenstance if your trading network is too small. If you try to pull off a direct trade with 10 neighbors, chances aren't good. If you can ask 100, your chances improve. If you can ask thousands, however, it's a slam dunk.

The barter clubs that developed in the Depression of the 1930s set up broad barter networks of needy people with little cash. They placed free "seeking trade" ads in club newspapers. Yet the mechanics of the process were difficult to maintain, and the clubs eventually died out.

Barter on a Network

Now there is an easier way to broaden your barter network—the Internet. The *net* in Internet, after all, stands for *network*. One of the most straightforward ways to seek a trade on the Internet is to place a free ad in the barter section of Craigslist.

Craigslist.com has a barter section in its "for sale" category, and a "housing swap" grouped with apartments and homes for sale or rent. The swaps are often for somebody wanting to trade a place in a city for a vacation spot on a lake, or vice versa. After all, that's the idea. One person on Craigslist wanted to trade a 14-acre horse ranch in Indiana for a city house near any city. "I'm open to a condo, house, townhouse," the ad read. "I just want to get on with a new life away from here."

There seemed to be enough ads of people wanting laptop computers, and those wanting to trade them away, that there were bound to be good matches. Sometimes it's a drywall contractor willing to do work for a truck. Other ads are for sound systems in exchange for an electronic gaming system.

Do a web search on barter, and you'll find plenty of sites. Some will not last long; others garner a strong reputation and stick around.

U-exchange.com is a site specifically set up to facilitate direct trades. As of 2009, it's been growing in use and reputation, having been written up by major media such as CNN, *The Wall Street Journal*, and *The New York Times*. The traders can be broken down to location, and you can even do a map search to locate all trades originating in your area.

Barter Globally? Maybe Not

With the Internet, you can perform a direct trade with anyone in the world. But do you really want to? Sure, the man in France says he has that rare Spike Jones record on a 78 rpm record. But is he really going to send it the same time you ship that spare laptop? Okay, maybe the computer isn't in quite the mint condition you said it was, either. In fact, you haven't been able to get it running since 1999 when it was apparently the only computer in the world actually hit by the millennium bug.

A coincidence of fraud? If life was fair, fraudulent traders would only trade with each other. But if only one side in a trade is committing fraud, the other side is getting screwed. Direct trades on the Internet can be nearly impossible to guarantee if you keep it all on the 'net. If you expand your network so far that you can't eyeball what you're trading for, then you really don't know what you're going to get. For most barter of goods, your best bet is to keep your trading partners within driving distance ... or be willing to catch a plane.

> **Balance of Trade**
>
> Just because there's no money trading hands doesn't mean you don't have to obey legal niceties. If you're trading valuable objects or service over the Internet, get the terms of the deal in writing. Make it clear what each side of the deal expects to receive, and if applicable, in what condition. Make the details of the transaction clear, and you have a better chance of coming out with a fair deal.

When a trade is not simply a swap of goods but an exchange of services— say a website design for help on taxes—the only practical way to complete the entire transaction may be over the Internet. It's important in those instances to not only have a clear understanding of what is expected from each side, but also solid and frequent communication.

It's not just the service exchanged that's most important in such deals. It's the relationship between the trading partners.

Building One-to-One Relationships

Building relationships used to mean being able to look someone in the eye, extend a firm handshake, and discern a trusting demeanor. But that's so twentieth century. Face-to-face contact, however important it may still be, is rapidly being replaced by being a friend on Facebook, communicating your character on MySpace, and tweeting your life away on Twitter. As uncomfortable as all that may seem to some, the web as a social network has become a fact of modern life and an important way for anyone doing barter to build relationships.

The more you know about people and communicate with them, the easier it is to do business with them fairly. Yes, you still have to be careful of scams. Almost any networking sight has cautions about what to look out for, as does Craigslist and other sites that deal with barter. Pay attention to those cautions.

Balance of Trade

When you do have someone send you an item in a barter transaction, get a tracking number for the shipment to assure delivery. Most shipping companies give you details on your shipment each step of the way: when it's been picked up, when it reaches a central hub, even when it's on a truck and headed for your door. The U.S. Postal Service doesn't give such details, however, but the delivery confirmation number can at least tell you it's on the way.

The social networks can let you find references for people you don't know, or you can have established friends introduce you to people they trust. Maybe you can't make it over to France to see if the guy really has that rare Spike Jones record. But checking your connections on the web, you may discover that you know someone who knows someone, who knows someone else, who has a good friend living in Paris who will gladly check the record.

And as you become active in barter, you build your own network of trading partners. Even if you can't look them in the eye, you discover there are some people whose e-mail is bond.

Judging Value

Say you did find someone who wanted to trade you an old grill for your old mower. Is it a fair trade? How do you judge the value of each item? Only the parties involved in the trade can truly judge the value of the goods involved. But remember, even if it's a cashless transaction, value is still determined by what the market will bear.

There are some basics to judging value, of course. This may involve determining its cash equivalent, like the Blue Book value of a used car. The condition of the car can subjectively add or detract from that starting estimate, and you come close to its true market value.

Ideally, the two items in an exchange are of similar market value, but that rarely occurs in a direct trade. It's not only the market value you have to consider, but the value of your need.

In trading a mower for a grill, to start with, it helps if both work. Besides determining that an object you're trading for works, however, you have to determine if it's going to do the job you need it to do. It may be a perfectly fine, but small gas grill, and you have a big family. You don't want to be flipping burgers two at a time. If it doesn't fill your need, then it doesn't have value to you.

On the other hand, if the grill is more than you hoped, only three years old with features that you don't need but wouldn't mind having, you'll take it. But will the other guy take your old mower that works great, but looks dull and dirty, and doesn't have powered wheels?

The question then becomes: how tall is his grass? If he's been having a hard time unloading his grill, and his wife and other neighbors are really on his case to get the grass cut, you've got a deal. The urgency of his need overcame the value of the object he was giving up.

Of course, if he had been able to perform an indirect trade, he may have had a better shot at getting something of higher value for his grill, and still getting his lawn mowed.

Indirect Trade

To overcome the problems of direct trade, communities, organizations, and for-profit companies have come up with a system of indirect trade.

Users or members of the system earn credit by "selling" goods and services not for cash, but for an *alternative currency* such as community dollars or trade dollars. The member can then use these trade dollars to "purchase" other goods offered within the trading network.

Why use an alternative currency when you can spend the dollars in your pocket? For one thing, you may not have enough dollars in your pocket. But you do have a spare lawn mower in your garage. You could try selling that lawn mower at a garage sale, but if there's a shortage of cash in the community, you may not get much for it. Yet members of the community may have plenty of stuff in their garages or services they can offer. A community that can generate its own dollars to keep track of trades within its local economy creates a way for people to help meet their wants and needs.

def•i•ni•tion

Alternative currency A method of keeping track of indirect barter transactions apart from cash. The limits imposed by direct trade are removed, and barter becomes more readily available.

In much the same way, businesses that are members of commercial trade exchanges have an excess capacity in their production or ability to offer services, or an excess inventory. They create their own currency with trade dollars and generate or expand an economy that could be otherwise stifled when everyone holds onto their cash.

While a barter network's credits are most often referred to as an alternative currency, it may be more accurate to consider trade dollars a complementary currency. Unless a community so isolates itself from the rest of the world and becomes self-sufficient, people still need cash.

A barter economy, then, doesn't replace a cash economy. Rather, barter is a part of the general economy, and is a way to preserve cash for other needs that can't be obtained by any other means. Barter takes the edge off by reaching into your reserves of stuff and time instead of your savings account and credit card limit.

Community-Based Trading

The driving force behind community-based trading is social need. We'll take a closer look at examples and the workings of community barter in Chapter 3, but in general, community trading networks arise as a grassroots effort to survive an economic crisis and to boost a local economy.

In a barter network that handles indirect trade through "community dollars," a key ingredient is to buy local. A U.S. dollar can go anywhere, and more often than not, leaves these shores. The same is true of all national currencies. But for a small town, every dollar that leaves the county, let alone the country, can have a negative impact.

A community dollar, on the other hand, is only accepted by other members of the community network. These dollars circulate, but only within the community. Where national chain stores can suck dollars out of a community and decimate local businesses, local stores benefit from an alternate currency that has to, by its nature, circulate locally.

Because only members of the local barter network accept community dollars, it is a restrictive kind of currency. You have fewer places to spend it. But for that reason, members will more readily part with community dollars to preserve their cash. A homeowner may think of putting off a remodeling project because money is tight, but he can go ahead with the project if he pays the drywall contractor in community dollars.

Indeed there is no advantage to saving community dollars, because the alternate currency can't earn interest in a bank. For a community looking to boost the local community on a grassroots level, that drive to spend is a key advantage.

There is also a noneconomic advantage to this currency. The more you search out local members of the network, the more you build relationships and the sense of community. A local currency can build a collective cohesiveness.

Time Is Money

Many community barter networks use a time-based currency as the means to their barter system. The unit of the exchange is the person hour. The person hour is paid for with *time dollars*.

def•i•ni•tion

Time dollars   Credit paid for hours of service in a time-based currency. Everyone's contributions are valued equally. A person who volunteers to work for another member within the system for one hour receives a one-hour credit. That credit, paid in time dollars and accounted for in time banks, can be redeemed for an hour of service from some other member of the system.

Time dollars, recorded in time banks, encourage reciprocal community service. Everyone's time earns the same rate of credit, regardless of experience or expertise of the individual.

Time-based currencies, or time banks, have been started in a number of communities across the United States, Canada, Britain, and at least another 20 countries. Organizers of these systems say a time bank not only works economically, but strengthens the fabric of community.

But such systems can be fragile. Their social goals can drive volunteers to the system, but the economic gains are not always enough to allow such systems to survive or reach critical mass.

Trade Tales

Edgar Cahn, author and lawyer who has worked for social justice since the 1960s, came up with the concept of time dollars in 1980 as "a new currency to provide a solution to massive cuts in government spending on social welfare. If there was not going to be enough of the old money to fix all the problems facing our country and our society, why not make a new kind of money to pay people for what needs to be done? Time Dollars value everyone's contributions equally." Cahn is the founder of TimeBanks USA (www.timebanks.org).

Time service exchanges, which began in the 1980s, struggled after initial enthusiasm and funding from foundations dried up. Since the mid- to late 1990s, there has been a resurgence in time banks.

Trade Exchanges: Barter for Profit

Unlike community dollars and time banks, which offer social improvements as major goals of their efforts, commercial trade exchanges set out to improve profits. Trade exchanges facilitate business-to-business indirect barter, keeping track of the exchanges through trade dollars.

I'll go into more detail on trade exchanges in Chapter 4. For now, let's just say there are some similarities to community barter organizations, but some key differences driven by the profit motive.

Businesses join a trade exchange to preserve cash and maintain cash flow. Instead of rummaging through neighborhood garages for old lawn mowers and gas grills, members of a trade exchange offer goods that aren't moving through regular sales and are perhaps stored in their warehouses, such as, say … lawn mowers and gas grills. These goods may be in better condition than what you find in your neighbor's garage. They may never have been used. But they're last year's model and just aren't moving.

What businesses offer in a trade exchange is *excess capacity*. It's better for a business to barter away what it can't sell in cash, and barter within a trade exchange is an easier sale.

def•i•ni•tion

Excess capacity   The difference between what a business has available for sale and what is actually selling. Excess capacity can take the form of goods in a warehouse that aren't meeting sales expectations, production lines running at less than full capacity, empty rooms in a hotel, or potentially billable time of a service provider that remains open.

Trade exchanges can prosper in good times or bad because excess capacity can be reduced but not eliminated even in boom times. Businesses are always looking for a way to preserve cash flow, and barter allows them to do that.

Because trade exchanges are for-profit companies, businesses pay fees to be members and conduct transactions. But trade exchanges also employ brokers to arrange deals that can reach thousands of dollars in value.

Perhaps most importantly, barter through trade exchanges allows a business to expand its customer base. Barter is not used to replace cash business, but to add new business. A company offering barter sales attracts other members of the trade exchange looking for places to spend their trade dollars.

Despite the profit motivation behind trade exchanges, they are similar to community barter groups in that they encourage businesses to buy locally (though not exclusively) and boost a community's economy.

The Least You Need to Know

- ◆ Direct trade depends on coincidence of need. You have to be lucky.

- ◆ Improve your luck by using the Internet to broaden your network of trading partners, but protect yourself against scams.

- ◆ Community dollars and time banks have a social as well as an economic purpose.

- ◆ Trade exchanges for business-to-business barter are solidly capitalistic, and can improve a company's bottom line.

Chapter 3

Community Barter

In This Chapter

- ◆ Community barter focuses on social needs and self-reliance
- ◆ Case study: Ithaca Hours, the most successful of community barter groups
- ◆ Community currencies boost local economies
- ◆ Case study: Hour Exchange Portland, which trades time, not goods

Barter in any of its forms is an economic alternative. Yet community-based barter is also a social alternative. The chief goal is not so much to strengthen profit by preserving cash flow, but to strengthen the sense of bonds that support a village, a town, a neighborhood, a city.

Community barter seeks to improve the vitality of an area as a whole, even as it allows individuals to improve their own economic standing, and if necessary, get through hard times.

In this chapter, we look at examples of two similar community barter groups, but with differences that impact their aims and results. In both cases, they offer alternative currencies to keep track of barter transactions.

Ithaca Hours

Ithaca, New York, besides being home to Cornell University, has become a standard bearer for community barter ever since it instituted its own local currency, "Ithaca Hours," in 1991.

Its website, ithacahours.org, explains the mission of Ithaca Hours as "a local currency system that promotes local economic strength and community self-reliance in ways which will support economic and social justice, ecology, community participation and human aspirations in and around Ithaca, New York. Ithaca Hours help to keep money local, building the Ithaca economy. It also builds community pride and connections."

It is not a surprise that Ithaca gave rise to an alternative currency system that promotes "economic and social justice." The city has a strong liberal tradition with a concern for social issues. Ithaca Hours has become a model for other communities looking to set up their own currency to keep track of the value exchanged in indirect barter. (Despite the name, Ithaca Hours is not a time-based currency. For that, we'll be going to Portland, Maine, later on in this chapter.)

Ithaca Hours fall under the category of *fiat money*, as do nearly all national currencies. The board of Ithaca Hours' corporation is the authority that sets the value of Ithaca Hours and approves its printing.

def•i•ni•tion

Fiat money Currency declared by an authority as legal tender, even though the currency itself has no intrinsic value, as does commodity-backed currency. In a barter system, trade dollars such as Ithaca Hours are authorized by the system's governing body—or for a commercial trade exchange, the company owner—to be accepted as tender for transactions between members of the system.

Unlike U.S. dollars, which can be accepted by anyone, and spent anywhere in the country and pretty much around the world, Ithaca Hours can only be spent with other members of Ithaca's community barter system. Not everyone in Ithaca is a member, but in 2009, over 900 participants accept Ithaca Hours for goods and services.

Some of these members also pay partial wages in Ithaca Hours. For the employers, it's a way to preserve cash and still pay a higher wage. Employees may prefer cash for their raises, but if the cash isn't there, they can still earn extra value for their work.

Is It Real Money?

In a practical sense, anything is money if you think it's money and have faith in its value, and the person accepting something like Ithaca Hours has the same belief and faith.

In a legal sense, the Internal Revenue Service thinks it's money, and will tax you on any barter credit you receive as income. 'Nuff said?

Actually, I can't say that enough. It comes up again several times in this book. Any type of barter credit, be it an Ithaca Hour or a commercial trade dollar, represents the value of what you earned by "selling" goods or services.

Balance of Trade

It's illegal to counterfeit barter scrip such as an Ithaca Hour. It may seem weird that an Ithaca Hour bill or other scrip can be protected by counterfeit law. But think about it. That scrip is a legal document, a contract, in essence, that allows the bearer to spend it with other members of a barter system. To counterfeit barter scrip is simply committing fraud.

The IRS flat-out states that barter income is taxable, though it also makes clear the Feds really aren't concerned about a casual one-to-one trade like that lawn mower for a gas grill exchange from Chapter 2. Time dollars or time credits managed by nonprofit time banks have also been treated as casual noncommercial trades and not taxed. More later in the chapter.

Barter credit, however, can work for you at tax time as well. It represents an expense for goods and services you bought, an expense that may be deductible.

The Worth of an Ithaca Hour

Not surprisingly, most barter scrip is linked to a national currency. In the United States, it's the dollar. An Ithaca Hour, when conceived by its originator, Paul Glover, was pegged at $10 U.S. That figure was picked because it represented the average hourly wage in Tompkins County where Ithaca is located. All currency in the Ithaca system are set as fractions of the Hour. A $\frac{1}{8}$ hour equals $1.25, for instance. A half hour, $5.

The system's organizers say Ithaca's scrip is called an Hour as a reminder that even commodities represent someone's labor, or the time needed to provide a skill or perform a service.

Glover, a long-time community organizer and 2004 presidential candidate for the Green Party in several primaries, was doing research into local economics in 1989 when he learned of an "Hour" note issued by a 19th century British industrialist. The note could be spent at the company store. Glover learned later that the British hour notes were based on "Time Store" notes, an experiment in labor-based exchange conducted in Cincinnati by anarchist Josiah Warren in 1827.

> **Trade Tales**
>
> Ithaca Hours replaced an earlier barter system there, a Local Exchange Trading System, or LETS. LETS are local, nonprofit barter networks where no printed currency is used to keep track of the value of trades. Instead, transactions are recorded in a central location open to all members.

But where Warren's Time Store notes and current time dollar systems equate everyone's value of one hour of time equally, no matter the effort or skill expended in that hour, traders in Ithaca Hours set their own prices as they would for a common currency. An hour's service may earn one, two, or three Ithaca Hours, depending on the seller's value of his or her service, and the buyer's willingness to pay.

Glover was moved to design an Ithaca Hour in 1991, and soon began convincing businesses to accept the scrip. Within four months, 90 people had joined, and exchanges were being made by businesses and individuals. The system grew until it was incorporated in 1998.

Boosting Local Economy

Dollars are said to have a multiplier effect when spent in a local community. Those dollars inserted into the community can be re-spent several times, increasing the overall economic impact of each dollar.

But each dollar spent at, say, a Wal-Mart or other chain store, doesn't make it back into the community where a particular outlet is located. Some will be paid for local wages and other direct services. But the rest will be sent to nonlocal corporate coffers.

This is where local barter currencies such as the Ithaca Hour have an increased local economic impact. Its organizers say several million dollars' worth of Ithaca Hours have been traded since 1991 among the thousands of residents and more than 500 businesses that are members of the system. The members range from a medical center and a credit union, to local farmers, restaurants, and individual craftsman. Nonlocal businesses are free to accept Ithaca Hours, but the only place they can spend those hours are back in Ithaca.

Keeping it local builds a network of "inter-supporting" businesses within the community and keeps the multiplier effect working locally.

The Ithaca Hours Model

Ithaca Hours is the oldest and largest of the community currencies in the United States, but its model has spread to a number of towns in this country and Canada. Some last for only a few years, but other local barter networks employing its own currency crop up regularly.

Because they are mostly run by nonprofit organizations, community currencies need an active volunteer core, membership fees (usually small), and often funding grants from outside sources. Because of the economic downturn that began in 2008, Ithaca Hours began receiving a large number of requests for information and is working on a start-up kit for communities to duplicate the system.

Time-Based Currency

Where Ithaca Hours uses the time of labor as an inspiration for naming its Ithaca Hours, actual time spent in service is the specific basis for time credits, or time dollars, exchanged in community time banks.

Time banks keep track of volunteer service credits, where each service provided receives equal value, an hour for an hour.

Hour Exchange Portland, Maine, is the largest and oldest of the time bank systems. It was founded in 1997 by local activist and physician, Richard Rockefeller, as a way for people to share their skills and talents in exchange for services they wanted or needed. For every hour of service provided, a member receives one time credit. The goal is for local individuals, organizations, and businesses to help meet each other's needs, be it helping a neighbor or working on a group project.

The emphasis is on community help, using time credits for services such as health care, clerical help, weatherization, and home repair. The goal, according to its organizers, is for members to "help rebuild and sustain neighborhood networks and strengthen community as a result of their activities." It also serves as an incubator for local micro-enterprises, helping launch small businesses by allowing them to spend time dollars on services from its members including marketing, web design, and business planning.

> ### Trade Tales
> With its emphasis on community service, Hour Exchange Portland has leveraged its impact on the community to allow members to spend time dollars for classes with Portland Adult Education. Time dollars can also be used to purchase tickets for theater, ballet, music, and other art performances. Tickets for performances are two time dollars. The price is in keeping with the organization's standard of equal value of time: two hours of service gets you into an approximately two-hour performance.

Making everyone's hours of service worth the same is a disadvantage from a business standpoint for professionals like doctors, lawyers, web designers, and architects. Even organizers admit it sounds a little crazy to say an hour's worth of a doctor's time is worth an hour of someone raking leaves.

But the system does allow those who normally charge higher hourly rates to set aside a portion of their time for charitable work—the exchange suggests 10 percent—offering their services for time credits. It's not quite pro bono in that the credits they earn can be used to get help around the office. More importantly, it allows people who wouldn't normally be able to afford professional services to pay for it with time credits they earned raking somebody's yard or going grocery shopping for an elderly member.

Are Time Credits Tax Free?

While the IRS has been aggressive in making clear that barter exchanges and alternative currencies are taxable, time credits appear not to fall under the same rules. Department rulings suggest that time banks such as the one in Portland, Maine, cannot be considered a "barter exchange," an organization or company that keeps formal track of the value of trades by its members. The IRS specifically states that the term barter exchange "does not include arrangements that provide solely for the informal exchange of similar services on a noncommercial basis."

The IRS has concluded that time banks keep track of "informal exchange of similar services," all of it on a noncommercial basis. That is, an hour of service for an hour of service. There is no dollar value placed on that hour of service.

It's all quite friendly, casual, and nonprofit. As long as it stays that way, time credits are also nontaxable—unless the IRS changes its mind.

Barter Bits

Time banks such as the one in Portland make it difficult to spend time credits on goods, but not impossible. The price of the goods, however, are measured roughly in the time it takes to make it. If a knit hat takes one hour to make, it's worth one time credit.

The Time Bank Model

Hour Exchange Portland reports it has more than 700 active members providing more than 1,600 services in 178 categories. In 2008, members exchanged over 11,000 hours of services in approximately 3,500 transactions.

The success in Portland has encouraged other time banks to form across the country and the world. But the idea for time credits began in 1980 when Edgar S. Cahn, co-founder of the National Legal Services Program and founder of the Antioch School of Law, came up with the idea as a new currency to counter major reduction in government funding of social welfare programs.

He developed the concept further in 1987 at the London School of Economics, and soon after began putting the time credits to use in the United States. There was a surge of interest originally, but a fading interest by the mid-'90s. A further development of the concept, however, and a time dollar convention in 1997 for new and surviving groups, helped identify what worked among the organizations that survived and new ones being formed.

Cahn then founded TimeBanks USA to act as the hub of a network of independent time bank exchanges around the country. In 2000, he published his book *No More Throw Away People*, described as an overarching framework for time dollars.

TimeBanks USA's website, timebanks.org, lists approximately 60 active time bank nonprofit organizations in the United States, and about 30 others around the world.

The Least You Need to Know

- Local barter networks that issue their own currency assure that "dollars" stay local.

- Despite the name, Ithaca Hours is value-based currency, worth $10 per Hour bill. Prices are set by the seller.

- Time banks trade time of service, with one time credit or time dollar worth one hour of service. Everyone's hour is valued equally.

- Time credits foster community service, but can be difficult to use for goods. But that makes them difficult to tax as well.

Part **2**

Trade Exchanges

A trade exchange is a commercial enterprise that manages a barter economy for business-to-business transactions. It can be local or regional, and networks with other exchanges across the continent. A trade exchange works because it allows businesses to go beyond the limits of "direct trade" by setting up a system of indirect trade using trade dollars.

In this part, we take a close look at how a trade exchange works and how a business can benefit by being a member.

Chapter 4

How and Why a Trade Exchange Works

In This Chapter

- ◆ Understanding the heart of the matter
- ◆ Using barter credit for better trades
- ◆ Even a barter economy requires currency
- ◆ Keeping account of barter credit

A trade exchange is the driving engine of a barter economy between businesses. Anyone can do direct trade if he or she happens upon the right trading partner. But finding that partner can be very difficult.

A trade exchange provides a range of trading partners, formalizes the trades, keeps accounts of transactions, and raises the utility of barter to a practical and profitable level.

In this chapter, you'll learn what a trade exchange does. You'll discover that a trade exchange functions as an alternate currency, where participants are no longer bound by one-on-one trading.

By utilizing a trade exchange, a business can pay for goods and services with "trade dollars." In doing so, they conserve cash while attracting new customers.

What Is a Trade Exchange?

A trade exchange is a membership-based business that enlists companies that agree to barter with one another, not by doing direct swaps, but instead by trading goods and services with one another in exchange for trade credit, or "trade dollars." There are approximately 400 trade exchanges in North America, according to the National Association of Trade Exchanges. Members of these exchanges total 350,000 to 400,000 businesses doing an estimated $3.5 billion to $4 billion annually in trade.

The purpose of the trade exchange is to take the limited possibilities of a one-on-one trade and transform it into a one-to-many trade. You're still trading for goods and services you need. But instead of an informal balancing of value for goods exchanged between two people, you use trade dollars. A trade dollar can't be redeemed for cash, but it can be spent with other trade exchange members to acquire goods. The trade exchange keeps track of how many trade dollars you have in your account.

Barter Bits

Most trade exchanges rely on paper trade drafts that the buyer signs, authorizing the transfer of trade funds. A few trade exchanges, however, do this electronically, just as a credit card works.

There are two advantages of a trade exchange membership: new customers and cash conservation. Members, eager to conserve cash for cash-only expenses, are motivated to seek out other members who also accept trade dollars. In doing so, buyers keep cash in their pockets, and sellers get new customers.

In a very real sense, the trade dollar is backed not only by the value of goods and services offered within the trade exchange, but also by the intentions and promises of the other members, who have agreed to transact with this alternate currency. The trade exchange's primary function is to give members as many trading opportunities as possible, and at the same time, account for these trade dollar transactions.

The Limits of Direct Trade

Direct trade between two businesses has an informality and simplicity that trade exchanges can't match. But it has its limits. Consider the following trade.

Let's take the case of "Sid the Sign Guy." Most of the signs Sid manufactures are interior signs. He also produces vinyl lettering that affixes to commercial vehicles. His business consists of 3,000 square feet, a drive-through entrance to accommodate vans and trucks, lots of fancy computerized sign-making equipment (bought and paid for), and five employees who are busy most of the time. There's one problem. His roof leaks.

Sid calls a roofer for a quote. The news is horrible. He needs a complete new roof. Cost: $10,000. Business is good, but not that good. Short of begging his banker for a loan or subsidizing his business with personal funds, what can Sid do?

Sid has an idea. What if he can *trade* with the roofer? Sid runs the scenario through his head. He has excess capacity, and computes his cost of vinyl and other raw materials at 30 percent. All his other costs are fixed: his payment to the bank, his labor, his yellow page advertising— he's paying those anyway. If he can just do the trade, his only out-of-pocket costs for doing $10,000 of signs for the roofer will be $3,000. He can handle that.

Sid approaches the roofer, named Ralph. Ralph the Roofer explains he doesn't need signs. If he was to do a trade, he'd do it with an orthodontist, because he's got two kids with crooked teeth. But no, he's all set on signs. Sid would have to spend cash.

Sid the Sign Guy is dejected. It rains badly the next week, all his equipment is flooded, his business is ruined, his wife divorces him, and he declares bankruptcy. Sid is last seen at a local filling station, asking for money, claiming he ran out of gas.

Breaking the Limits

But suppose Sid is a member of a trade exchange. The exchange facilitates Sid the Sign Guy trading with Ralph the Roofer. Through a trade exchange, Sid isn't going to do a direct trade with Ralph. Rather he's going to give him "trade dollars" that Ralph can spend with, you guessed it, Orville the Orthodontist!

Sid the Sign Guy has been selling to other members of the exchange, accumulating trade dollars in his account. All these customers have been *found business*. Sid recalled one customer who had driven from two counties over. He had explained he was in the septic tank cleaning business, and he, too, had filled idle time with new customers and earned trade dollars. Everyone, it seemed, was motivated to spend trade dollars with fellow members and conserve their cash.

def•i•ni•tion

Found business　A new customer for your business. Generally, you want to use barter to expand your business, and not have existing customers switch from paying cash to paying on trade.

Sid continued to make sales through the exchange. As his account got more and more trade dollars in it, he became a better spender. He learned to work closely with his trade broker, who apprised him of new members and opportunities. He spent his trade dollars to eat out, go to the eye doctor, and hire an accountant. None of his purchases had been large, until the roof.

When Sid discovered his roof leaked, he searched out Ralph the Roofer. Ralph's company performed the work, and then Ralph had Sid sign a trade draft which he sent to the exchange for credit. As Sid's account was debited $10,000, Ralph's was credited the same amount. Ralph spent $6,000 trade to get his kids' teeth straightened, leaving him with a $4,000 trade dollar balance.

Hey, This Is Money!

You're no longer silently pondering, are you? In fact, you're having an "Ah-ha!" moment. You're standing up and yelling, "Hey, this sounds like money!" It sounds like money because it is money.

Money in All Its Forms

As we saw in Chapter 1, money can take many forms. Colonists and Native Americans used wampum. Other societies have used sea shells and other objects as a means of keeping account. When cash became scarce in the 1920s, some used "Depression Dollars." Today, there are "community dollars" in some cities where folks swap babysitting services for lawn mowing, all on a point basis. The point is: when cash is tight, people seek out and invent new currencies.

Trade exchanges are like community dollars on steroids. Community dollars are great for what they do, exchanging personal services such as babysitting and mowing lawns. But they cannot help Sid the Sign Guy barter for a $10,000 roof. Only a trade exchange can pull off a deal like that. In fact, trade exchanges do much larger deals than that.

To sign up new members, to hire brokers, and manage the operation costs money. Nobody's going to do it for free. Trade exchanges make money by charging members an entry fee and by charging a commission to their members.

In Sid's case, he pays a 10 percent commission when he buys. That said, Sid did the following simple arithmetic to determine how much he had saved by trading:

Cost of goods doing $10,000 of signs:	$3,000
10 percent commission paid to exchange:	$1,000
Total out-of-pocket cash costs:	$4,000
Savings in cash:	$6,000

Why Spend Trade Dollars Instead of Cash?

If you're in business, you know the importance of cash flow. You need cash to pay your cash vendors. The utility company isn't going to take trade, nor is the company that holds the mortgage on your house. It behooves you to spend trade dollars whenever you can, because in an active exchange, trade dollars can be easier to obtain.

We just saw a scenario in which Sid the Sign Guy spent $10,000 trade with Ralph the Roofer. By seeking out and spending trade dollars with Ralph, Sid was able to retain $10,000 cash. But he still had a cost of goods and commission due to the exchange, so he actually had $4,000 cash out of pocket for the roofing repair.

Here's a rule of thumb: In the cash world, it's hard to get new sales but easy to spend the money. After all, when you spend cash, you don't have to ask the seller if he "accepts it." In the trade world, the reverse is true: it's easy to get the sale, but harder to spend. Yet, the motivation is always there for a savvy trader. Each time he spends trade dollars, he conserves cash, and at the same time, virtually guarantees himself a new customer from the trade exchange will walk through his door.

A Trade Exchange Manages the Currency

When a trade exchange begins, no one has any money. Not Sid, not Ralph, not Orville. If no one has any money, how can anyone buy? A trade exchange has two accepted ways of getting money into its members' hands:

- It can buy inventory from members for resale, or;
- It can allow members with in-demand products to spend in the negative.

If the trade exchange lets Sid the Sign Guy spend trade dollars he has not yet earned, it's a safe bet other members will at some point need signage, and the loan will be repaid. But what if the trade exchange loans $10,000 to Doug the Dog Psychiatrist? Chances are Doug will never get any business, even on trade. That means there's $10,000 out there, chasing goods and services that are valueless.

A trade exchange with a few hundred members could end up handling millions of dollars of cashless transactions, issuing credit and acting like a bank.

Barter and the IRS

Trade exchanges and the IRS have been buddies since August of 1982. That's when trade exchanges were recognized as third-party bookkeepers, same as banks, savings and loans, and other financial institutions. In fact, on the last day of March, as required by law, owners of trade exchanges must dress in the Official Banker Attire of gray pinstripe suits, and at 11:59 P.M., just before the official deadline, electronically transmit Form 1099-B to the IRS. Reporting is based on total sales for the previous year.

Barter Bits

According to the IRS, "a barter exchange is any person or organization with members or clients that contract with each other (or with the barter exchange) to jointly trade or barter property or services. The term does not include arrangements that provide solely for the informal exchange of similar services on a noncommercial basis."

Just as your bank must report the amount of interest earned, so must a trade exchange report the barter income of its members. It sends an aggregate sales total for corporations and individual sales for sole proprietorships. These are submitted using federal taxpayer ID numbers, or social security numbers. When you join a trade exchange, the sales representative asks you to sign Official Tax Nuisance Form W-9.

Let's go back to Sid the Sign Guy. He made a number of barter sales to different members of the exchange. Each time Sid made a sale, he deposited trade dollars into the trade exchange "bank." When he purchased the new roof, he withdrew those funds. In spending with Ralph the Roofer, Sid enjoyed a totally deductible expense. That's because the roof was a part of the building the business owned.

Not so with Ralph. He used $6,000 in barter to purchase orthodontic services. That's personal income. Ralph should include this on his personal tax forms.

Balance of Trade

If you join a trade exchange, or any third party who facilitates barter among members, and the representative does not ask you to sign a W-9, run for the hills. This individual is known as a "trunk trader," and is running an underground economy. When sales are not reported to the IRS, you're inviting an audit.

How Trade Dollars Are Transferred

By now, you're probably wondering how these cashless transactions happen. Exactly how did Sid the Sign Guy get trade dollars into the account of Ralph the Roofer?

The vast majority of money exists in a virtual world. It takes form in various types of accounts. These accounts can be checking accounts, savings accounts, mutual fund accounts, and more. Even the bank carries only a small percentage of deposits in actual cash. Trade dollars are the same. They exist in members' accounts. They exist as credits and debits.

Before Ralph the Roofer started work for Sid the Sign Guy, he verified his membership by asking to see a nonexpired membership ID card. He then called his trade exchange for an authorization number to get the okay to do $10,000 of work. He wanted to verify Sid was "good for it."

Balance of Trade

If a buyer is either delinquent on her cash fees to the exchange, or she's spending more than her established line of barter credit, the exchange might refuse to issue an authorization number, thus nixing the deal. The exchange is more likely to offer a larger line of credit to a business that it perceives as able to generate enough barter sales to pay back the trade dollar loan.

When Ralph the Roofer got the authorization number, he entered it on a trade draft that had been given to him by the trade exchange. Trade drafts are three-part, with one copy retained by the seller, one going to the buyer for his records, and one going to the trade exchange (sent by the seller).

A trade draft is always the "proof of the pudding" for a trade exchange. Disputes occasionally occur between members, and the trade exchange hates to play referee. If a buyer becomes dissatisfied at a later date and wants her trade dollars back, she's out of luck if she signed a trade voucher. She can no more get her trade dollars back from her trade exchange than dollars from her bank.

When Ralph sent a copy of the trade draft to the exchange, it debited $10,000 from Sid's barter account, and credited Ralph $10,000. Sid and Ralph each received a statement at the end of the month. Trade exchange statements are just like those from a bank, but they have two columns: one for trade dollars and the other for cash owed to the exchange.

Like a bank, trade statements are balance forward. That is, they transfer the ending cash and trade balances and transfer them to the beginning of the new month. In this way, Sid and Ralph can see what their trade balances are, and how much money they owe the exchange. Many exchanges allow their members to check their balances online, just like banks.

What People at Trade Exchanges Do

There are two primary jobs for the staff of a trade exchange. One is to grow the exchange, to sell memberships. The other is to "stir the pot," to broker deals and encourage buying and selling.

Brokers are the face and voice of the exchange to its members. They are on the phone, tracking down purchases, arranging deals, connecting buyers and sellers. Because it's not a perfect microcosm of the cash world, there is not a balance of types of members. Trade brokers are constantly trying to "spend out" those members with high balances and get trade dollars to those with low or negative trade balances.

Trade Tales
In some trade exchanges, a trade broker and salesperson selling memberships can be one in the same. But usually they're different people. The salesperson is expected to grow the membership by enlisting diverse businesses that engage in trading. Most exchanges charge an entry fee, from which the salesperson's pay is drawn.

Brokers must know something about all their accounts. They have to know gross margins, the problems of various businesses, and the challenges. Above all, they have to gain a sense of the needs of their customers. They have to know who to offer the golf equipment to, who might be interested in advertising on radio, and who can use a supply of water jugs.

In doing all this, brokers use the phone, the Internet, mass e-mails, newsletters, and face-to-face meetings over a cup of coffee. Some exchanges maintain a showroom as a place for members to put their wares on display for other members to buy.

Savvy members work regularly with the brokers to make the connections they need in order to make effective use of barter, to find the deals, and to seize opportunities.

All that activity helps keep an exchange active and economically healthy. It also helps to attract new members. Every business has attrition, and unless it's growing, it's not vibrant.

Some exchanges charge an entry fee; for others, new members join for free. The latter exchanges are content to get a new trader and the commissions from their trades.

The Value of a Trade Dollar

An economic system is able to function because of two principles: faith and trust. When you bought this book, you decided it was worth the asking price. But for the transaction to have occurred, the bookstore had to believe in the economic system. It had to have faith in the issuer of the money, and trust that the money could be re-spent. A trade exchange is built on the same foundation.

But that faith and trust the bookstore showed is based on a perceived value of the U.S. dollar. For much of its history, the dollar was backed by gold and silver, but now it is backed by the health and production of the U.S. economy. When the economy weakens, the dollar weakens.

In much the same way, the value of a trade dollar is based on the economy within the trade exchange. The trade dollar is tied to the U.S. currency, but its true value is in the goods and services offered by members of the trade exchange. When a trade exchange has few members, the value of a trade dollar is limited. When a trade exchange attracts numerous members offering a wide variety of goods and services, the value of the trade to a business owner increases.

A trade exchange not only keeps account of the trade dollars being spent, it also regulates those dollars as with any currency. It determines who can get a loan and who cannot. It is the president, Congress, chairman of the Federal Reserve, and the treasury secretary all rolled into one. If the trade exchange allows too many dollars into circulation, inflation and shortages can occur. Too few, and members won't have any trade dollars to spend.

However you slice it, members must have confidence the economy is being competently run. This is an ongoing job for the trade exchange.

The Least You Need to Know

♦ A trade exchange enables you to conserve cash by using trade dollars instead, which are easier to attract than U.S. dollars.

♦ Use barter to attract new business.

♦ A trade exchange manages an alternate currency.

♦ Barter is taxable. When you join a trade exchange, the sales representative will ask you to sign a W-9. If he or she doesn't, don't join the exchange.

Chapter 5

What to Look for in a Trade Exchange

In This Chapter

- ◆ Know who you can trade with
- ◆ Make sure the exchange's direction is positive
- ◆ Get to know the brokers
- ◆ Get the tools you need to succeed from your trade exchange

Trade exchanges come in all flavors. There are basics common to all. Yet, each exchange operates differently, with its own philosophy and set of strengths and weaknesses.

The number of members an exchange has is important, but not make or break. Some exchanges publish a large directory but don't have that many active traders. You want to make sure there are, or will be, enough traders in your own backyard.

Before joining, try to figure out where the trade exchange is headed. Look for local commitment to growth and excellence.

Then look at the quality of brokering that's offered. Regardless of membership numbers, a good broker can maximize your sales and purchases through barter.

There are bells and whistles to look for, too. A trade exchange should invest in ways its members can more easily transact. There are high-tech and low-tech ways of doing this.

Insist on a List

When you join a trade exchange, there are two simple questions to ask yourself: (1) Will the exchange be able to send me customers? and (2) Will there be places for me to spend my trade dollars?

Balance of Trade

When you look at a membership list, make sure the pie is not split too many ways. If there are 20 chiropractors listed, and that's what you do, the potential for additional sales, even on barter, is not very good.

Some exchanges don't even print a directory, nor is one offered online. Be wary. Don't settle for a long list of categories. You want to see the directory of actual members. Generally, the more members there are, the greater your opportunity, but there are caveats.

Lots of Members May or May Not Equate to Opportunity

Prospective members always figure they can tell how good a trade exchange is by weighing the directory to see how many members it has. This might be an indicator, but be skeptical. Trade exchanges are notorious for fluffing their directories by listing the same members under multiple categories. Check the list and then ask how many active traders are in your area.

Remember, the person trying to sell you a membership is most likely compensated by a sales commission. Make her earn her keep. Ask some tough questions.

One such question is, "Can I call some of the members before I join?" Of course, if the exchange makes 99 percent of its members happy, the salesperson will worry like crazy you're going to call someone in that 1 percent. That's why you should talk to a cross section of members and consider their responses as a whole.

Don't Be Marooned

Some membership bases are concentrated, while others are scattered over a wide geographical area. You're not going to drive 10 miles to get your car washed. Nor are you going to travel 30 miles to get your dog groomed. Be sure trade members are close enough for you to spend your trade dollars.

You'll also want to make sure you'll be able to attract sales, for the very same reason. Let's say you own a small diner, or you're a massage therapist, or you're a real estate agent, but you're in a town 30 miles from the barter action. Unless there are other members nearby, you might be waiting a long time for your first sale.

Although someone in your area has to be first, you don't want to be the "first and only." Make sure the trade exchange you join has made a commitment to a concerted sales effort in your area.

With every rule there is an exception. Perhaps you're off the beaten path, but you operate a quality destination restaurant. Or you own a marina or run a golf course. Or you sell jewelry. Traders will seek you out, and assuming you feel you can spend the trade dollars, by all means, welcome your new customers with open arms.

Sadly, a few trade exchanges don't care where they go to expand their membership bases. They're entirely sales driven and offer very little in the way of brokering. They'll sign up almost anyone they can, regardless of whether they'll be able to match them with buyers and sellers. If you're prepared to function as your own broker in an exchange like this, that's fine. But know you'll have to work a lot harder to spend your trade dollars.

Multiple Offices Can Be Important (or Not)

Joining a trade exchange with multiple offices can be pretty impressive. For one thing, it can show the exchange has staying power and credibility. For another, it's nice if you travel a lot.

But for most members, how big a trade exchange is around the country doesn't count for much, unless, of course, you have goals for wide product distribution. No matter what anyone says, the vast majority of trade happens within local areas, not city to city.

Sometimes what seems to be a smaller exchange might be able to offer more members you can actually trade with. If one exchange has 10,000 members but only 100 locally, and another has 200 local members but none anywhere else, it may make sense to join the "small" exchange.

Be sure to look at who you can sell to, and who you can buy from. Sometimes, all it takes is one or two members to make it all worthwhile.

Discover Secret Members

All trade exchanges keep certain members under wraps. There are a number of reasons some members go unpublished. When you join, make it a point to dig up some of these hidden gems.

You might ask yourself: "Why would anyone want to be unpublished?" There are a number of reasons. Usually, it's because some sort of hard good is involved, where the seller has to carefully monitor his or her barter sales. Or the seller might be able to offer part of his or her inventory on trade, but not all of it.

For example, a furniture store might not want to be published because it would invite every Tom, Dick, and Harry to swoop down and try to barter for everything in the store. This would leave the store trade rich, yet cash poor. By being unpublished, the owner can identify, say, a bedroom suite that has sat on the floor too long. He calls his broker to push that particular item.

Media, too, usually goes unpublished. A radio station doesn't want a client, who already spends cash, to flip through the directory, come across its listing, and exclaim, "Hey, I already advertise there. I'd like to switch my account to barter!" By choosing not to be published, the radio station can protect its cash, while getting the business of advertisers who had never spent a dime.

What you should know about a trade exchange goes deeper than looking at a list. It means asking your *sales rep* or your *broker* where the hidden gems are. With a little prodding, she'll tell you. This is valuable information as you register your requests with your broker in the coming months.

def•i•ni•tion

Sales rep, broker   In a trade exchange, a sales representative sells memberships to the exchange. The broker, on the other hand, helps to arrange trade deals between members of the exchange, particularly large deals.

Find Out Where the Exchange Is Headed

Make sure you look for a trade exchange that's headed in the right direction. This can often be ascertained by talking to the person in charge. Whether large or small, there should be someone local with a vested interest in the business.

If you're referred to the "main office" in another city, be concerned, especially if the brokers are located there, too. No matter what anyone says, your account cannot be effectively handled by a broker who is not even in your city.

Balance of Trade

From the mid 1980s to the end of the 1990s, one exchange, in a large metropolitan area, maintained a client base of about 10,000 members. Then it sold to a tech company that figured everything could be handled on the Internet. Brokering staff and local management was stripped. Within 10 years, the exchange became a shadow of its former self, with fewer than 500 members in its original area.

Look for a trade exchange that has a stable or growing membership base. There is attrition in all membership-based organizations, so a trade exchange has to constantly be out there signing new members.

Get In on the Ground Floor

Sometimes your best opportunity for joining an exchange lies in its infancy. Although you might not be certain of its long-term viability, by becoming a charter member, you can enjoy some real advantages. Remember, even the best exchange around started with no members.

Barter Bits

When you join a brand new exchange, you should be able to get in for free, or next to it. You also stand to get a lower commission and yearly dues. Your faith in the new exchange can be handsomely rewarded.

Before joining, try to figure out if the exchange has made a commitment to your business community. Look for an actual office, rather than just an Internet presence. Double check to make sure the exchange sends out 1099s, as required by law.

Look for other signs of professionalism such as a website, brochures, office staff, and reputation. Even if they can't yet show you a big fat directory, try to get a gauge of the exchange's future success. Then bet on the come, but do it sensibly. Don't do so much trade that it will be catastrophic if the exchange peters out.

Put a Pencil to Fees

What's the difference between paying a 10 percent commission and a 13 percent commission? Most members figure the answer is easy: 3 percent. Figure again. It's a 30 percent difference in the commission you pay. If you transact $20,000 of barter in a year, that's a $600 cash difference.

This is not to say that a 13 percent commission is unfair, but if you've got a 10 percent deal, that's even better. Some exchanges charge a commission on the buy, others on the sell. Still others charge on the buy and sell. Make sure the numbers make sense. Don't be afraid to negotiate, especially if you sell a product the trade exchange is looking for.

Also, make sure you don't get hit with unexpected fees. Know your monthly charges. Are they in cash or trade? What about a renewal fee?

Finally, some trade exchanges charge interest (in trade) on deficits. Make sure it's a reasonable rate, and remind your exchange that if it wants you to pay them when you're negative, maybe it should pay you when you're positive.

Look for a Good Broker

Although the list of traders is important, most prospective members become too enamored by it. They should still be asking a "who" question, but the "who" question they should be asking is, "Who is my broker?"

If you're contemplating joining an exchange, ask who will be assigned as your broker. If the answer is "no one," or "someone at the home office," it's unlikely that trade exchange will be able to help you grow your business.

When you talk to your broker, ask about the likelihood of getting new sales. How does he or she plan to promote your business? What is the broker's advice on whether your business should be published? What pitfalls should you look out for if you join? In short, your broker should have a basic understanding of your business: when you should trade, and what you should trade.

Barter Bits

Nothing beats a face-to-face. You can best size up a trade exchange by visiting its office. Introduce yourself to the owner or general manager. Talk to the brokers. As you get to know each other, your trading relationship will blossom.

Does the Exchange Offer What You Need?

Do this simple exercise. Open up your checkbook and assess where you're currently spending cash. See if the exchange can set you up with advertising, accounting services, signage, window washing, asphalt work, or anything that might pertain to your day-to-day operation. Then ask about trade opportunities within those categories.

Don't limit your inquiries. Ask the broker about other ways you might be able to spend trade. Where can you spend trade personally? What about vacations? Do they have that optical company you need? How about someone to mow your grass? In other words, assess your broker's ability to satisfy your needs, before you sign on the dotted line.

A Trade Exchange Is Defined by Its Brokers

If a trade exchange suffers from high broker turnover, its members suffer. Each time you're assigned a new broker, that person must go through a learning curve. Not only must he learn about you, but he's got to do the same with a couple hundred other businesses. It can take months before the broker can effectively match up buyers and sellers.

New brokers are initially "order takers" rather than "order getters." As they learn their client base, they tend to be unsure of who's trading and who is not. Overwhelmed by requests, they resort to dishing out phone numbers, rather than making calls on behalf of those making requests.

When you visit a trade exchange, look for its broker (or brokers) to be swamped. They should be melded with their phone and computer. They should confidently pull up members' accounts on their computer. They should make tons of outgoing phone calls, too. That shows they're selling stuff and that they're reaching out to build relationships.

Conservative or Wheeling and Dealing?

No two trade exchanges are alike. Each is a different culture, where the amount of trade activity is dictated by the philosophy of its management. When you consider joining a trade exchange, know what you're getting into.

Some exchanges are conservative in nature. That is, they purposely keep a tight rein on the amount of trade dollars in their system. In other words, they don't allow their members to spend what they have not yet earned. With fewer trade dollars "in circulation," it's harder to sell, but easier to spend. It's a matter of supply and demand. This can either work for or against you, depending on what you do.

Let's play out a scenario. You own a miniature golf course. Other members, with limited reserves of trade dollars, might not be compelled to buy from you. They don't have the trade dollars to spare. They're saving them for "needs," rather than "wants." If you're the miniature golf guy, and you're joining an exchange with a really tight currency, don't expect to do millions in sales. But when you do make sales, it will be easier to spend.

Trade Tales

An office machine dealer had successfully done business through a trade exchange for years. Although it had a fairly high cost of goods, it routinely spent its trade dollars for an assortment of like-kind goods and services. It was then approached by a competing exchange where members had large trade balances. The result was an influx of sales, totaling over $50,000. At first, the company was elated. Only later did it realize it was much harder to spend these trade dollars. It took the company three years to spend out.

Other exchanges fall on the opposite end of the spectrum. They have more trade dollars circulating within their systems. The result is members are more freewheeling with their spending. This can be advantageous if you own the miniature golf course: you'll attract more customers, and your cost of goods is zero. But if you sell appliances and your cost of goods is high, be careful. You don't want to get swamped with too much trade.

Look for Reasonable Pricing

If a trade system has too many trade dollars in members' hands, you'll know it. When there's too much currency in any economy, what happens? Prices rise. This happens with some trade exchanges, too.

Nobody expects a trade exchange to be a discount house. After all, there's always going to be someone in the cash world who will sell for less. Remember, too, that some high-priced items with narrow margins will rarely be available on trade, and if they are, they'll fetch a higher price. No matter. Overall, you want the prices in your exchange to be reasonable and not sky high.

Consider the Extras

You already know your exchange should supply you with a member directory. But an online one can be a nice convenience. Most exchanges have websites that let members access the directory and look up phone numbers.

Ideally, you'll be able to go online and look up your statement and transaction history. And when you're the seller, you'll be able to get an online authorization.

Look for periodic e-mails from your trade exchange, too. If you need sales, insist on being included. If you're in a buying mode, open up those e-mails to discover new opportunities.

> **Balance of Trade**
>
> Remember, the bells and whistles of an impressive web page cannot take the place of committed local management and talented brokers. The human touch counts the most.

Low Tech Can Be Good

The fact is a surprisingly large chunk of an exchange's membership rarely goes online. They're too busy running their businesses. These members value other means of communication, such as a monthly newsletter.

Some other exchanges send out monthly packets that include fliers from members, promoting their willingness to accept trade. Others even send out routine faxes to their members, knowing they're not going to get deleted by a spam filter.

A Barter Showroom Is a Place to Spend

Still other exchanges operate barter showrooms. Usually adjacent to the exchange's offices, the showroom is a convenient place to spend some of your trade dollars.

Don't expect any showroom to be equal to the department store at your local mall. Instead, you'll find a smattering of merchandise put there on consignment by fellow members. Don't judge the exchange entirely on the basis of its showroom, however. Good trade exchanges are better at putting together deals than they are at retailing.

Does Your Exchange Let You Meet and Greet?

Barter really cooks when you can meet fellow members. Look for an exchange that facilitates member introductions. Some exchanges conduct mixers, lunches, or social events.

Trade Tales

One exchange invited its members to enjoy a ballgame on a party deck for the local minor league team. Approximately 100 members showed up. Among those who attended were a doctor who performed vasectomies and, you guessed it, a man who wanted one. The arrangements were made the following week.

Some other exchanges coordinate elaborate trade shows in ballrooms or gymnasiums, especially before Christmas. Members sell their wares to attendees, also fellow members. Offerings can be anything from mink coats to video games. Whenever you're given the opportunity to meet other members, do it. You're likely to find a buyer or a seller.

Ask About Two Important Departments

As an exchange grows, it becomes necessary to compartmentalize some of its functions. If you're joining a large exchange, you may want to ask about two departments: (1) the travel department and (2) the media department.

A separate travel broker can be a real plus when it comes to booking a vacation or business trip. Accommodations are usually readily available on trade, but it takes a special person to keep it all straight. Ask about availabilities. Chances are you'll be able to spend your trade dollars to visit a sunny island in the Caribbean, or go skiing in Utah.

Balance of Trade —————————————

Trade exchanges offer travel, but they're not travel agencies. They usually have a nice selection of properties, but if you're looking for high-demand dates, you may be out of luck. Properties usually black out times they expect to be filled to capacity.

Larger exchanges sometimes have media departments also. Media can be the bread and butter of a trade exchange. Because it's a perishable inventory, much as an unsold hotel night, media is generally pretty available on barter. Ask about media opportunities and get to know this specialized broker.

The Least You Need to Know

◆ Assess a trade exchange by looking at its directory. But the "list" does not tell you everything. Some members are not active; others are unpublished.

◆ Find out where the trade exchange is trending. Local commitment and professional brokering are critical to any exchange.

◆ Trade dollars in most exchanges can be readily spent. Yet, this is not always the case. Before you join an exchange, know what you're getting into.

◆ Success in a trade exchange depends on professional brokering. Establish a relationship to be "in the know."

◆ Evaluate how easy it is to conduct transactions. There may be online directories and statements, or low-tech ways, such as mixers and trade shows.

Chapter 6

Making Barter Sales and Purchases Around the Country

In This Chapter

- ◆ Know how trade exchanges trade with one another
- ◆ Move excess inventories to other markets
- ◆ Trade an IOU to another exchange
- ◆ Learn how other exchanges can help you buy on trade

A trade exchange may be able to help you trade around the country. You'll want to know how they do this, so you can determine if you want to make intercity trading a part of your marketing plan.

You can move inventories or excess product if your broker barters them to other exchanges. Be sure to make the process as easy as possible.

But not all inventories need to be shipped. Some can simply be mailed in an envelope, in the form of scrip, gift certificates, or some other form of IOU.

Most exchanges have made arrangements so you can buy from others around the country. Hotels and restaurants are used by everyone. Depending on your business, however, you might want to barter for an inventory you can turn to cash. Or, you can obtain advertising to help you penetrate new markets.

Trade Exchanges Trade with One Another

The trade industry has for years envisioned a universally accepted trade dollar. This has not happened.

Yet, there are three ways exchanges make it possible for you to trade around the country:

- ♦ Belonging to a multioffice or franchised operation
- ♦ A direct trade agreement with another exchange
- ♦ Membership in a national association of exchanges

There are pluses and minuses for each, and it's a good idea to ask questions.

Multioffice Exchanges Can Open Doors

If your exchange is a part of a multioffice group or a franchised operation, you can automatically buy from and sell to other members, regardless of location.

If you join, ask about trading availability and if they maintain trading relationships outside their own system. The more you know about where you can trade, the better.

Exchanges Trade Direct with Each Other

Another way your local trade exchange might expand your universe of buyers and sellers is to create a reciprocal agreement with another exchange. Let's say your broker gets a $5,000 vacation package for you from an exchange in Florida. He will subsequently debit that amount from your account. And he will credit the exchange in Florida.

But let's say your exchange buys five more vacations, all worth $5,000. Your exchange now "owes" the one in Florida $25,000. That exchange may temporarily suspend sales until your exchange can sell something to Florida.

If the exchange you belong to is "in hock" with lots of other exchanges, it may work against you if you're trying to buy. But it can work for you if you're trying to sell.

A Trade Exchange of Trade Exchanges

The third way a trade exchange can help you open inroads in other markets is by being a member of a national association. These associations have developed a trade exchange whose members are all trade exchanges. This ostensibly allows members of any one exchange to trade with members of any in the system.

But there are limitations here, also. If an exchange gets too negative in trade, its ability to make purchases on your behalf are limited. You may end up getting lots of trade dollars you can spend within your local exchange, but not elsewhere.

Attract Customers from Around the Country

Many exchanges are equipped to help you sell to other markets. This is irrelevant if you own a local service company or provide a product that can't be shipped. But if you're a manufacturer, distributor, retailer, or liquidator, a trade exchange can help.

Let's say you sell snowboards and have successfully traded through your local exchange. You do more than retail. In fact, you have also purchased large inventories of snowboards at the end of the season and put them on the Internet.

Barter Bits

Sometimes a member of a trade exchange has a quality offering, but for some reason it hasn't sold. Maybe it's a car, boat, forklift, or piece of equipment. If you have something like this, tell your broker. It may sell quicker than you think.

But there's a problem. Your local exchange has 400 to 500 members, of which only a dozen or so ever hit the slopes. And you've already sold to them. So how can you increase your barter sales? Combine this with another fact of life: there are other trade exchanges out there that have members who snowboard, but they don't have any product to offer them.

Sit down with your broker. Explain that you've saturated the local barter market, and then ask him to push your snowboards to other exchanges. Don't worry, you won't have to join these other exchanges or pay additional fees. Your broker will make all the arrangements.

Give Your Broker Something to Pass Along

If your broker's on the ball, the first thing he'll do is call his colleagues at some of the other trade exchanges. They will, in turn, promote your snowboards to their members. A lot of information can be lost in the shuffle. That's why you'll want to design an attractive e-mail that can be forwarded by the other trade exchange to its members.

Have your broker ask if the other exchange could use a free sample. If so, ship it out. Nothing reminds a broker more of a product offering than something sitting in front of his nose.

Barter Bits

There's a reason you're bartering. It's because you have excess inventory you've been unable to sell for cash. In addition to giving your broker the marketing tools he or she needs to sell your product, be patient. Still, it's not a bad idea to be a squeaky wheel of sorts. Check in periodically with your broker to see how it's going.

Be Prepared to Fill the Order

As snowboards are promoted to members of other trade exchanges, be ready to field their members' phone calls and requests for information.

Because they're spending trade, most trade customers are more flexible. Still, treat them with the same respect you show cash customers. Get their orders out expeditiously, and once you satisfy them, they'll likely spread the word to their cash-paying friends.

Accounting for trade transactions from other exchanges requires special attention. Be sure to communicate with your broker throughout the process. Just because members from another trade exchange call you, it doesn't mean they are authorized by the other exchange to spend. Before shipping the product, call your broker, to make sure you get your trade dollars.

Balance of Trade

In trade transactions, the buyer typically pays for the shipping, in cash. Don't send out inventory without first getting a UPS or shipping number. Unfortunately, some buyers will spend their trade, and try to skip on the cash.

Large Inventories Can Move, Too

Maybe you have a semitrailer full of snowboards. Rather than selling them one by one, you'd like to trade the entire inventory. Not all exchanges are capable of handling these transactions, but a good many are.

Barter Bits

Here's a good way to see if your barter broker can sell large inventories to other exchanges. Ask him what large inventories he has successfully moved. Then ask about details relating to shipping and bills of lading. If you get a quizzical look, that exchange might not be prepared to transact big deals.

Give your broker as much information as you can, pertaining to model numbers, quantities, and how many can fit into a truck. The more information you can supply, the better. Be up front if your product is refurbished, discontinued, or lacks a warranty. Your broker will then be able to shop your offer to other exchanges, who in turn, will present it to their members.

It is entirely possible your snowboards will be purchased by someone whose business is snowboard related. For example, a ski resort that owns rentals would be an ideal candidate. But it's also possible the buyer could be some sort of liquidator or middleman.

> **Balance of Trade**
>
> If you sell a large inventory, make sure you don't end up competing against yourself. Ask where the seller plans to sell your product. If it's to someone you already do business with, back away from the deal.

Consider Trading an IOU

Let's say you don't sell snowboards; you sell cheesecakes. You're in a similar predicament. You need more trade dollars, but have saturated the local membership with cheesecake offerings. You're capable of shipping your cheesecake worldwide, but frankly, the potential for more barter sales seems to be limited.

Get with your trade broker and see if he or she can get another exchange interested in your cheesecakes. You can't exactly ship a truckload of cheesecakes to the other broker and have them land on his or her desk. Do this instead: have your broker get the other trade exchange to purchase, say, a $20,000 "block" of cheesecake credit. Then, you can simply create a separate ledger. As members from the other exchange call you with orders, you'll deduct it from the original balance.

> **Balance of Trade**
>
> When you're buying gift certificates, understand it's just like an IOU. It's only as good as the company that issued it. If you sit on a certificate for two years, and you try to redeem it after the issuer has gone out of business, your broker will probably not give you back your lost trade dollars.

You might also be able to sell $20,000 of cheesecake gift certificates to the other exchange. Then as they're redeemed, you account for them. The point is to create a system to keep track of what's left on the original balance.

Get Retail Instead of Wholesale

You've probably noticed a huge advantage. Normally, if a company sold $20,000 of cheesecakes in one swoop, it would have to price at wholesale. Not so in this example. Individual members from the other trade exchanges would not be buying in quantity, so they would expect to pay retail.

Trading Advertising and Travel

Maybe you would like to barter advertising or accommodations. Both lend themselves to trade with other exchanges. There are two big advantages: (1) there is little incremental cost in making additional sales and (2) there are no shipping charges.

Trading Advertising

Let's play out a scenario. You own a biweekly magazine whose area is national and whose target market is salespeople. It's a well-put-together magazine, but advertising revenue is down. Working with a well-connected trade exchange can help you fill up some space.

Offer a block of advertising to your trade exchange. Let's say it totals $50,000 in value. The exchange will first check to see if any local members would be interested in all or part. If not, an experienced broker can run the advertising opportunity by other trade exchanges. You now enjoy the prospect of attracting a whole new group of advertisers.

 **Balance of Trade**

The first rule of organized barter is: don't let it interfere with your cash business. Whenever you issue a block of credit or any type of promissory note, be sure to include the restriction that it cannot be bartered to a cash customer.

Trading Travel

Let's go with another example. You manage a resort and convention center in Florida. Your peak times are full, but overall, your occupancy rate is 70 percent.

How much business can a local trade exchange send you? After all, members in your own backyard are unlikely to take a vacation so close to home. The best plan of action is to sit down with your broker and ask about offering your excess rooms to other exchanges around the country.

Trade Tales

An exchange traded a block of hotel credit to another office. It resulted in a company trading for 100 rooms that otherwise would have been empty. The property traded a continental breakfast and some refreshments, but it was cash for lunch and dinner. It more than covered its out-of-pocket cash expenses for accommodating the group.

Chances are good your exchange will be able to promote your property to thousands of businesses that belong to other exchanges around the country. Some of those members may wish to book a family vacation. But there's another, greater potential. You might snag a booking for a company that wants to treat its employees to a vacation/training weekend. Just be sure you don't trade rooms that otherwise would go for cash.

Spending Trade with Other Exchanges

With your broker's help, you can spend trade dollars for thousands of goods and services far from home. The easiest to barter for, in descending order, are: (1) travel, (2) media, (3) inventories, and (4) special requests.

Travel on Trade

As we've seen, travel on barter is a natural. An otherwise empty room costs the owner of a hotel very little to fill. Trade exchanges therefore find it relatively easy to sign up and then trade accommodations.

However, a trade exchange is not a travel agency. It is inherently limited by the number of properties that barter. Also remember most hotels will black out certain dates they expect to be sold out. If you have no flexibility on when you're going, your broker has less of a chance of being able to satisfy your request.

Also, it helps to be flexible on location. If you say to your broker, "I want sun and fun, during the month of May," there's an excellent chance you'll go on the vacation of a lifetime. It is way better than saying, "I want Peoria, Illinois, on the night of May 14, off the interstate."

Don't always expect a cash equivalent price either. If you ask 10

> **Barter Bits**
>
> There are three components to travel. First you have airfare. Then there's the room charge. And finally, there's food. Aim for the accommodations and food. With fewer unsold seats, airlines don't usually barter.

guests at a hotel how much they're paying, they'll give you 10 different answers. That's because some of them went online and bought an unsold room right at the last minute. Others walked in off the street and paid rack rate.

The trade price will usually be somewhere in between, depending on the property. Remember, you already enjoy a lot of leverage when you spend trade dollars. You don't have to get the rock-bottom price to get a great deal.

Buy Media Around the Country with Trade Dollars

The next easiest thing to get from other exchanges is media. This is especially enticing if you own a (surprise!) hotel and resort. You can, in essence, trade empty rooms for outdoor, broadcast, and print media—to fill up those empty rooms!

Remember, if you currently spend cash with someone, it's unlikely you'll be able to trade for it. But if you're willing to deal with new sources, there can be huge opportunity. If you're seeking to promote beyond your local area, definitely ask your broker about trading with other exchanges.

Keep an Eye Peeled for Inventories

There are lots of inventories for which there is no cash buyer. In these instances, a seller will often consider an offer of trade dollars. If you and your broker are "in the know" concerning the offers of other trade exchanges, you could make hay. Sometimes it's a remarkably good inventory, sitting there because no one has been creative in finding a buyer. You can be that person.

Trade Tales
An alert broker came across an offer from another trade exchange. It was three semis full of decking, in a storage yard in the middle of nowhere. The broker managed to get a hold of the specs, and it was gold. He bought it from the other exchange at a discounted price and offered it to his member, who doubled his money, in cash!

Some outstanding deals lie dormant because of two issues: (1) inability to conduct a visual inspection of inventory and (2) shipping. Most members are simply too distracted or impatient to work with their broker to coordinate the details.

Balance of Trade

When trading with a member of another exchange, someone may suggest you actually join that organization. Don't. Your exchange's lifeblood is commissions. If you join the other exchange, bad blood could result.

Remember, in the barter world, the buyer typically pays for shipping. You don't want to get stuck with a shipping bill for a distressed inventory that ends up being too distressed. Do your due diligence.

Work with your broker to coordinate shipping. There's a vast difference in cost among shippers, so it's a good idea to get a number of quotes. Also, keep in mind that some shipping might be available on barter. Don't overlook these opportunities.

Find Special Requests

If you can't find an item you want in your trade exchange, it always makes sense to call your broker. Sometimes another exchange has exactly what you're looking for. Just as your exchange might be top heavy with snowboards or cheesecakes, another exchange might be long on something you're looking for, say, a gas grill.

Your broker may find it difficult, however, to search high and low for one item for one member. She has only so many hours in a day. If she can't find it within a reasonable period of time, it does no good to bug your broker. Sometimes cash is the only alternative.

The Least You Need to Know

- Trade exchanges work in different ways to trade with one another. If your exchange is not a part of a group, find out how they implement intercity trading.

- Discover new markets by having your broker promote your business to other trade exchanges. Be sure to develop a system of handling orders.

- Sometimes, you can sell another exchange a block of credit redeemable at your business, redeemable at retail.

- Purchasing opportunities abound with other exchanges. Work through your broker for travel, media, inventories, and special requests, some of which you can turn to cash.

7

What Makes a Good Trader?

In This Chapter

♦ Following the exchange's rules

♦ Treating fellow members fairly

♦ Paying your bills—barter isn't free!

♦ Using common sense and empathy

It benefits you to be a fair trader. Success in a trade exchange depends on reciprocity—between you and the exchange, and between you and your fellow members. Fair traders get "the good stuff" from their brokers. They are apprised of opportunities others are not. Here's how to stay on the good side of an exchange and your fellow traders.

Abide by the Exchange's Rules

A trade exchange is busy signing new members, putting trades together, managing the currency, and accounting for transactions. Even a modest-sized trade exchange can process $10 million of barter each year. To juggle these tasks, your trade exchange must maintain order. It must also standardize procedures having to do with recording transactions and issues dealing with fairness. You want to conform to these standards.

You know some business owners who, no matter what, always try to take advantage of the other guy. All trade exchanges have rules pertaining to fair play so some members don't take advantage of others. Breaking these rules can lead to short-term gain, but long-term losses.

It can be tempting to pay your trade exchange "next month" instead of now. Not paying your transaction fees invites your trade exchange to devalue you. In doing so, it will likely offer you less service, along with less accessibility to the hard goods everyone values.

Yet fair trading cannot be defined just by reading a rule book. Common sense must prevail. You've got to treat your fellow members fairly and with empathy. Do this and they'll treat you the same.

Trade Transactions Are Serious Business

Just because it's not cash, some of your fellow members deal with trade dollars in a cavalier manner. They treat trade dollars as "funny money." Trading can be fun, but it's not "funny."

> ### Trade Tales
>
> A former member of a trade exchange in Ohio went on a spending spree, charging over $4,000 trade in one month at 13 restaurants, taverns, and entertainment venues. Incredibly, he did this without ever presenting a membership card; he was just a good fast-talker. In truth, the member's card had been revoked for not having trade dollars and being delinquent in transaction fees. This put the trade exchange in a difficult spot with some of its best clients. By deciding to not honor the sales, it created a rift with a number of its members who had made the ill-advised sales.

One way to trade unfairly is to not follow the rules and procedures when transacting. Members are supposed to identify themselves with a valid, unexpired membership card. Yet some are careless in not carrying it; others don't have a card because it's been revoked. Sellers are playing with fire when they fail to ask for a valid, unexpired ID card. They also stand the chance of getting stuck when their goods walk out the door.

Check to Make Sure

There's another component to making sure trade transactions are authorized. It's the authorization number. When a buyer approaches a seller, he should not only show a current ID card, but the seller should call the exchange to get an authorization number, once he knows the amount of the pending sale.

Trade exchanges have different rules pertaining to authorization numbers. Sometimes it's required on all purchases over a set amount, say, $50. In other cases, it's required for all transactions, regardless of the amount.

Some exchanges offer an automated service 24/7. Whatever practice your exchange uses, be sure to follow protocol. You not only protect yourself, but you also avoid getting into a dispute with the trade exchange's management.

Napkins Are for Wiping Your Chin

You'd be surprised how many members think it's fair to ignore the proper paperwork when it comes to transacting with fellow members. Instead of using an approved three-part trade voucher, some members use scraps of paper, or even the backs of napkins.

This usually works and no one gets hurt. But what happens when there's a dispute a month later? Did the buyer, in fact, authorize the transfer of trade dollars? Remember, a signed trade voucher is "proof of the pudding." If there isn't one, there is no proof. It puts your trade exchange in an unfair situation, having to decide who's right between two of its members who can't agree on a price.

It's also not fair to turn in your trade vouchers late. Most trade exchanges guarantee a signed, authorized trade slip will be honored for up to a week, or maybe a month, after the transaction. But what happens when the seller sits on the trade slip?

> **Trade Tales**
>
> A contractor who was a member of a Florida trade exchange didn't pay much attention to his statement because he "always had enough trade to spend." Yet, shoddy procedures resulted in the member discovering he had not sent in vouchers for contracting work he had completed *three years* earlier! The vouchers totaled over $5,000 trade dollars, from six different buyers. The problem was two of the buyers were no longer in business, and one more didn't have any trade dollars available to spend. When three of these transactions weren't approved by the trade exchange, he got upset and nearly quit.

Be sure to send in completed trade vouchers to your exchange in a timely manner. Remember, just because a buyer has the trade dollars in his account right now doesn't mean she'll be good for it six months from now.

Don't Recycle Barter Scrip

In Chapter 4, I told you how trade transactions don't always happen with a three-part trade voucher. Sometimes a trade exchange issues "scrip." Scrip takes the form of certificates representing, say, $5 or $10 increments. Businesses that accept scrip are sometimes listed on the back of the scrip certificates. In other cases, people who have received scrip can find out who honors it by looking at a specially issued directory or going online.

Scrip is issued by the trade exchange so members can give trade dollars to people who are not members. You can give scrip to anyone, even your paperboy at Christmas. He might spend it at the pizza joint, for example. The pizza joint is then supposed to send it back to the trade exchange to receive credit.

The operative words are "supposed to." What happens when the pizza place stockpiles all the scrip it gets, from the paperboy and other recipients of scrip? Then he bundles it together and spends it with the pressure washer, who turns around and spends it with the dry cleaner?

Passing along scrip is obviously a way some members avoid paying the exchange a commission. This is not recommended, not only because it's not fair business, but it will ultimately backfire. The exchange will find out about it. Your broker won't be happy, and you won't get the good stuff.

Play Fair with Other Members

Most of a trade exchange's rules pertain to how members treat one another. They are not to overcharge, they shouldn't go part cash except under certain exceptions, and they must make their goods readily available to other members unless they're on "standby." Enforcing these provisions among hundreds of members can be a daunting task.

Most trade exchanges continually battle overcharging on the part of a few of their members. Members are sometimes tempted to overcharge because they might offer a product that is in high demand, or they're the only one selling it on barter. Whereas overcharging is sometimes condoned (see the concept of "parity" in Chapter 9), it is not acceptable to arbitrarily add a surcharge because it's on trade.

Overcharge and know this: if your trade exchange finds out about it, it won't come to bat for you when you encounter the same thing. Nor will you find out about the unpublished offerings every exchange has, but doesn't tell everyone. Still worse, you run the risk of actually being thrown out of your trade exchange.

Part Cash, Part Headache

Most trade exchanges have rules that define when a member can ask for *part cash*. While these exchanges recognize the occasional need for some sellers to charge part cash in certain circumstances, part cash should not routinely be expected.

def•i•ni•tion

> **Part cash** When a seller splits what he or she charges in a barter transaction to part trade dollars, part real cash. The practice is frowned upon by trade exchanges.

Trade Tales

A Connecticut trade exchange had a wholesale food purveyor selling to restaurants on trade. It allowed a part cash component because the wholesaler had an extremely tight gross margin, around 10 percent. The trade exchange went along with a program where the restaurants paid part cash. The restaurants were, in fact, thrilled with the arrangement.

Deep down, everyone selling through a trade exchange would like to receive enough cash dollars to cover "his nut" or out-of-pocket costs. By the same token, everyone wants to spend at 100 percent barter. Clearly, if everyone charged part cash, there would be no full trade opportunities when purchasing.

Trade exchanges diligently police part cash transactions. They do so because if buyers encounter part cash when they try to buy, they'll be more likely to do the same when selling. This can become a cancer if the exchange doesn't pay attention. Don't be a part of your trade exchange's problem. Sell at full trade, and you'll get full trade in return.

Be Available for Trade

When you join a trade exchange, one of the rules is to generally make your goods and services available to other members. Yet, certain members make a habit of constantly being unavailable. These members are known as contractors.

If you're a contractor, we're not talking about you personally. We're talking about *other* contractors that want to buy stuff on trade, but when someone wants to buy from them, they don't return their calls.

Saying you're open to accepting trade, and being available, is one rule you don't want to break. Nothing exasperates your trade broker more than when you make him or her look bad by being continually unavailable.

Whatever business you're in, if you can't afford to trade fairly, then don't trade. Your trade exchange might not be thrilled with your decision, but you won't have burned any bridges, either.

Treat Your Trade Exchange Right

Part of being a fair trader is treating your trade exchange the same way you would like to be treated. To that end, there's one rule that is at the top of every exchange's list. It's the one forbidding direct barter among members. If two members of a trade exchange have a preexisting trading relationship, that's one thing. But if a member peruses the directory and then approaches members with the expressed purpose of conducting direct barter, this will likely enrage the trade exchange.

The lifeblood of a trade exchange is its transaction fees. These fees can range from 10 to 15 percent. When a member trades directly with another member, it avoids those fees. If the trade exchange finds out, it will quite possibly ruin the relationship. At the very least, it's a great way to go to the "bottom" of the list.

Balance of Trade

Do not barter directly with another exchange member. Two members purposely did a direct trade in Pennsylvania, totally bypassing commissions on a $16,000 transaction. The exchange owner found out about it and demanded a commission from each member. The members complied.

Create a Win-Win

It's easy to see how some members are tempted to "break the rules" by direct trading. Let's face it. A commission of a few thousand dollars is a significant amount. Instead of trying to bypass the system, it's a better idea to work within the system and to call your trade broker.

Trade Tales

A trade exchange in Michigan secured an inventory of chairs worth $90,000 for one of its members, a nonprofit corporation. Shipping was going to cost $4,000. If the exchange charged its customary 10 percent commission, along with the shipping charge, the deal wouldn't have happened. Instead, the parties negotiated a reduced commission of $6,000. This made the deal possible.

A frank conversation and negotiation probably makes winners of you both. When deals get really large, most trade exchanges do a little give and take. They don't advertise this, but many sharpen their pencils on their commissions.

Make an offer. If you've got an especially large transaction pending, and the commission is going to be $5,000, tell them you want to pay half. Chances are your commission will be a lot less than if you had said nothing. And you wouldn't have had to break the rules to get it.

Don't Play One Exchange Against Another

In some markets, there is more than one trade exchange. There is nothing wrong with joining more than one, but if you do, don't leverage one exchange against the other. In the long run, this will probably get you in trouble with both.

Barter Bits

In the Phoenix area, there are a total of five trade exchanges. In Toronto, there are 12. Yet, in some cities with over a million people, there are none.

Here's what some members of multiple trade exchanges do. Let's say they need an excavator to complete a project worth $8,000. They submit the request to their broker in Trade Exchange A. Then they give the same request to Trade Exchanges B, C, and D. They now have four brokers working on the same project. In fact, the brokers are likely calling the same excavators, who may also be members of several exchanges.

The member who made the multiple requests usually goes with the first broker who put the deal together. But what about the other three brokers, who are still toiling away? Does he even bother telling them he already found what he was looking for?

This tactic might work for awhile, but it won't pay off in the long run. Once a broker discovers he has been used and abused, the next time that member makes a request, guess what? His request gets second priority! It gets conveniently buried on his broker's desk.

The Equivalent of Credit Card Juggling

Just as some people can't resist having 10 credit cards in their pockets, others can't resist joining a bunch of trade exchanges either. There's nothing inherently wrong with having 10 credit cards, as long as you pay them off. There's nothing wrong with joining 10 trade exchanges either, as long as you pay them off—that is, as long as you're not negative with each of them.

For a trade exchange to function, some members must have negative trade balances, just as others have to be positive. The fact is, after you have established a history of making sales, your trade exchange might extend you a barter "line of credit." In other words, you could be allowed to spend in the negative.

Trade Tales

One company that installed windows and doors was a member of six exchanges, four in one market. It was negative with all of them, totaling $150,000 of indebtedness. Facing cash and barter obligations, the business had to protect itself from its creditors through Chapter 11 bankruptcy. Thankfully, the business recovered and was able to pay back the trade dollars owed.

Let's say you're substantially negative with Trade Exchanges A, B, C, and D. At some point, you won't be allowed to go any deeper. Unable to spend, the exchanges will continue to send you customers who expect you to accept trade dollars. You will have mortgaged your future by overspending in the present. Now you're paying the piper. Trade dollars aren't free.

Negotiate Your Entry Fee

Being a fair trader doesn't mean you go along with everything your trade exchange suggests. For one thing, you're still playing fair if you negotiate your fees.

There are three types of fees likely assessed by your trade exchange. There's the entry fee, monthly fees, and the transaction fees or commissions. Trade exchanges won't tell you this, but each fee can be negotiated.

If you're considering joining a trade exchange, it's a good idea to call the highest possible person on the totem pole. He or she can give you the most latitude in your sign-up fee. Although some exchanges don't even charge a sign-up fee, most do. However, they consider the sales department a break-even affair. That is, virtually all the money generated by entry fees goes to pay the sales staff. The exchange's primary interest is getting new traders.

Most exchanges also assess a monthly fee. Or they may charge you a renewal after one year. Sometimes these fees are in cash; other times it's in trade dollars. Usually, they are in the range of $20 or $30 per month. This might not sound like much, but taken over time, it adds up. You're fair in asking for a deal.

If you can't get the exchange to waive these fees, see if they'll convert them to trade dollars. You have nothing to lose by asking.

Should You Negotiate Your Transaction Fees?

Yes, negotiating your transaction fees is totally fair. But you should know that much of your success in doing so hinges on your product offering. If you're a financial consultant and the exchange already has five other financial consultants, it has little motivation to cut the commission you pay on transactions. But if you sell something the exchange either doesn't have or has in a limited supply, that's a different story. Your business represents increased trade volume for the exchange, not just redistributed trade volume.

There's another way anyone can fairly negotiate fees. If you want to shave a point or two off your commission, ask your trade exchange if they'll put you on auto-pay with your credit card. If your exchange knows it will never have to chase you down, it will probably give you a deal.

If you negotiate your fees too low, however, you run a risk. Let's say there's one new garden tractor available in the entire exchange. It's springtime and the grass is growing. Your exchange can sell it to any of 50 members. Who do they call? The member who negotiated a 5 percent fee, or someone paying 10 percent?

Unless you're perceived as a fair and valuable trader, it probably won't be you. Fairness on commissions is a two-way street. Both parties have to make money.

Stay Current

Fair play in barter means paying your bills. Trade exchanges are in some respects not in the "barter business" as much as they are in the cash fees business. They understand the value of barter, but are the first to understand "cash is king."

The most important person at your trade exchange is your broker. Your broker's salary is based on the payments you make. If you fall behind on your fees, and your broker doesn't get paid, who do you think will get the best service, you or someone else?

If you do somehow fall behind on your cash fees, there is a way out. And it doesn't involve hiding or avoiding phone calls. Call your broker at your first opportunity. Work out a payment plan and stick to it.

> ### Trade Tales
>
> Years ago, when a fledgling trade exchange suffered a computer crash and was unable to send out statements for three months, one member helped out by actually *prepaying* his cash fees, to the tune of $5,000. This member is still on top of the trade exchange's list when it comes to "getting the good stuff."

Your trade exchange will still consider you to be a fair trader, especially if you continue to make trade sales to other members. This at least generates other cash fees for the trade exchange.

Follow the Golden Rule

It makes sense to treat your fellow members as you would have them treat you. Not only is this fair trading, it's also smart trading. Being a fair trader goes beyond following each and every bylaw. It means using common sense and having empathy for your fellow members.

Sometimes members who have just joined don't have a sense of how the barter game should be played. They inadvertently offer deep discounts, thinking this is the road to success.

> **Balance of Trade**
>
> Belonging to an exchange doesn't mean you can trade every job. A screen printer joined a trade exchange in Pennsylvania. He was immediately approached by another member who talked him into slashing his price on a large order. On a $24,000 trade sale, the screen printer had over $20,000 cash tied up in the shirts. The screen printer quickly learned that in the future, he could afford to trade some jobs, but not others.

Fair trading means allowing other members to enjoy a fair margin. If you dicker down to the bare bone, the seller might sell to you once, but never again. If you do the same with other members, you'll quickly find your purchasing opportunities limited, because a trade exchange's membership base is also limited.

Understand it's fair for the radio station to tell you it can't trade the week before Christmas. Know the resort hotel is on firm ground when it says it cannot trade the New Year's Eve gala, when it expects to sell each and every ticket for cash. And common sense dictates you don't swarm a restaurant that has only 40 seats with a party of 20 on a Saturday evening. In short, fair trading means allowing other members to protect their cash business.

Trade Tales

A high-end restaurant with an extensive wine list joined a trade exchange in Michigan. The wait staff was trained to sell bottles of wine for patrons to take home. When a trade customer came in and was similarly pitched, he obliged and took away two cases of fine wine. The server thought he did a great job, until the next morning, when the owner discovered his reservoir had been depleted to satisfy the thirst of just one trade member, who really knew better.

Springs Are for Mattresses

You put springs in a mattress. You don't "spring" trade on an unsuspecting seller. Not letting the seller know you're on trade, and then hammering out your very best cash price, defeats one of the core purposes of organized barter—for the seller to get a fair price.

You should always identify yourself first as a member of trade. In many instances, trade has to be pre-approved by a specific person, usually the owner. In doing so, he might not have to pay a commission to a sales-person, thus making trade possible. Or maybe only certain inventory can be sold on trade. There may be other restrictions or limitations. Either way, springing trade on members is unfair, and in the long run, will not get you what you want.

Here's a Tip: Tip!

Most traders are good tippers because they know many people in service industries depend on tips for their livelihoods. They also enjoy the advantage of not having to spend cash. Yet, there's always someone who ruins it for everybody else. If just one trade member stiffs a server at a restaurant, you can bet the owner will hear about it. This reflects on the trade exchange and can even impact the owner's willingness to barter.

If you give trade dollars to employees, make sure they know what is expected of them. Let them know they should tip at least 20 percent to servers, drivers of limos, hair stylists, and massage therapists. Remember, servers are not members of the trade exchange, so a tip in the form of trade dollars doesn't work.

Your Broker Is a Not a Telepath

It's never fair to change your trading status without telling your broker. Let's say you want to go on standby status, or not accept any more trade sales until you've had an opportunity to do some purchasing. If you just stop trading and don't tell anyone, your broker will continue to send you business, which you'll have to refuse.

This is clumsy for you, a waste of time for the buyer, and counterproductive for your broker. This also makes your broker look bad in the eyes of other members who were sent on a wild goose chase.

The Least You Need to Know

◆ Follow a trade exchange's rules; otherwise, as a member you can inadvertently invite chaos. Trade dollars and the rules governing their usage should not be treated in a more cavalier manner than cash.

◆ The better you treat your trade exchange, the better it works for you.

◆ An exchange's fees can be negotiable, saving you cash. But you have to begin the negotiation.

◆ Fair trading leads to profitable trading.

8

Maximize Profit, Minimize Taxes

In This Chapter

- ◆ Too much in trade sales can be costly in taxes
- ◆ Trade purchases can be deductible
- ◆ Barter strategies to minimize taxes
- ◆ Playing too loose with direct trade

Sometimes when people talk about trade exchanges and barter, the matter of taxes gets all lopped together. They fail to make a distinction between one-on-one barter and organized trade exchanges. The uninformed hears the word "barter" and figures it's all a part of the "underground economy." It's true that some people finagle the government out of billions of dollars of taxes by direct trading. For example, a house painter trades with a dentist, and both parties fail to report any income.

Trade exchanges are different.

Trade dollars are accounted for, and taxed, in exactly the same manner as cash. The Internal Revenue Service (IRS) considers a trade dollar equal to cash for income purposes. But it must also equate trade dollars to cash when it comes to expenses. With proper planning, trade dollars don't have to work against you at tax time. In fact, they can even help you minimize taxes. Not like the painter and the dentist did, but by using trade dollars to generate write-offs, depreciation, and donations.

Finally, some people mismanage accounting of trade dollars and invite audits, penalties, and interest. Others, not members of trade exchanges, cheat the government out of billions of dollars of tax revenue each year. However you trade, it's best to do it above board.

Be Aware: Too Many Trade Sales Can Cost You in Taxes

Remember, when you conduct a sale through a trade exchange, it's just like cash, at least from an accounting perspective. If you make a sale for $5,000 barter dollars, it's the same as if you deposited that amount in the bank. Let's say you make another $5,000 sale, and another, and yet another. You have $20,000 trade dollars and, oops, it's December 31. The year is over.

So what are the tax ramifications? Not good, unless you have offsetting expenses or write-offs in the cash world. Think about it. What is your tax obligation if your business has money in the bank that it didn't have in the previous year? It's no problem if it's cash, because, after all, you have the cash to pay your tax liability. But if you're trade rich at the end of your tax year, you could end up being cash poor.

Most businesses plan to make a profit, but not so much that Uncle Sam and the governor get it all. That's why, if you've had a really good year, you probably go out and buy a piece of equipment, write off an old debt, or perhaps pay yourself a bonus. Getting caught with a ton of trade dollars at the year's end could show you making a large profit, but with little cash on hand to pay the taxes.

At the end of every tax year, the average trade exchange sees a flurry of activity from members who are eager to expense out some of their trade dollars. Members sometimes go on sprees, sometimes pre-purchasing advertising, printing, or other needed services.

Balance of Trade

Remember, if you purchase goods or services on trade before you have actually received them, if the seller doesn't make good or goes out of business, don't expect the trade exchange to bail you out by reversing the transactions. Make sure the seller is reputable before authorizing a transfer of a significant amount of trade dollars.

Plan your trade income, and limit it if necessary. Better yet, make strategic barter purchases that you can write off before the end of the year. If your trade balance is on the high side, approach the end of the year with an eye toward making purchases of advertising, equipment, and maintenance, or any needed item that can be written off.

Get an Accountant Who Understands Trade

One way to make sure you properly plan your trade sales and purchases is to find yourself an accountant who understands the nuances of a trade exchange. It's amazing how many tax professionals get flummoxed when presented with trade dollars. They sometimes think it will mean more work for them, or they over-think it. Or they heard somewhere that people who barter are more likely to be audited.

Barter Bits

No one is ever audited solely because they're a member of a trade exchange. They run the risk of being audited, however, if they totally ignore trade dollars when they prepare their taxes, as these numbers have been electronically reported to the IRS by the trade exchange. All members should routinely incorporate trade dollars income, and expenses, into their regular financial and tax reporting.

If your accountant doesn't understand trade, find one who does. Call your trade exchange for a list of accountants and CPAs who are members. They'll help make sure you take full advantage of barter opportunities, as they help you balance your trade income and expenses.

Sometimes businesses visit their accountant only when taxes are due or there's some emergency. Make a habit of regularly sitting down with your bookkeeper and going through the statements you receive from your trade exchange. Together you will be able to identify your purchases that are deductible.

There has been some disagreement as to whether the commission you pay to the trade exchange is always deductible. If it's on the sale, there's no problem. It's a cost you incur for getting a new customer. If it's on the buy, and for a personal purchase, it could be argued that it's not consistent for your company to pay the commission.

Pay Yourself Trade by Creating a Sub-Account

It's amazing how many times new members balk at the prospect of spending trade "personally." They somehow think barter purchases have to be relegated to business-related purchases. But isn't payroll a legitimate business purchase? In fact, isn't payroll, specifically your own payroll, the reason you're in business to begin with? And if you can take a trade dollar out of your company, rather than a cash dollar, doesn't that make sense, too?

Again, let's compare trade dollars to cash. If you own a business, and you decide to buy a pizza for your family, you don't pull out the company's checkbook to pay for it. Instead, you'll probably pay for it with a personal check or debit card. In the cash world, when you give yourself a paycheck, funds are transferred from your company account into your personal account. That way, your pizza doesn't get mixed up with your office supplies.

You can do the same with your trade dollars. Maintain an account for your business, but also ask your trade exchange to create a sub-account with your name on it, under your social security number, into which trade dollars can be transferred. As an employee of your own company, you periodically transfer trade dollars into this new account, as needed.

Pay Uncle Sam and the Governor

A sub-account has your name on it, and your social security number. When you pay yourself by transferring trade dollars into this account, you are subject to the same withholding obligations as when you pay yourself cash. In other words, you should build it into your existing taxable income. This will be reflected later when your company issues a *W-2 tax form* to you personally.

Since you are already reporting trade dollar income on your W-2 form, there will be no need for your trade exchange to double-up and report the same numbers on a *1099 form*. Your trade exchange has paperwork you can complete so that it won't be obligated to send you a 1099 form on the same earned income that was already reflected on your W-2.

> **def•i•ni•tion**
>
> **W-2 tax form** The form prepared by an employer and given to an employee listing wages earned during the year, along with federal and state taxes that are withheld, along with social security tax information. This information is also submitted to the IRS.

> **def•i•ni•tion**
>
> **1099 form** Similar to a W-2 but meant to report various types of income other than wages, salaries, and tips. If your company issues you a W-2, it cannot also issue a 1099. A 1099 is tendered for an independent contractor, nonemployee, or other types of vendors.

Don't Go Hog Wild Spending Trade Personally

Some members are tempted to go on a spending spree when they join a trade exchange. This is fine, *if* their business can afford it and *if* they have the cash to cover their taxes. Consider the case of a member who has a taxable income of $150,000. That puts him in a 28 percent tax bracket. But now he takes an additional $50,000 of trade income. This jumps him into the 33 percent tax bracket. He must pay this rate not only on his trade income, but also on each dollar he earned!

Putting off is not the answer either. Some members are tempted to create a sub-account for themselves, but never transfer trade dollars into it from the master account. In other words, this member's personal account is perpetually "in the negative." He doesn't deal with the eventuality of income because it's a "loan."

Balance of Trade

Every rope has an end. If you borrow money, or trade dollars, from your company and never pay it back, the IRS may at some point declare the loan as income, with taxes and penalty immediately due.

It is okay to borrow from your company, but if it's a loan, it has to come due at some point, and not 100 years from now. You must also pay your company a reasonable interest rate. Otherwise, the IRS could construe your personal sub-account that is perpetually negative as a sham, a way of simply avoiding income tax.

Barter Strategies That Can Minimize Taxes

Because trade dollars are governed by the same accounting procedures as cash dollars, they can also be used in the same ways to shield income. A savvy trader not only finds barter purchases that are related to her business, but she also digs deeper. She digs into capital purchases, real estate, and charitable giving.

Let's contrast two buyers of copy machines. They both own restaurants. One is not a member of a trade exchange; the other is. They both need identical copy machines. The cash buyer scours the Internet and finds his machine for $7,000 cash dollars. The trade member gets hers for $10,000 trade dollars. Who got the best deal?

Someone not steeped in barter is likely to think it's obvious: the buyer who spent the $7,000 got the best deal. After all, that was the lowest price. But let's take a closer look.

Remember, the trade customer didn't really spend $10,000 cash dollars. She spent what she had *into* $10,000 of restaurant meals, or about $3,000 cash (assuming a 30 percent food cost). Add in a 10 percent commission to the exchange ($1,000 cash dollars), and the trader still spent only $4,000 cash for her copier. This is a way better deal than her cash counterpart, who spent $7,000 in cash.

But it gets even better. Don't forget, the trader has a receipt for $10,000 dollars. She's got a larger number to start with on her depreciation schedule. It's true that Uncle Sam is always tinkering with tax code, especially depreciation schedules. But one thing is clear. *Section 179* of the IRS code is going to be around for a while.

def•i•ni•tion

Section 179 This section of the U.S. Internal Revenue Code lets a taxpayer deduct the cost of certain types of property as an expense, rather than requiring the property become capitalized and depreciated. Section 179 limits this to tangible property having to do with conducting business, not real estate.

Because depreciation schedules are totally fun, let's run them for our two buyers: the first for $7,000 in cash, and the second for $10,000 in trade.

Depreciation for $7,000 Cash Purchase

Year	Depreciation	Net value
1	$1,167	$5,833
2	1,400	4,433
3	1,400	3,033
4	1,400	1,633
5	1,400	233
6	233	0

Depreciation for $10,000 Barter Purchase

Year	Depreciation	Net value
1	$1,667	$8,333
2	2,000	6,333
3	2,000	4,333
4	2,000	2,333
5	2,000	333
6	333	0

The business that spent $10,000 in trade, rather than $7,000 in cash, not only paid less in terms of actual cash for the price of the machine because of barter, but she also enjoyed a sweeter tax advantage.

Real Estate Trades Mean More Depreciation

For the serious trader, real estate offers even more in terms of saving on your taxes, especially if you're into income properties, either residential or commercial. Let's face it. There are a lot of motivated sellers out there. Some of them can be induced into taking trade dollars for all or part of the asking price.

There are three ways trading can help you on your taxes. First, you shield your income with depreciation. Second, you get to deduct expenses of maintenance and repair. Third, you magnify these two advantages by doing it all on trade. You're spending trade dollars that don't really cost you a dollar.

Trade Tales

A restaurant that was a member of a trade exchange found itself gen- erating nearly $100,000 trade dollars per year. Instead of going on stand-by, the owner began investing his trade dollars into income proper- ties, an endeavor he was not unfamiliar with. Over the next two years, he purchased over $300,000 of properties, keeping his crews busy, while creating a tax shelter at the same time.

Let's say you spend $50,000 trade on a property. As you depreciate it, the first 10 years of a schedule might look like this:

Depreciation on $50,000 Property Purchase

Year	Depreciation	Net Value
1	$1,439	$48,561
2	1,818	46,743
3	1,818	44,925
4	1,818	43,107
5	1,818	41,289
6	1,818	39,471
7	1,818	37,653
8	1,818	35,835
9	1,818	34,017
10	1,818	32,199

For a taxpayer in a 28 percent bracket, this represents a tax savings of $509 each year. Over the course of 27 years, that comes to a cool $13,000 in cash. The original cost of the property was $50,000 trade. But remember, that cost him only what he had *into* $50,000 of new sales. What's the bottom line? It's possible our trader got the house for nothing!

Similar tax savings can be realized if you buy commercial property. Either way, when you use trade dollars instead of cash in real estate, your depreciation goes into overdrive. You get cash deductions for having spent trade!

If you invest trade dollars for maintaining and repairing your property, you also enjoy deductions. Most trade exchanges are able to offer a host of labor-intensive services on barter. These may include garbage pickup, painting, drywall hanging, signs, roofs, snow plowing, and asphalt maintenance. Again, you get *cash* deductions for having spent *trade*.

Use Trade Dollars for Donations

There's another, more altruistic way to minimize your tax bill. It's to donate trade dollars to your favorite nonprofit. Many trade exchanges allow nonprofits to join for free. Chances are good you can make a difference for your favorite nonprofit, and your pocketbook, at the same time.

To gain a deduction, you can donate trade dollars you haven't even earned yet. Let's assume it's December 31 and you've discovered you've had a really good year. To partially negate your tax obligation, you could go to the bank and withdraw a pile of cash. Then you could give it all away. But that wouldn't make sense, especially if you belonged to a trade exchange.

Depending on how much trade you do, you might be able to get a trade dollar "loan." You could donate trade dollars and in the eyes of Uncle Sam, it will have been identical to donating cash. You get your deduction, and you get it this year. But beware. You may owe taxes next year, when you actually earn the trade dollars.

Some Charities Enjoy Special Status

There are lots of different kinds of charities. Your bowling league might be "nonprofit," but it doesn't qualify for charitable deductions. But if a bowling league serves disabled bowlers, that's a different story.

State and federal governments sometimes elevate the status of certain types of nonprofits by establishing special benefits to donors. These usually come in the form of offering *tax credits*, rather than simple *tax deductions*.

def•i•ni•tion

> **Tax credit**   A one-for-one dol-lar reduction in your total tax bill. A **tax deduction,** on the other hand, simply reduces your taxable income.

Many states offer tax credits, up to certain amounts, when you give to certain preferred charities. These charities usually serve the disabled, or are associated with education. Again, when you give trade dollars, rather than cash, you get a double whammy. You save cash on your taxes, while having donated trade. To find out what kind of charities qualify, it's best to consult with your tax advisor.

It's Easy Being Green

Ever notice how every few years, the federal government offers tax credits for certain types of investments? In order to promote certain industries and economic activity, the taxman can become extraordinarily generous.

There are many green purchases that qualify for significant tax credits on your income tax. For example, if you spend trade dollars to upgrade your heating and air conditioning system to an Energy Star–rated system, you could qualify for a 30 percent tax credit, up to $1,500 cash.

That means if you spend $5,000, either in cash or in barter, you could get a $1,500 tax credit. If you're that restaurant owner we were talking about, and your food cost was 30 percent, and you spent trade for a modernized heating unit, guess what? You just got your HVAC for free!

There are other opportunities out there. Sometimes the federal government gives tax credits for hybrid cars; other times it might be efficient water heaters. Green seems to be where it's at right now. Tax credits of up to 30 percent exist for solar and wind power, geothermal heat pumps, and insulation.

Many of these products can be obtained with trade dollars. But things change. It's always best to consult your tax advisor before charging headlong into purchases that could give you tax benefits one year, and nothing the next.

Play by the Rules

There's not a bank, or a trade exchange, that doesn't have a few participants who find themselves in tax trouble from time to time. These fall into two categories. Either they're incompetent in matters of accounting, or they are dishonest in such matters.

Ignorance (or Incompetence) Is No Excuse

Some people start up home-based companies and join a trade exchange. Most have a clue; others do not. You can tell them when they sign up that trade dollars represent taxable income. You advise them to deduct business expenses. You tell them to treat trade dollars just like cash. With some people, this goes in one ear and out the other. Incredibly, some members totally ignore trade dollars altogether when preparing their taxes. They think because it's not cash, it can somehow be off the books.

Ignoring trade is a great way to invite an audit. Whereas simply being a member of a trade exchange will never get you audited, ignoring trade sales could. At the very least, it could subject you to late fees and penalties.

Sometimes people join with the best of intentions. They plan to incorporate trade into their taxes, but they somehow forget to tell the exchange a tiny piece of relevant information, such as, "I changed from a sole proprietorship to a corporation three years ago."

Trade Tales
One member was aghast when she received a not-so-nice letter from the IRS. It seems her taxpayer identification number did not match the one she gave her trade exchange. For three years, the exchange had reported all her sales on her FedEx account number. This was funny in one way, but not so funny in another.

This puts the trade exchange in an untenable position. It cannot buy a time machine and revise three years' worth of 1099s. Instead, the member, by not paying attention, has turned something that should have been simple into a mess that only an accountant can figure out.

Others Push the Envelope

Some members take it a step further. They cheat on their taxes in the cash world and the trade world also. One of the most common ways is they buy something on trade, such as a mink coat, and figure, "Hey, this sounds like a business expense!"

It's not, and the trade vacation to the Caribbean isn't either, in spite of the fact that a discussion at dinner included the comment that the corporate minutes really should be up to date.

Personal income should be accounted as such, whether in cash or in trade. Whereas trade dollars can be used effectively to create deductions, you should consider barter to be a marketing tool, rather than a way to beat the tax man.

The Real Underground Economy: Direct Trade

One-on-one trade, not conducted through organized trade exchanges, is what sometimes gives barter a bad name. Social scientists and economists can only guess how much direct barter happens. The vast majority of this trade remains a part of the *underground economy*.

def•i•ni•tion

Underground economy   Transactions, both legal and illegal, that are either cashless or unreported. This includes all commerce where taxes and/or regulations are being avoided. It can include a vast array of activities, from painting houses to running drugs. The underground economy is generally smallest in countries where taxes and regulation are the lowest.

Direct barter has been facilitated by many online auction and classified services that include "barter sections." Even the most well-known services encourage people to barter everything from professional services to lawn mowing, new and used goods, and all kinds of personal and business property. These transactions, facilitated by the Internet, could account for billions of dollars of unreported income.

Because all trade exchanges send out 1099s, they are not a part of this underground economy. Yet, many individuals and businesses trade direct, paying scant attention to taxes. When the carpet cleaner accepts restaurant gift certificates in exchange for cleaning the restaurant's carpet, what normally happens? What should happen?

What normally happens is the carpet cleaner, in essence, received income for his efforts. So did the restaurant owner, but in his case, he could write it off as a legitimate expense of doing business. Either way, neither party is likely to have reported the transaction to the IRS or state taxing authority.

Direct trade, because it is usually "off the books," can also catch up to you when it comes time to get a loan from the bank, or when you sell your business. No bank or buyer is likely to take a "second set of books" seriously.

> **Balance of Trade**
>
> Many people conduct one-on-one trading and fail to include these transactions on their taxes. But there is a major pitfall. For one, what happens if one party fails to live up to his end of the bargain? There is no back end, no overseer, as is supplied by a trade exchange.

The Least You Need to Know

- Trade exchanges are obligated to send out 1099s to their members, accounting for trade dollars same as cash.

- Avoid having too many trade dollars at year's end. Monitor your barter, and take advantage of deductions.

- You can spend trade dollars personally. Payroll is a legitimate expense. Take trade, but account for it properly.

◆ Trade dollars can be used to create deductions by purchasing capital equipment, real estate, and products where the government offers tax credits or deductions.

◆ Trade exchanges make accounting easy, if you pay attention. Beware of the pitfalls of direct trade, and be sure to pay your taxes.

Part **3**

Barter Strategies

We've covered the basics so far, but how do you really take advantage of barter? Whether you're in a trade exchange, are using community dollars, or just trading direct, there are strategies you should know to improve your trades.

Smart and creative trading can help you even out the rough spots that occur over time and maximize profits when times are good. By building relationships with fellow traders and trade exchange brokers, you'll discover opportunities you never realized were out there—opportunities that don't exist in a strictly cash economy.

Chapter 9

When to Trade and When Not To

In This Chapter

- ♦ Trade while profitable
- ♦ Determining the cost of your trade dollar
- ♦ Timing: trading when you have excess capacity
- ♦ Getting what you need from your trade exchange

Before you start trading through a trade exchange like there's no tomorrow, do your homework—or there may be no tomorrow for your business. Barter through a trade exchange can improve your cash flow, but it can't be a complete substitute for cash. This chapter tells you how to examine your company's financials, your cost of goods, and your capacity.

You then need to take a look at your local trade exchange to make sure the market it runs benefits you, and if its brokers will work to get the best deals for your business.

Your trade exchange will tell you only part of the story. Its brokers are too busy putting deals together to help each member understand the nuances of organized trade. Like the old gambler, you have to "know when to hold 'em, and when to fold 'em." It's the same in barter. You have to know when, and under what circumstances, you should trade, and when you should walk away.

If You're Drowning, Barter Can't Save You

If your head's underwater, the only thing you need is air. You don't need, say, a ham and Swiss on rye. Every need, other than breathing, is of no importance.

By the same token, if your business is going down for the third time, you don't need barter. You need cash. You need cash to pay the power bill, payroll, and the raw material that goes into your product.

The Donut Shop

Let's pretend for a second. You own a donut shop. You've been trying to get out of debt for two years now. You're struggling to make payroll; you haven't taken a dollar out personally for months; and you're behind on your taxes. Oh, and you joined a barter exchange a few months back, hoping it would help save your business.

Balance of Trade

A business that's not making money has to limit its purchases to survival items. All available cash is earmarked for necessities such as utilities, labor, and inventory. It doesn't have cash for advertising, capital improvements, or income for the owner. The barter shopping list shrinks, making success in a trade exchange almost impossible.

A barter customer walks in and places a $50 order. Later that day, another one comes in, and another, and later on, yet another. Over the course of the month, you discover you've made $3,000 of barter sales. You begin to celebrate.

Not so fast. You call your broker and ask what you can get on barter. Because of your poor cash flow, your options are limited. You find out you can't pay your food purveyor in trade. The power company isn't on trade; nor is your landlord. Your broker says they signed a new restaurant on trade that serves a killer ham and Swiss on rye. But you don't need a sandwich; you need cash.

You go back into your office and try to figure out a way to make payroll. By trading, you did nothing except hurt your cash flow.

Same Donut Shop, Minus the Holes

Now turn the situation to the profitable side of the ledger. You own the same donut shop, but things have been getting better. Business has been trending upward for the last two years. After some lean years, your business has become profitable and is giving you a nice income.

You joined a trade exchange a few months ago, hoping to increase your business even more. Your sales rep was right: new customers appeared from nowhere, spending barter dollars generously. Last month you did $3,000 of additional business.

With the increased business, you decide it's time to spend some of that new income. You call your broker at the trade exchange. She tells you about a company that seal-coats asphalt. You agree your parking lot could use some sprucing up. Your broker goes through a list of other availabilities, all of which you could use: landscaping, window washing, employee bonuses, radio advertising, an all-inclusive vacation, and finally, a great new restaurant near your house. Your broker tells you they serve a great ham and Swiss on rye. You go back into your office and dream of sandwiches on barter.

A profitable business is able to more easily put trade dollars into its operation, and profit into the hands of its owner. The business that makes money buys more on trade because it has enough cash to cover its base needs. As the shopping list grows, so do the opportunities to spend trade dollars to improve the business.

Are All Goods Created Equal?

If you ask most people what weighs more, a ton of lead or a ton of feathers, only small children will be fooled. Obviously, both weigh the same: a ton.

Ask a similar question, this one pertaining to barter: What's more valuable, a ton of carpet or a ton of carpet cleaning? This time there is a difference. The carpet is clearly more valuable. Carpet and other *hard goods* are more valuable in a trade exchange because the seller has a higher cost of goods, so it's generally harder for the trade exchange to sign them up. Carpet cleaners, on the other hand, sell their excess time, so it's easy to sign them up.

When the carpet cleaner or chiropractor makes a sale through barter, he doesn't have a lot of cash invested into his new sale. What they offer are *soft goods*. The carpet cleaner must pick up the additional cost of chemicals, gas for his van, and labor. On a $200 sale, he might have $20 in chemicals, $10 in gas to get to the job, and $30 in labor, nothing if he does the job himself. That totals out to $60. In this scenario, his trade dollar cost is 30 cents.

def·i·ni·tion

Hard goods   Products or services that are of high demand and low margin. Hard goods are, as a rule, harder to find in a trade exchange.

Soft goods   Products or services of minimal cost to the seller, but which are sold with a high markup. Such products are generally easy to offer for barter and easy to find in a trade exchange.

The chiropractor fares even better. He accepts a new trade customer and schedules the new customer in time he already has. He's already paid for his x-ray machine, his receptionist, his rent, and his advertising. The chiropractor's cost of trade dollar: virtually nothing.

What Does Your Trade Dollar Cost?

Computing the cost of a trade dollar is usually simple. If you own a restaurant and your food cost is 30 percent, your trade dollar cost is 30 cents. If you own a donut shop, your main costs are sugar, flour, and grease. However, you sell the used grease to some guy with a bio-diesel car. So maybe your trade dollar cost is 20 cents.

Yet many businesses commonly overestimate their costs of generating a trade dollar. Usually, they fall into the trap of adding in fixed costs, such as rent, utilities, advertising, computers, and the cost of maintaining the kitchen sink. All these costs are fixed. They must be paid whether the business is trading or not. Therefore, they should not be used when computing the cost of a trade dollar. Only variable costs count.

Barter Bits

Incredibly, a few businesses enjoy a "negative" cost of a trade dollar. That is, they not only don't have a variable cost of goods, but they get additional cash from the buyer. For example, a professional sports team not only puts fannies in empty seats (costing nothing), it also entices those fannies to get up and spend cash at the concession stand.

Sometimes business in the same industry can each have a dramatically different cost of goods. Take two electrical contracting companies. One pays its electricians for a set 40-hour work week, even if they work 38 hours in some cases. To trade those two unbilled hours costs the company nothing, so the trade dollar cost is zero. If the company pays labor costs incrementally, however, by the time it figures labor, withholding, and workers' compensation taxes, the trade dollar cost could zoom up to 50 or 60 cents.

Here's a list of some businesses where it doesn't cost much to generate a trade dollar:

Chiropractor:	$.00
Consultant:	$.00
Real estate agent:	$.10
Radio station:	$.00
Hotel:	$.10
Restaurant:	$.30

Here's a list of some businesses with a higher cost of generating trade dollars:

Furniture store:	$.60
Office equipment:	$.60
Appliance store:	$.85
Automobile dealer:	$.90
Home improvement:	$.80

Is a High Cost of Goods Reason Not to Trade?

Not every trader has a low cost of goods, or small amount of cash invested into a trade dollar. Yet, properly managed, many of these businesses gain other advantages that are not so obvious.

Let's say you don't clean carpet, you sell it. In the cash world, if you're saddled with slow-moving inventory, you might have to severely discount the carpet. Beyond the obvious (that you have taken a loss), heavy discounting can denigrate the value of your other stock. Or you may end up cannibalizing yourself, as a customer buys the discounted carpet instead of a higher-priced one on the floor. By offering specific slow-moving carpets to your trade exchange, you won't have to resort to price cutting. You will not only get a better price, but it was inventory you weren't going to replace anyway.

Another advantage that goes to sellers of certain hard goods is a secret—literally. Most exchanges don't publish the names of all their members. If the trade exchange values what you sell, guess what? You'll be more likely to get first dibs on other hard goods. Put yourself in the shoes of the trade exchange. There's one tire dealer, and everybody wants tires. Who's going to get them? The low cost-of-goods member who can be made happy with almost anything, or you, the carpet dealer?

> **Balance of Trade**
>
> If you deal with narrow margins, and your cash flow is bad, be careful with indiscriminate trading. If you fall in love with simply getting more barter sales, without regard to replacing your inventory, you may find yourself trade rich, but cash poor.

For some businesses, barter is totally out of the question. If you own a service station and you're making a nickel a gallon, trading gas will drive you into bankruptcy. It is also generally unwise to trade lumber, new computers, new automobiles, and other products that offer less than a 10 percent gross margin. Don't expect to be able to buy these items on barter, either.

Trade Tales

One member of a trade exchange owned a car wash, which is a soft good. But he also sold gas, which is an extreme hard good and would normally be untradeable. Needing more trade dollars, he ingeniously combined the two: he sold $100 packages that included $75 of car washes and $25 of gas. His cost of goods was still very reasonable, yet members were able to get gas on trade, as long as they got their cars washed!

Hold the Presses: What About Parity?

Did I just say not to trade new cars? I didn't mean that. All trade exchanges, whether they like it or not, must allow their currencies to be subjected to the laws of supply and demand. That is, when a product is scarce, enterprising members find a way to bid the price up.

Take the case of a new car. What if someone with low cost of goods, say an owner of a health club, is willing to pay double trade dollars to the car dealer? What if the car dealer accepts? This is against the rules of most trade exchanges, but does it happen? You bet. Some exchanges turn a blind eye to this behavior and then run the transaction. Other exchanges huff and puff and threaten to veto the deal, but then run it anyway. Others have institutionalized this economic fact of life and call it *parity*.

Parity, whether tolerated, con-doned, or encouraged, allows the dealer of appliances to sell at "sug-gested retail," which in the cash world would be complete fantasy. Nevertheless, parity pricing lets certain items become available on barter that otherwise would not.

def•i•ni•tion

Parity For trade exchanges, it is a transaction that allows a buyer to offer a purchase price in trade dollars signifi-cantly above an item's market cash value.

A Lesson from Econ 101: Excess Capacity

Remember Econ 101? The professor was always throwing graphs and curves at you. You never knew why, but it seemed every concept was illustrated with widgets, and widget factories. No one knew what a wid-get was, but they were selling like hotcakes!

Say you actually own that widget factory. The demand for widgets is huge and growing, and your factory is working at full capacity. Your raw material cost is small, but if you accept just one more order, you will, like the overeating Monty Python character, explode. Okay, maybe not, but you will have to add another shift and build a new wing onto your factory. By producing just one more widget, your factory will absorb enormous incremental production costs. The cost of making one more widget goes through the roof.

Beware of a Falling Profit Margin

Most businesses are not in this situation, but a few are. Let's say you own a home improvement company, and you install windows and doors. Your installers will riot if you make them work any more hours. If you hire another crew, keep them busy full-time, and buy an additional truck just to accommodate a few trade customers, you just shot yourself in the foot.

Or what if you publish a magazine? You determine the amount of advertising you need versus editorial content to cover costs and earn a profit. But when an issue is chock full of advertising, it's like the widget factory. If you sell just one more ad, you'll have to either: (1) bump another advertiser, or (2) add four pages to your magazine, with most of it unsold. Your profit margin drops.

Trade Only When It Fits You

Never be intimidated by a trade exchange that tries to get you to barter time or space when you have none available. If you're the owner of the magazine with hardly any empty space, tell the exchange you'll trade on a "space available" basis. Or, if you're the contractor, accept trade during the times of year when things are slow. In that way, you prevent income from dropping through the floor in slow times, without under-cutting cash sales when times are good.

The key is to not let barter dollars interfere with cash dollars. Frankly, cash has to come first. Trade should always represent incremental sales, when you have the excess capacity to handle them.

When you're spending your trade dollars, be aware that other businesses may similarly put restrictions on when and what they trade.

A radio station might limit your ability to advertise during December, or a resort might not let you trade during spring break.

Rating Your Trade Exchange

In determining how much you should sell through a trade exchange, you must get a feel for what you can buy. Not all trade exchanges are equal. Some exchanges have lots of goods and services available, and competent brokers. A few others are nothing more than an answering machine in somebody's basement. The sales representative from the trade exchange might tell you what you need to know, but chances are you'll have to dig deeper.

There are two ways to rate a trade exchange. One is to evaluate your fellow members. The other is to evaluate the people who run the exchange. With both, it's an ongoing process.

Bigger Is Not Always Better

As you trade through an exchange, you'll find out size does not matter. There are a few large exchanges that count many hundreds of businesses as their members, yet most are on *standby*. Others can produce a long list of active traders, but they're all dog psychiatrists and astrologers, or stuff you don't need.

Here's something else to look out for when determining when to trade. Some large exchanges have plenty of members, all eager to sell, but they're so geographically spread out, most purchases are not practical. After all, you're not going to drive two hours for a donut and coffee, even if it is on trade.

def•i•ni•tion

Standby When a business decides it has too many trade dollars in its account. It chooses not to accept any more trade sales until it spends some.

A few other large exchanges appear to have everything in place, but seem possessed by signing new members. They don't service the ones they have. Their members are left twisting in the wind, with little or no understanding of how trade works after their sales rep departs and their initial enthusiasm wanes.

What's important to know is actually pretty basic: can the exchange send you customers, and can you spend its money? If a trade exchange's members put out good offerings, and you can get them to buy from you, you'll want to ramp up your activity. If not, you might want to think twice about accumulating too many trade dollars.

Insist on a List

No trade exchange publishes its entire membership list. Regardless of size, it should still put out a directory, either hard copy, online, or both. This makes it way easier to navigate your trade purchases.

> **Balance of Trade**
>
> Make sure your trade exchange isn't inundated with businesses in your category, especially if demand might be limited. The sales pie could be split too many ways.

When you peruse the directory of your trade exchange, keep an eye out as to whether the businesses listed are ones you would likely buy from. If a trade exchange refuses to share a directory, there might be a reason. Either it doesn't have what it says it does, or it doesn't want you talking with the other members.

Know the People at the Trade Exchange

When it comes to knowing when to trade, people are more important than a list. The heart of a trade exchange is the brokers it employs. Without brokers, a trade exchange is simply a list of businesses. There is no cement, nothing binding them to fair trade or to trade at all. Brokers sell your product, and they help you spend your trade dollars. Without them, members revert to what they're accustomed to, spending cash.

A broker should have a sense of the local market, and a basic understanding of your business. When you call a broker, he or she should not just spit out a list of businesses and phone numbers. A good broker massages the deal, and sees it through. Trade doesn't happen all by itself.

If your broker does not perform these tasks, it could be cause to limit your sales through your exchange. On the other hand, if your broker assists you in spending trade, you may want to increase your activity.

It's a good idea to be a squeaky wheel, but a nice one. A broker should handle no more than 200 accounts, but sadly, overload is all too common in the industry. If a broker handles too many accounts, time spent with any one account is limited. Schmooze your broker, and you'll be more likely to find out about the good stuff.

Balance of Trade

Beware of trade exchanges that exist solely on the Internet. If there's no local presence and no broker to help you, spending your trade dollars will likely be difficult.

The Least You Need to Know

◆ If your business is in trouble, you can't save it through barter. But if you've reached a certain level of success, a trade exchange can improve your business and enhance your lifestyle.

◆ Before your first trade, compute the cost of your trade dollar. Small margins need planning and close monitoring.

◆ Trading is dependent on having excess capacity. You should never bump a cash customer to make way for barter.

◆ Make sure the members in your trade exchange have products you can use. Rating your exchange is important and ongoing.

Chapter 10

Building Relationships: Advanced Schmoozing

In This Chapter

- ◆ Expand your choice of goods through good relations
- ◆ Make life easy for your trade exchange
- ◆ Develop friendships with members
- ◆ Know that attitude is a self-fulfilling prophecy

A trade exchange's membership base is not a true reflection of the cash world. Rather, it's composed of those businesses a trade exchange happens to sign up. For example, an exchange might have six dry cleaners but no dentists. In another exchange it's the reverse. Not many dry cleaners, but dentists are growing on trees.

An effective way to get goods that are not as plentiful as others is to become friends with your trade exchange. It's a good idea to establish a relationship with the owner, sure. But more importantly, get to know the brokers. They're the ones who can get you what you want.

Relationship building doesn't stop at the exchange. Make friends with other members. You get the inside track on goods that other members may not even know about.

Through it all, attitude can make or break you. A positive attitude when you're buying is important. Don't apologize for spending trade.

Barter Is a Limited Universe

The categories of businesses represented in a membership base of a trade exchange can sometimes become skewed. Sure, there will be lots of things you can buy, everything from restaurant meals to eye care. But if you're looking to walk into a big sporting goods store and take your pick of whatever's on the shelves, think again.

It's difficult for a trade exchange to sign certain categories because they have become the domain of the big box stores. Think back. Twenty years ago, how many locally owned sporting goods stores were there? How many are there now?

Barter Bits

When I began my barter career in 1980 in my hometown of Kalamazoo, Michigan, there were nine locally owned new appliance dealers. With big box stores dominating the market, today there is but one remaining.

The same goes for appliance stores, men and women's clothing, jewelry, shoes, furniture, movie theaters, bookstores, and more. There are even chain funeral homes. So what distinguishes businesses that trade? Typically, it's ones where there's local ownership.

When the supply of certain items is limited, it's important to get "in the know" so you're tipped off when they become available. Sometimes it's as simple as reading an e-mail from your exchange and being the first to act. But more often than not, it's getting that phone call from your broker. It's the one that starts out with, "You're the first person I'm calling on this."

Forge Relationships

To get great service from your trade exchange, you have to first be a fair trader. But there's more to it than that. It's also important to build a relationship with your trade exchange.

This includes getting to know the owner or manager of the exchange and also the brokers. There are different reasons to schmooze each.

The Owner Approves Loans

In establishing a relationship with the head honcho, you're speaking to the person who can make or break you when it comes to allowing you to "spend in the negative" or extend a trade-dollar loan. Most exchanges try to abide by a quantitative formula when computing your trade dollar line of credit. This is usually based on past sales, perceived futures sales, payment history, and credit rating. (For more on trade-dollar loans, see Chapter 14.)

But there's another factor that comes into play: does the exchange know and trust you? Just like the small-town bank, a trade exchange will more likely make a loan to a business it knows and trusts.

Make a point to introduce yourself to the owner of the trade exchange. Tell him about what you sell, your plans, and why your business is stable. Tell him how you look forward to selling to other members, and how you will always play by the rules. Treat him like your banker because, in a way, he is.

Brokers Rule

Brokers often feel underappreciated and misunderstood. That really shouldn't come as a surprise. They're usually juggling upwards of 200 members. Some are bugging them to get more sales. Others are inundating them with purchase requests. A broker's life can be quite harried, with the only constant being interruptions.

There are times when something really neat comes across your broker's desk. Let's say the sales department just signed up the best steak house in the county. For this month, the broker has been allotted $3,000 of certificates. Who does the she call?

Your broker will call people on her VIP list. Those will be the clients who trade fairly, pay their cash fees, have not overspent, and are valued as members. In building your relationship with your trade exchange, you want to prove you are to be valued.

There is no magic formula for building a trusting relationship with your broker. Start out not by talking just about you. Ask about your broker's interests, her husband and kids, and how the little league game went the night before. In a day replete with people talking about themselves and *their* needs, this can be a welcome change of pace for the average broker.

Some members think they can best get their way by being demanding. This is counterproductive. Brokers make and receive dozens of phone calls each day. It's natural they put off the ones they don't care for.

Do Lunch

Put yourself in the shoes of your broker. One thing that should be evident is she's stuck in the office for most of the day. Brokers love to get out. Consider asking your broker out for a business lunch and pick up the tab.

Your broker will probably share a few war stories at first. But then she'll open up about new trading opportunities she hasn't shared with everyone. You're sure to pick up on some of those trading "goodies."

Get Your Broker into Your Place of Business

When a broker visits your place of business, she can get attuned to some of your needs. Just by looking around, trade opportunities will pop into her head. Sometimes these can be invisible to you, but your broker sees things with fresh eyes. She might notice your parking lot needs striping, or your ceilings cleaned, or a back door needs to be replaced. She can go back to her office with the project of fulfilling your needs.

By the same token, your broker might notice something you never considered trading. Perhaps you aren't using a piece of equipment. Or you have a delivery vehicle you don't use anymore. By being there, your broker can put all the pieces together.

Don't Be a Stranger

Just as it's good to get your broker out of his or her office, it's also a good idea to drop by the trade exchange's office from time to time. While you're in, you might meet the other personnel, including the travel broker, if they have one.

> **Balance of Trade**
>
> Unfortunately, some members wear out their welcome. One member became infamous. He would repeatedly invade a broker's office and plop down, reading a newspaper. Removal of the chair, so he had no place to sit, became the only solution.

Before you leave the exchange's office, don't forget to pay a visit to the person or department responsible for accounting. Sooner or later, you're going to have a question about a transaction. Making a friend now could save you time later.

Be Clear on the Importance of Communication

Disenchantment with a trade exchange usually comes in two forms. One is the complaint of not having enough business, and the other is too much business. Neither problem would occur if someone had bothered to build a lasting relationship on the front end.

If you're not getting enough customers, don't just sit there. Call your broker. Ask to be featured on the website or newsletter. See if you can get a mailing list. In short, be proactive in helping your broker get you new customers.

If you're having trouble spending your trade dollars, the same rule applies. Communicate. It's amazing how many times a member complains about not being able to spend trade, yet doesn't open up e-mails, read mailings, and can scarcely find his membership ID card.

Returning Calls: The Best Relationship Builder

Nothing wastes your broker's time more than a member who does not return calls. Let's look at how your broker tries to do his job. An owner of an office furniture company calls looking for a drywall contractor. The broker wants to expedite the job. He doesn't simply dish out a phone number to the inquiring member. Instead, he gleans the basic details of the job: how big of a job and when it has to be completed. He then calls a drywall contractor who needs trade.

But the contractor doesn't call back. After another day passes, the broker makes another call. As days pass, the broker not only gets frustrated, he's also looking bad in the eyes of the office furniture company. In the meantime, yet another member calls and wants to place a large order for office furniture. The broker hesitates to call. The office furniture guy is frustrated with trade, waiting to get his drywall done.

Even if the drywall contractor had called and said, "I'm booked for cash for the next month, but could take a trade job after that," then at least the broker would have known where he stood. He could move on to another contractor, or worst case, informed the office furniture company that no drywall contractor was presently available.

Let's follow this example to its logical end. A year later, the exchange comes across a $10,000 inventory of drywall mud. The drywall contractor, who had previously not returned his phone calls, now has a positive trade balance. But so does another contractor.

The drywall contractor may be a great fellow. He might run his crew efficiently and everyone loves him. But his broker does not share the love. Who do you think is going to get the phone call?

Make Your Broker Look Good

Sometimes if you do a small favor for your trade exchange, it can really help build the relationship. Let's take another example. You're the owner of a sandblasting company. Business has been crazy. In fact, you and your employees are working 60 hours a week, with no letup in sight.

The phone rings. It's your broker, asking if you can sandblast a set of antique hubcaps. Your trade balance is healthily positive, and you really don't need the job. But your broker explains it's for a really important client. It's the office furniture company.

Looking at it from the short term, the easy answer might have been, "No, I don't have time." But the relationship-building answer would be, "Okay, I think I can squeeze it in."

The damage done by the unresponsive drywall contractor has now been partially mitigated. By doing a favor for your client, you also did a favor for your broker. So again, something really nifty pops up on trade. Who's going to get the call? And the next time *you* need something, your broker will jump through hoops.

Making Your Broker Look Bad (Don't Do This)

To their detriment, some sellers play games, and in the process, make their exchange look bad. Here's what they do. When another member approaches them to buy something on trade, they say something like, "I have 10 zillion trade dollars in my account! I need half cash!"

When this happens, more often than not, the member is actually *negative* in trade. By claiming to have an inordinate amount of trade, he has put his trade exchange in a bad light. Trade exchanges find out about this unfair posturing. It's yet another short-term strategy some members take that backfires.

Telepathy Doesn't Work

Direct communication with your broker will save a lot of problems. Yet, some members rely on telepathy. This is especially irritating when a member goes on standby and neglects to mention it to the trade exchange.

When a broker receives a member request, there are times she has to work on assumptions. She assumes certain members are wide open for trade, because that's been their history. Let's illustrate. A member has lost his directory (they're always doing this), so he calls the exchange. His kid's soccer team just won a big game and he would like to take them all out for pizza. Where should he take them?

The broker knows a great pizza place that has always traded, so she gives the client the name and address of the restaurant, assuring him all he needs is his membership ID card. So the member packs the kids into his SUV and carts them all to the pizza place, only to find that the pizza place has put out a cardboard sign that reads, "Trade limited to $20 right now."

Barter Bits

One way some sellers can control their trade is to issue a limited amount of gift certificates each month, and give them to the trade exchange. As the amount of purchases increases, the seller simply gives more certificates to the exchange.

The pizza place blew it, big time. Because his cash flow was poor and his trade balance had gotten a bit high, he figured he could just invent his own rules. Plus, he didn't bother to tell the trade exchange. He embarrassed the buyer with all the soccer players. He also alienated his broker.

If your trading status changes, make sure you communicate with your broker. In all likelihood, she'll help you spend out, and if you do need to place restrictions on trade, you can work together so no one gets upset. You will have maintained a solid relationship with your trade exchange.

Volunteer to Be a Referral Source

Trade exchanges are constantly trying to sign up new members. You can earn a lot of good will if you help them do that. Let your exchange know you will gladly field phone calls from potential members asking about trade. To someone "on the fence," this can really help out. This will help solidify a positive trading relationship with your exchange.

Get to Know Other Members

Whenever and wherever you can, get to know other members. In doing so, you discover trading opportunities, both to buy and to sell. Many exchanges offer the chance to meet and greet other members at social occasions. You definitely want to do that. But take it a step further. Make it a point to make friends with other members, and teach them how to use trade if you need to.

Let's illustrate. You called your broker and told her your business needs a new roof. She warmed up a roofer and referred him to you. He gives you a quote; it's for $10,000. But the contractor is hesitant. He says he "needs the cash."

Tell the contractor you understand his hesitancy. Then ask why. Perhaps he'll explain that he's new to trade and a $10,000 barter arrangement seems like an awful lot.

Build a relationship and you increase your potential for trade. In all likelihood, the roofer doesn't understand trade exchanges the way you do. So help him understand how barter can benefit his business.

Start off by asking the business owner what he needs. At first, he'll probably mention impossible items such as gasoline and taxes. If you dig deeper, however, you'll probably discover places he's currently spending cash, and where he could do it on barter.

By developing a relationship with your exchange and other members, you're already pretty familiar with what's available. Ask the contractor if he ever rents commercial equipment and then tell him where he can do it. What about the signs on his trucks? Might he have an interest in doing some advertising on trade to attract cash customers? Tell him about the potential of paying trade dollars to his employees. Then tell him you haven't even started.

The list goes on and on. Get your contractor friend to open up about discretionary items, and personal needs. Perhaps he's planning a vacation. Did he know he can go to an all-inclusive resort on barter? Talk about eating out, dental and eye care, and all the things you have available in your exchange.

By helping a hesitant seller discover all he can buy with his trade dollars, you've helped yourself, sure. But you've also helped the contractor expand his business.

> **Trade Tales**
>
> One member became a roving emissary for his trade exchange. He actually visited accounts that had, for one reason or another, become inactive. In helping them to spend, he also got them to sell again. This helped the exchange, but it also helped him.

> **Trade Tales**
>
> One member of my trade exchange happened to mention to another that college tuition was available, through another exchange, at a liberal arts school in the Midwest. He took the information and ran with it. The member's daughter ended up going there on trade.

Don't Force Yourself on the Seller

Building a relationship with other members is based on the giving of factual information. Some members have been known to stretch the truth when it benefits them. Be sure to realistically portray what you can, and cannot, get on barter.

Also, make sure the deal is good for the seller. Allow her to have a margin where taking trade makes sense. No one should barter an item that has an 80 or 90 percent wholesale cost of goods, and then pay a commission to the exchange for the privilege. Remember, you're already getting a good deal because it's barter. Dickering on barter is not kosher.

> ### Trade Tales
>
> One of my members, a printer, was in search of a premium he could insert into boxes of completed printing. He settled on $5 gift certificates good at a local bakery. The bakery not only did a sale for $1,000 of certificates, it also saw dozens of new people come in to redeem them. The owner of the bakery estimated new cash sales to have exceeded what she received in barter.

Nothing makes your fellow member happier than getting a little extra cash. As you spend trade dollars with them, assure them you'll spread the word about their businesses to your cash friends.

Let's say you've taken some friends out golfing. If you see the owner of the course, remind her you're introducing three people, not members of the exchange, to her golf course. If they have an enjoyable experience, they'll be back, spending cash.

Spend Cash with Fellow Traders—Really

Here's another way to strengthen relationships with your fellow members. Spend cash. This might seem antithetical to barter, but it's not. Everyone enjoys receiving cash from time to time.

This is especially true if you frequent a business, say, a restaurant, over and over. By occasionally parting with your cash, and making sure the owner knows about it, you can score some unexpected points with the seller.

Build a Network Within a Network

So where does all this relationship building lead? You know, you making friends with your broker and with the other members? It leads to a network within a network. It leads to fair trading and to knowledgeable, communicative members taking care of those of the same ilk.

It's a key reason some members always seem happy with organized barter, while others are not. Let's say something bad happens to a member—for instance, someone jacks up a price on him. For some, their first inclination is to respond in kind. They do the same to some other unsuspecting member. When this behavior is discovered by the trade exchange, guess what? At the very least, the unfair trader goes to the bottom of her broker's list. Worse, it gets him expelled.

But with the network you build in an exchange, you seek out others who trade fairly. You may avoid the business that doesn't, but you don't let that experience poison the well in your dealings with businesses you trust.

Attitude Makes or Breaks You in Trade

Trade dollars will always remain a secondary currency. As such, you sometimes have to employ a little "salesmanship" when you spend them, especially on large purchases. If a member is tentative when spending trade, the seller will sense it. Bartering success will be limited.

This concept of "selling" when buying is foreign to some. After all, if you pull out a $50 bill, you stand the chance it will be snatched out of your hand.

Yet, some members, when making a large barter purchase, say something like, "I've got all this trade. I was wondering if I might interest you in taking some." Then they wonder why the seller doesn't jump out of his or her shoes to take barter. Trade dollars are money. There's nothing to apologize for. Contrast this with, "I'd like to be your customer. Trade has been great for me. What can we work out?"

Barter Bits

I once had a member who, through his power of persuasion and positive attitude, arranged to spend $12,000 for a slightly used pontoon boat. This wouldn't have been so unusual if the seller had been an existing member. We did the paperwork afterward, and the individual who sold the boat successfully spent his trade dollars on remodeling for his home.

Tell the buyer about your positive experiences. Not only have you attracted new customers, you've also been able to spend your trade dollars on an assortment of goods. Give examples. You spent $5,000 trade on printing; you hired a janitorial company; you took your family on a vacation at an all-inclusive resort.

Don't dwell on one negative experience. If you're in trade long enough, someone will try to cheat you, either with a high price, inferior workmanship, and especially not showing up. But that happens in the cash world, too. And you still accept cash, don't you?

The Least You Need to Know

- A trade exchange can offer a wide variety of goods and services, but some categories are limited because they've been taken over by big box stores and diminishing margins.

- When you develop a solid friendship with your trade exchange, you're more likely to be "in the know" when it comes to trading opportunities. Make sure you get to know the exchange's ownership, brokering department, and salespeople.

- There are certain things you can do to strengthen these relationships. Above all, communicate; return your calls. Do a favor for your broker from time to time.

- Whenever you can, build friendships with fellow members. Attend member events; be proactive in getting to know them. Don't shy away from mentoring other members.

- Trade dollars sometimes take a little work to spend. Maintain a positive attitude with fellow members, and you'll be much more successful.

Chapter 11

Paying Employees in Trade

In This Chapter

- ◆ Barter and your employees: is it a match?
- ◆ Selling the concept to your employees
- ◆ Implementing a plan
- ◆ Keeping on top of it

You may already pay your employees by giving them a perk, discount, or other advantage that is not cash. Many companies do this. A restaurant owner might let his employees "eat free." A driver of a beer truck might be able to take a case of beer home each week.

What if you sell a product that your employees don't want or need? By joining a trade exchange, you can still pay them in kind—by using trade dollars! In Chapter 12, you'll learn how to get other businesses that are not members to accept trade dollars. But you can also get your current employees and new hires to love trade, too.

Is Your Exchange Consumer Friendly?

Before you present the idea to your employees that they should take part of their income in trade dollars, you've got to make sure it's in their best interests. If the trade exchange is poorly operated, neither of you want a headache.

Some Problems with Exchanges

Some exchanges are well run, but they're new. They don't yet have enough consumer goods available to be worthwhile for your employees. This doesn't mean, however, that it's a bad idea for your company to join a new exchange. They still could have products your business can use.

Some trade exchanges specialize in business-to-business transactions. They offer little in the way of goods and services your employees can use. They may be great in media, large inventories, or real estate, but they don't have much to offer by way of consumer goods and services.

Be aware some exchanges' memberships are too spread out. This can make spending hard. Your employees will not be willing to travel to cities 30 miles away to wash their cars! Make sure there are enough members in your area to make it all worthwhile.

Finally, a trade exchange that promotes itself by printing a thick directory doesn't necessarily mean its members are actively trading. Many of them might be on "standby," unwilling to accept more barter sales until they are able to spend their credit. That's why it's a good idea for you to be the guinea pig. Do some trades through your company. Start a *sub-account* for yourself. Get a sense of who's trading.

def•i•ni•tion

Sub-account An account created from a main trade exchange account specifically for individuals, not other businesses. Trade dollars are periodically transferred into sub-accounts from a business's main account.

While you're at it, rate the quality of service offered by the trade exchange. Do the brokers help you buy and sell? Are there quality offerings at good prices? The answer should be "yes" to both these questions.

Your employees will also appreciate special promotional opportunities to spend their trade dollars. Many exchanges maintain showrooms where inventory is made available for trade dollars. Other exchanges conduct expansive trade expos where members are invited to make barter purchases from one another.

An exchange in Chicago coordinates an annual gift show, where more than $1 million in trade dollars changes hands in half a day. Inventory ranges from toys to mink coats, from video games to gift baskets. Sub-account members are always invited to these affairs.

Look for these types of purchasing possibilities.

The Exchange Should Make It Easy

So how will your employees be able to spend trade dollars? Certainly, it should not be from your company's account. If your employees spent from that account, it would be chaos. However, there is a way. Virtually all trade exchanges offer sub-accounts.

Companies that provide sub-accounts to employees typically transfer a set number of trade dollars each month. Or sometimes they transfer variable amounts, depending on the employee's performance or goals met. Just as the main account, sub-accounts receive monthly statements that indicate how many trade dollars they have available to spend.

No way should you pay an entry fee for creation of a sub-account. It necessitates hardly any work on the part of the trade exchange. Most exchanges recognize this and encourage companies to set up sub-accounts for their employees because trade activity is increased. Don't be surprised, however, if the trade exchange charges your company a nominal monthly fee, either in cash or trade, to cover handling and postage.

> **Balance of Trade**
>
> A trade exchange shouldn't charge much to start up a sub-account for an employee, but that doesn't mean it will waive its commission. In most cases, it is the main account that pays the transaction fee, upon making the transfer into the sub-account. The sub-account then pays no commission.

Are Your Employees Suitable Traders?

If you have 50 or 100 employees, managing that many sub-accounts will be almost impossible. Within a group that large there will be a few who won't want to make trade dollars work, and a few who will abuse their privileges. Sub-accounts work best, and are most manageable, when limited to around 10.

Before you get your employees involved with your trade exchange, make an educated guess as to whether they will be able to actually use trade dollars. If they're all ready to retire and have frozen-in-concrete purchasing habits, it probably won't be a fit. But if they need stuff and are willing to commit some effort to making it work, they'll be asking for more trade dollars before you know it.

Sell Your Employees on Using Trade

As the owner of a business that accepts trade dollars, your willingness to accept these dollars hinges on one key premise: that it's newly found business. Your employees feel the same way. They're unlikely to welcome trade if they perceive them as simply a replacement for cash they already had. Make sure they understand this key point of organized barter.

Let's say you approach an employee who's making $20 per hour and say, "Let's change your pay scale to $15 cash and $5 trade. Doesn't that sound great?" Chances are you'll be met with an icy glare. Your employee will have already calculated there will be less money to put in his gas tank, buy groceries, and pay the mortgage.

Let's change the scenario around a bit. Instead you say, "Business has been slow, and there's no money to give you a cash raise." Your employee is disappointed. But then you add, "But I can give you a $5 dollar an hour raise with trade dollars!"

See the difference? Now the response will be totally different: "Sounds good! What are trade dollars?" Now it's your turn to tell a receptive employee about his or her raise in pay, and how trade made it possible.

New Hires Can Be the Most Willing

Let's face it. We're all facing challenges with the economy the last couple of years. Whereas it can be difficult to get new sales, it's an employer's market when it comes to hiring. There are lots of qualified, motivated people out there wanting to work.

These people, some without a current job, will be excited to gain employment and accept trade dollars. It is at the beginning stages of employment that a person is most likely to agree to accept trade dollars.

Build Excitement—Have a Meeting

Sometimes the best way to kill an idea is to have a meeting. Not so with barter. As your employees become aware they'll be earning trade dollars, announce that you'll need about a half hour of their time. If possible, invite someone from the trade exchange. Cater in some refreshments (on trade). Have the person from the trade exchange give examples of what your employees can buy on barter. Explain how they can use their ID card to make purchases each month. Then hand out the ID cards.

Be sure not to oversell barter. Trading for certain hard goods can be difficult because they have small margins. Brand new computers and plasma TV sets, for example, are tough. So are items that have become the domain of the big box stores, where local ownership is rare.

You'll also want to make the point that trade dollars require a little effort to spend. Remind your employees it's important to read e-mails from the exchange, and to contact their broker if they can't find something.

Keep expectations realistic. If you do this, you and your employees will likely enjoy a longtime relationship with your trade exchange.

Ironically, some employees actually prefer trade dollars to cash. This, in spite of the fact that trade is accepted less universally. But that's precisely the point. Trade dollars cannot get buried into the family budget and

Trade Tales
One employee of a company in Missouri spent his trade dollars for a once-in-a-lifetime trip to Alaska. The trip included accommodations, restaurants, sightseeing tours, and fishing excursions. The person came back eager to accept more trade dollars as a part of his pay!

eaten up by house payments, utility bills, and insurance. Instead, in the eyes of some, trade dollars have to be spent for restaurants and entertainment. These employees especially love trade.

Put Your Plan into Motion

One of the first questions you'll ask yourself will be "how much trade should I be giving my employees?" This depends on a couple of factors. One is the cost of your trade dollar. You can be more generous if you earn your trade dollars by selling something with a low cost of goods. If this is you, you can afford to be Santa Claus.

The next question has to do with what you think your employees are worth. Once you've determined that, you'll want to arrange for monthly transfers into the accounts of your employees. There's no law they have to be the same amounts either. You'll obviously give the new intern less than your most experienced, competent worker.

Build Incentives with Trade

Many companies that belong to trade exchanges find success in using trade to create incentives. For example, you might consider awarding $1,000 in trade to the top-performing salesperson, and $500 trade to the second-place finisher.

You might also consider using trade dollars to purchase fun prizes that create a buzz. Some companies purchase golf clubs, restaurant gift certificates, or weekend getaways. Then they fashion a contest to give away the prizes. This can really affect your bottom line. However you slice it, trade dollars can create the motivation you're looking for.

Enhance a Benefit Plan with Trade

Just when you thought the trade was solely all-play, here's some news you can share with your employees. Trade dollars can also be a part of a serious benefit plan. Maybe you're unable to offer a comprehensive medical insurance plan. But that doesn't mean you can't offer an alternative, made possible because of barter.

You'll want to check with your trade exchange first, but chances are good you'll be able to offer your workers dental, eye care, chiropractic services, massage therapy, and even acupuncture. You can even add a corporate health club membership on trade.

As you add benefits, you'll want to be sure to talk with your accountant about making them tax-free. Trade dollars are accounted for in exactly the same fashion as cash. For example, if regulations permit you to expense cash to buy a company dental plan, you can do this on trade also.

Barter Scrip for Transient Employees

Perhaps you own a company where you hire temporary or seasonal employees. If your turnover is high, you might not want to entrust these people with a membership card. For all you know, a few of them might go on a spending spree, spending more than they're allotted.

There is still a way to pay the temporary employee. Most exchanges offer a scrip or gift certificate program. Scrip is simply trade dollars put into dollar bill form. It's a way you can give, say, $100 to an employee, perhaps in increments of $5. These certificates can be spent at certain listed businesses. When the person spends all the scrip, there is no more. This way, it's not possible for the person to spend more than he or she has.

 Balance of Trade

You've probably heard the expression "to be your brother's keeper." When you start up a sub-account, you are responsible. If the account goes negative and then disappears, the trade exchange justifiably comes back against you. You'll have to cover the trade dollars.

Keep Barter Excitement High

You want to make sure your employees continue to be excited about trade. As long as they're taking trade for part of their pay, it benefits your company. If your employees become disenchanted with trade, however, they might put their hands out for cash. You don't want that.

So you'll want to stay on top of it. You'll need to know if your workers are effectively spending their trade dollars. The statement your company receives should include the trade balances of your employees. If it doesn't, call your exchange periodically. Make sure your employees are in fact spending the trade dollars they've been getting.

If an employee is accumulating trade dollars, ask him why. Perhaps it's not a problem and he is simply saving for a future purchase. But if he has been thwarted on purchases and no longer values his trade dollars, you'll want to intercede.

Barter Bits

Most exchanges offer hard copies of directories, but these are often out of date. They're used primarily for promotional and sales purposes. Virtually all exchanges offer member listings online. Make sure your employees are apprised of these opportunities.

Make sure your employees have access to a current directory and they're receiving e-mails from the exchange that promote hot barter offerings. In general, they should receive the same communications you do. If there's a trade gift show, they should be invited. If new inventory has arrived in the barter showroom, they should know.

Be the Company Store, If You Dare

Here's a creative way of paying employees in trade. Take care of their personal emergencies and then do a payroll deduction! This is not for the faint of heart, however.

Let's say you're in the restaurant business. Your dishwasher is a good dishwasher, but has had continuing financial problems. His car has broken down, again. You might consider picking up a used car on barter and letting him pay for it, over time, with a payroll deduction.

Trade can literally save the day when comes to your employees' unexpected problems. Trade can also take care of hiring an attorney, finding an apartment, or cleaning up after a flood. Just be sure your employee sticks around long enough to pay you back!

Don't Forget Uncle Sam

Trade dollars, in whatever form they take, are subject to the same taxation laws as cash. If you have an employee and issue him a W-2, you cannot also issue him a 1099. Therefore, as you pay an employee trade dollars, you must "gross up" the wage, so that when you withhold the tax from it, you come up with the original amount of trade dollars you gave your employee.

This book is not intended to be a treatise on accounting principles. Suffice it to say trade dollars should be treated exactly as if they were cash. Your accountant should be able to figure this out. If not, call your broker and get the name of one who can, and spend trade dollars at the same time!

Sub-Accounts Shouldn't Be Second-Class Citizens

Make sure you tell your trade exchange that you value your employees. You expect your trade broker to do the same. Brokers sometimes fall into the habit of dealing only with the owner of a business (you). They forget sub-accounts because they're not as visible; they're not the ones making decisions on product offerings. Nor do they pay the bills. Yet, one of your main outlets for spending trade is your payroll. Make sure your exchange understands this.

At the same time, you should remind your employee that trade is a two-way street. It requires effort on the part of the trade exchange and the member. If the card holder doesn't put any effort into spending, trade will be unlikely to work.

The Least You Need to Know

- ◆ Make sure your trade exchange has enough to offer your employees.
- ◆ Teach employees the basics of trade; don't oversell it.

◆ Parlay your barter payroll plan into goals, productivity, and an improved bottom line.

◆ Making barter work is an ongoing process for both you and your employees.

Chapter 12

Barter Beyond a Trade Exchange's Membership

In This Chapter

- Referring businesses to trade
- Using trade to collect bad debts from nonmembers
- Utilizing trade to pay off debts to nonmembers
- Trading with nonmembers to generate cash

You share a goal with your trade exchange. Both of you want to add new members. An expanding membership base means more places to spend your trade dollars. So motivated, it's not a bad idea to call your trade exchange from time to time to "see who the members are." This is a fine idea.

Yet, successful trading is not a product of simply finding out who's on the magic list. Rather, it's a matter of understanding a trade system can include anybody who agrees to participate. Trading is like fly-fishing in a fast-moving stream. The fish in it now are different than five minutes ago. And five minutes from now, some of the current fish will have swum downstream and will be replaced by even newer fish.

So who are these new "fish"? They're everybody. They're your current vendors and ones who would like to be. They're down the street and across the country. Some may owe you money; others you might owe. And there are others who can give you cold hard cash!

So grab a fishing pole. Let's find a stream!

Help Your Exchange Sign Up New Members

Many members simply wait for the sales staff of the trade exchange to go out and sign new members. They eagerly await e-mail alerts or the publication of a new directory to see who these new members are. The most successful traders, however, work hand-in-hand to sign up new members.

Is there a business you'd like to buy from that's not a member of the trade exchange? Call that business and warm them up. Tell them about trade and the new customers they'll attract. Then call your trade exchange and tell them who it is.

Trade exchanges' best advertising is word of mouth. When you warm up a potential member for them, it makes their sales effort infinitely easier. They love members who give them referrals, and they'll compensate you for it.

Most trade exchanges offer a referral fee when you get them a new member. That doesn't mean just giving them the name of someone you would like to see on trade. It means talking to, and warming up, that potential new member, and telling them of the advantages of joining. Don't try to close the sale. Don't inundate the prospect with information either. Keep it simple, pique their interest, and then let the sales department at the trade exchange do the rest.

All trade exchanges covet members that sell high-demand products more than ones that are low-demand. If you get your trade exchange a furniture store, tire dealer, or nice restaurant, these businesses sell more than low-demand products. Be sure to ask for an increased finder's fee when you get a choice account.

A more direct way of introducing a new prospect to a trade
exchange is to actually make
an introduction. Many trade
exchanges conduct weekly or
monthly mixers. Invite a friend
who is not yet a member. She'll
get to talk to a roomful of traders
who already know how to make
organized barter work.

Barter Bits

Most trade exchanges
offer a referral fee of
$100 to $200 for get-
ting them a new mem-
ber. Usually this is in barter,
but occasionally you'll find
a trade exchange that will
cough up the cash.

Other exchanges conduct trade fairs or expos where members sell their
products on trade. These are perfect opportunities to invite prospects
to become familiar with trade.

Convince Your Cash Vendors to Accept Trade

Let's face it. Trade is intended to be a way a business can get new business, not to replace current cash. So how can you spend trade dollars
with someone you're currently spending cash with? It depends on the
relationship. It also depends on whether you want to play hardball or
not.

Let's again take the case of Sid the Sign Guy. You know Sid from
Chapter 4, "How and Why a Trade Exchange Works." Because of Sid's
high fixed cost, high gross margins, and excess capacity, he has great
motivation to spend trade dollars whenever he can. Sid currently con-
tracts for his printing with Pete the Printer.

Sid the Sign Guy currently spends $5,000 per year with Pete the
Printer. Sid is perfectly happy with Pete's printing, but would like him
to accept trade dollars. Yet, Pete is unmotivated to do so. After all,
he is already getting cash from Sid and is quite comfortable with the
arrangement.

To get Pete to accept trade, Sid can explore a few options. The first
involves the proverbial iron fist inside the velvet glove. Sid can tell Pete
that, although he is happy with the quality of his printing, he owes it
to his business to spend trade dollars. Sid would go on to explain that
there are other printers in the trade exchange. If Pete wants to retain
his business, he has to join the exchange and accept trade dollars.

If Sid is feeling more accommodating, instead of playing hardball, he could offer Pete another choice. Pete must still join the exchange, but he would be asked to trade every other job. This would allow Pete to maintain half his cash business and trade for the rest.

Finally, Sid could tell Pete he will continue to spend $5,000 in cash each year. But anything after that would be barter. Sid could get some print jobs that were on his "wish list," and Pete wouldn't have to convert one dime of cash into trade.

When you try to spend trade dollars with someone who's not yet a member, know this: if the seller thinks he's going to get cash, he probably won't trade. Be unequivocal in your offer.

Use Trade to Collect Bad Debt

You've probably had the following experience. The mail comes. In between a charge card solicitation and the utility bill is a letter from the court. Not just any court, but the bankruptcy court. As you open the letter, you know it's a filing from someone, not a member of the exchange, who owes you money.

Let's again use the example of Sid the Sign Guy. Sid also received a letter from the court. It turned out one of his cash customers, The Buckeye Bar & Grill, had gone out of business, straight to *Chapter* 7. There had been warnings. Over the months, the restaurant had gotten further and further behind on its bill. Sid liked making signs for The Buckeye Bar & Grill, and he trusted them. Now he was getting "rewarded" for his trust. He was getting stuck for $4,000.

def•i•ni•tion

Chapter 7 Filing bankruptcy under this chapter does not involve filing a plan of repayment to debtors. Instead, nonexempt assets, if any, are sold off with proceeds split among the company's creditors. Usually Chapter 7 businesses have little if anything to offer creditors.

What if Sid had taken another course of action, say, a year ago? He could have called The Buckeye Bar & Grill and suggested a barter arrangement whereby he would receive gift certificates equal to the amount of indebtedness.

At the time, The Buckeye Bar & Grill had the capability of serving meals. They just didn't have any money in the checkbook. Also, by giving $4,000 of certificates to Sid, it cost the restaurant only about 30 percent, which represented their food cost.

Sid could eat only so many hamburgers and drink so much beer, so he traded the excess certificates to his local trade exchange. This would have been an easy trade.

Trade exchanges are always looking for restaurant meals to offer their members. They are, after all, constantly being challenged by a shrinking universe of locally owned restaurants. The Buckeye Bar & Grill actually had decent food, and the trade exchange would have been delighted to sell the certificates, crediting Sid's account.

If Sid had collected by accepting trade from this nonmember, he would today have $4,000 trade dollars, which he could have spent at hundreds of businesses. No, it wasn't cash, but it was a lot better than receiving nothing.

Real Live Goods from Real Deadbeats

Sometimes a collection effort requires you take physical possession of a product. For example, let's say a snowboard distributor owes you $10,000 in cash. Collect snowboards, and then call your broker at the trade exchange. The exchange may have a ready buyer, perhaps a ski resort, or it might like to place the boards in its showroom (if it has one), or it may want you to sell them at a trade show it has planned.

If you acquire goods you're not familiar with from companies that owe you money, don't panic. You might not be an expert at snowboards, but because of the nature of trade, you can sell them on trade when your creditor couldn't for cash.

Barter Bits

If you get your trade exchange involved in moving and storing merchandise, or in placing it in its showroom, your trade exchange will have additional costs and risks. It will probably want a markup on the acquired goods.

Leverage Barter Collecting Debt

Yes, when collecting debts, you should get cash whenever possible. Don't be too quick to offer barter as a way out. But when barter is the way to clear a debt owed to you, don't be afraid to leverage the value of trade to get more than the dollar amount.

I go into detail in Chapter 14 on ways you can leverage barter to improve your take in a transaction. For now, simply put, when someone already owes you cash, you might very well ask for—and get—a multiple in trade. This is especially true if the company that owes you cash has a low cost of goods.

In Sid's case, he was owed $4,000 cash from the nonmember Buckeye Bar & Grill. What if he had asked for $8,000 of restaurant gift certificates to settle the bill? Chances are the restaurant would have still gone along with the deal: it was still cheaper than spending $4,000 cash because the restaurant had empty tables and its food cost was 30 percent. Even on $8,000 of certificates, the cash-out-of pocket investment for the restaurant is only $2,400.

Sid now has double the trade dollars than what was originally owed him in cash. Not only did he get a great return on his money, he won't have to worry about receiving notices from the bankruptcy court.

Some Collecting Caveats to Remember

Even the best laid plans can go sideways. When you collect someone else's product you later sell through a trade exchange, there are a couple things to remember.

Don't forget that an IOU is only as good as the person who issues it. If you sell an IOU or gift certificate to the trade exchange, and the issuer immediately goes kaput, your trade exchange is going to come back on you. It's going to want you to refund the trade dollars to the people who bought the worthless certificates.

Here's another caveat. There are laws pertaining to "preferential vendors" in the event of bankruptcy. They were put into place to stop financially distressed parties from paying off friends and relatives, and then sticking everyone else. These laws allow the trustee to demand, under certain conditions, that recent payees return their payments to the court, if collected within 90 days of the filing.

> **Balance of Trade**
>
> Know your bankruptcy laws. A member of a trade exchange in California collected a boat worth $12,000 from one of his accounts. When he tried to sell it for trade dollars to another member, he discovered a bank still had a lien on it. This negated the entire deal.

Role Reversal: Paying a Debt

Let's say the roles are reversed. Instead of being the creditor, you're the debtor. In fact, your business is struggling. How can you get others who are not members of your trade exchange to accept trade dollars in lieu of cash?

If you're in a hole, there are two businesses you should be trying to make happy. One is your bank, and the other is your trade exchange. This is because your trade exchange is your bank of last resort. It will put faith in you and perhaps give you a trade dollar loan (see Chapter 4), if you are current on cash fees and if you sell a product that's in demand by other members.

Be Honest

We know you're honest, but in order to pay off creditors with trade, it requires brutal honesty. It means leveling with your creditors about the condition of your company. Most creditors are willing to work with you if you communicate with them. They're not stupid. They would rather get trade than nothing.

Assuming you have the trade dollars to spend, or you have a line of credit with your exchange, your job is to get your creditors to understand organized barter. Tell them trade dollars is all you have, and a cash payment is impossible. Only a fool for a creditor is going to refuse to consider your offer.

To get your creditor to accept trade, she first has to have no doubt you're broke. If she believes there is any chance whatsoever she'll be paid in a timely matter with cash, she will not agree to your proposal.

Trade Tales

A collection agency in Cleveland was dunning a Kalamazoo, Michigan, restaurant for several thousand dollars on behalf of a Fortune 500 company. The restaurateur, a member of the local exchange, asked if it would consider trade dollars instead of cash. It turned out the collection agency was a member of an exchange in Cleveland. It accepted the trade dollars and paid off its client in cash. The restaurant retained thousands of dollars in cash.

You have to tell her you have many creditors, and the first ones to act will be the ones who get paid. Explain the dire nature of your payables. Give your creditor a deadline, too. If she doesn't take the trade dollars, you have another creditor waiting in the wings.

The next step is you have to get your creditor to understand and appreciate organized barter. Call your trade exchange and speak with the best salesperson they have; then make an appointment. Lay it out on the table. Ask your creditor if she wants to get paid, today no less!

Trade Tales

A hotel in Chicago, strapped for cash, asked the local trade exchange to call its creditors who held invoices more than six months old. It offered trade payment in the amount of the invoices. The project worked so well the hotel was able to liquidate $1 million in debt, using rooms that otherwise would have been empty.

The Benefits to Your Creditor

Your creditor probably uses services commonly available on barter: printing, maintenance, vehicle repair, and maybe even signage from Sid the Sign Guy. She also wants to get the whole matter off her desk, and at the same time, would like to retain you as a future cash customer.

Accepting trade dollars instead of cash not only wipes off the debt, but leaves your business in a stronger financial position, which bodes well for both sides of the transaction.

Get Cash When You Trade

Now consider yourself the owner of Kate's Cakes. For years, you've been trying to get the pastry contract with the downtown convention center. The convention center does most of its own catering, but does not attempt pastries, cakes, and croissants. A competing bakery currently has the contract. You've tried to nab the account, but you've been unsuccessful. The convention center appears satisfied with the current arrangement.

How can you use your membership in a trade exchange to snare that business? And how would you like to get some cash while doing it? There is a way.

Doing the Math

Determine approximately how much the convention center spends on baked goods. Let's say you figure it's about $25,000 per year. Tell the convention center you would be willing to do it for $15,000 cash and $10,000 worth of hotel room gift certificates and then take the certificates to your trade exchange. Because it's a high-end hotel, the trade exchange will likely buy them from you for face value. You now have trade dollars to spend on whatever you wish.

Why would the convention center go along with your plan? It's simple. Just do the arithmetic. Let's say the hotel has 200 rooms and maintains an 80 percent occupancy rate. That means it's filling, on average, 160 rooms per night, leaving 40 unfilled. Multiply 40 rooms × 365 days × $150 per night, and you end up with $210,000 worth of unsold rooms for the year. Do you really think giving you a mere $10,000 worth of those empty rooms is going to cost the hotel any money?

> **Balance of Trade**
>
> Hotels are often allowed to exclude certain nights or times of year from trade. "Blacking out" those times they expect to have no vacancies protects their cash flow. Most exchanges can live with some restrictions.

There are many advantages for the convention center to change vendors and buy its specialty baked goods from Kate's Cakes. It slashed its cash out-of-pocket from $25,000 to $15,000, saving a cool $10,000. It also enjoys a future cash bonus, as the guests the trade exchange sends over will undoubtedly spend cash for meals, room service, and sundries.

Having Your Cake and Eating It, Too

This three-way relationship worked for everyone. The convention center saved $10,000 a year by filling up empty rooms; the trade exchange was pleased because it made a nice hotel available to its members as it generated commissions; and finally, you got a prestigious new customer.

But you accomplished even more. In the eyes of the buyer, you did not discount or denigrate the value of your product. You still charged $25,000, albeit some of it was in barter. You also "covered your nut" or out-of-pocket cash costs. Finally, the transaction with the convention center may have been "part cash and part trade," but what you traded to the trade exchange was 100 percent trade.

> **Balance of Trade**
>
> The media is especially sensitive to client complaints involving "rate integrity," or charging less to some advertisers than others. By including a trade component, instead of discounting, they can avoid this perception.

After all is said, you have one final advantage. After your one-year arrangement expires, there's a good chance you can convert the contract to full cash, assuming the people at the convention center like your delicious baked goods!

The Least You Need to Know

- If you want new members to trade with, help the sales department at the trade exchange find them.

- If a company not a member of your exchange owes you money, you can use trade to make a collection before the business files for bankruptcy.

- If your business is hurting, consider organized barter to pay off some debts with nonmembers and stay afloat.

- There are ways barter can lead to big cash deals. All it takes is a little partnering with your trade exchange.

Part 4

Advanced Trade Techniques

Now we're getting into some serious trading. The advanced strategies discussed in this part require a good deal of creativity and work, but the return can be major, even phenomenal.

Two of your major partners in these strategies are media and travel industries. Both have times of excess capacity that can be leveraged into profitable deals. Yet there are risks and pitfalls you need to avoid. Enter this part with care.

Chapter 13

Trading Up

In This Chapter

- ◆ Utilizing media and travel—the stalwarts of barter
- ◆ Using barter to leverage big deals
- ◆ Trading up using trade dollars
- ◆ Turning a little cash into a lot of barter

For the advanced trader, there are ways you can parlay small barter deals into really big ones. Call it "trading up." Do it right, and you can realize some surprising profits.

To succeed at trading up, you don't have to own a big business, but you have to accept a simple premise. That is, it's possible to trade an item for something of a greater value and then do it multiple times.

Trading up might sound simple, but you'll probably need to work with two traditional barterers: media and travel. You'll want to understand what motivates these industries and why they represent opportunities for you.

Direct trade has its limitations. But if you're a member of a trade exchange, you'll be able to trade up better than relying on direct barter alone. A trade exchange can minimize your risk and maximize your number of barter opportunities.

To trade up, you have to find ways to turn cash into trade dollar multiples. You need to find out what products are in demand in your trade exchange and then see if you can buy them—from liquidators, through auctions, or sales of distressed inventories. Finally, you may want to do something your trade exchange might not be crazy about—that is, buy trade dollars from your fellow members.

Trade in Increments

Investors are always told to "buy low and sell high." This conveys, however, a get-rich-quick mentality. The saying should really be "buy low and sell just a little bit higher." If you do that enough times, you will ultimately reach your goal.

When people advise you to buy low and sell high, they're usually referring to cash—buy something for $20 and sell it for $30. Buying low and selling high sounds simple, but it can be hard to do.

If you understand barter, this process can be easier than you think because barter doesn't require you to spend scarce cash. Take the case of one Kyle MacDonald. MacDonald succeeded in trading up, not to "a deluxe apartment in the sky," but to a comfortable Saskatchewan farmhouse—all for the price of a red paperclip.

No Money, No Job, Only a Paperclip

In 2006, Kyle MacDonald was a 26-year-old college student in Montreal. With no job and little money, he took a look at his assets, which included a red paperclip in his desk drawer. Tired of renting, he decided to trade the red paperclip for a house!

MacDonald realized no one would do an even trade of a house for a paperclip, so he decided to trade the paperclip for something, anything, of greater value. He posted his paperclip on the Craig's List barter section, and lo and behold, traded it for a pen that looked like a fish, which

he traded for a hand-sculpted door-
knob, which he traded for a camp
stove, and so on. Some of Kyle's
trades were fairly bizarre. One of
them involved trading a year's lease
for a home in Phoenix for an after-
noon with Alice Cooper. His last
trade was no less remarkable, as he
bartered a small role in a Hollywood
movie for a Saskatchewan farmhouse.

> **Trade Tales**
>
> After MacDonald completed
> his barter journey, the city
> constructed a huge red paper-
> clip in front of his house, com-
> memorating his achievement.
> He commemorated it in his
> own way, by having a jew-
> eler turn a red paperclip into
> a wedding ring.

Learning from MacDonald

Aside from the feel-good aspect of MacDonald's quest, his tactics
can teach us something about trading up: he didn't always trade hard
goods for other hard goods. He'd have been stuck forever. Rather, he
would make huge leaps by enticing people to "overpay" with a soft
good. But they were happy to do so because it didn't actually cost them
any money. MacDonald's last trades illustrated this. He had secured
a speaking role in a movie, which had not cost the movie producer a
dime. Yet it had a high perceived value by the owner of the house, who
gladly traded it to MacDonald so he could be in the movie.

It should be noted that there were no "losers" in any of MacDonald's
deals. On the surface, some didn't seem to receive equivalent value, but
they really did. They gave up items or services they weren't even using
or that they had very little cash into.

Nobody expects you to put together 14 trades to get where you're
going. Actually, sometimes all it takes is one or two trades.

It's hard to put together a multilevel barter deal without including at
least one of two industries: media and travel. They not only trade with
each other; they'll trade with you.

Media and Travel: Barter Junkies

Media and travel have always traded heavily. Just turn on the TV and
watch *The Price Is Right*. The show mainly consists of plugs for prizes,
interrupted by excited contestants jumping up and down. Many of these
plugs are for travel.

Trade Tales
Incredibly, the first radio trade was probably consummated in 1920. Radio station KDKA in Pittsburgh had promised to report the 1920 election results live, but faced the prospect of a lot of dead air. KDKA traded for phonograph records from the Hamilton Music Company to play music during long lulls in the coverage.

If you watch carefully, you'll notice the game show host is often giving away travel. He extols the pleasantries of some hotel you've never heard of before. Just as the hotel gains notoriety, the show also has a nifty prize to give away. No one had to spend a dime either. The show had programming to fill; the hotel had rooms to fill.

The media and hotels like to trade for two reasons. First, they both often have unsold time and space. Second, they need to buy lots of stuff.

Your local radio station, for example, must pay for maintenance of their physical facilities, along with printing, bumper stickers, and prizes to give away on air. By the same token, the hotel industry loves to trade empty rooms because it, too, has a myriad of costs, ranging from advertising, roofing repair, copy machines, parking lot maintenance, and zillions of other needs.

You can capitalize on the tremendous advantage that barter offers to the media and hotel industries. You're a smart trader and can enjoy *leverage*.

def•i•ni•tion

Leverage As used in barter, the advantage gained when a seller of a soft good willingly pays more in trade than a prevailing cash price. This process allows the buyer to "trade up" into items of greater and greater value.

Media and hotels have very little out-of-pocket cash when they fill their time and space. They sometimes actually prefer to pay two, three, and even four times the amount in barter than spend any cash. When you use this to your advantage, you enjoy leverage.

Not all the media and hotels will trade, and not all will offer you leverage. The key is to figure who will. Then call them.

Radio Stations: Prime Trading Partners

Radio stations are a prime target for leveraged deals. This is because it doesn't cost them any additional cash to run more commercials. Radio stations know the meaning of barter.

Some radio stations are abhorrent to spending cash. So much so, they'll gladly pony up multiples of trade to pay for what they need.

Balance of Trade

There is a caveat when it comes to radio stations trading. You'll never get one to trade if it has no excess air time, is asked to convert cash into trade, or is in danger of fostering a "barter reputation" when its willingness to barter becomes so well known that potential cash advertisers all want to barter.

Stations in extremely small markets, however, frequently don't trade, at least not with local businesses. In "one-horse" towns, the only station is by definition also the "number one" station. It has little incentive to trade.

On the other end of the spectrum, most highly rated stations in large markets don't trade either. These stations stuff every nook and cranny of airtime with cash business, much of it from national advertisers.

Corporate Policy Can Kill Trade

Finally, stations that were consolidated into large groups during the 1990s curtailed their trading, primarily because of corporate policy and tight accounting controls.

When a radio station is purchased by a new company, policy can dictate that barter is eliminated, not because it wouldn't be beneficial but because of a reaction to prior abuses.

Trade Tales

In 1985, an owner of a radio station in Indiana traded air time for his wedding, including the reception, bridal gown, tuxedos, liquor, honeymoon, and even the band that played at the reception. The station was subsequently sold to a large media group that banned all trade.

Some local operators "over-traded" their stations, using trade for the equivalent of liquor and fast cars. These abuses led some consolidators to consider barter too difficult to police. So they indiscriminately drove a stake through the heart of trade at all their stations.

The Most Likely Candidates

The best radio stations to approach on barter are those in the "middle of the pack." Search out stations in mid-sized markets, with average ratings. These stations have competitors, unsold advertising time, and are not a part of large groups. These stations are motivated to trade and have the autonomy to do so.

Not surprisingly, consolidation in reverse is now making barter more commonplace among many stations. Some of the highest-profile attempts at consolidation failed, and large radio groups have begun selling off a significant number of their stations to smaller groups. This has allowed for more local autonomy, including the decision to barter.

Don't Forget the Other Media

Radio stations have a tradition steeped in trade. They discovered early on that unsold airtime is the ultimate perishable inventory, and it costs them nothing to fill it. But there are other media that enjoy similar advantages—billboards, other broadcast media, print, and the Internet.

Again, it's best to approach a company that has a local decision maker. For example, some billboard companies are owned by regional or national concerns. Yet, in many markets, there are smaller billboard companies, locally owned, which have unsold boards. When you're searching for leverage, it's always best if you can contact a local decision maker.

The same goes with other broadcast media. They'll trade too, especially smaller cable operators. Competition is fierce for broadcast advertising revenue, and there is almost always unsold airtime.

Magazines, coupon clippers, and secondary newspapers are also good sources of barter. They often will barter advertising on a *space available basis*.

def•i•ni•tion

> **Space available basis**   Newspapers and magazines will sometimes barter ads on a space available basis, or when they have space that otherwise would have to be taken up with free promos or filler copy. If this is not the case, depending on the formatting of the publication, to run one more ad might entail adding four pages to the press run.

Usually, it's difficult to get a city's main newspaper to trade. Big papers traditionally didn't have to trade, and they commanded top dollar for ads. This has changed, yet the mentality of papers is generally not to barter.

The new kid on the block is the Internet. Web advertising is dominated by huge search engines such as Google and Yahoo. These entities will be difficult to approach on trade, but you might find certain banner advertising available, particularly if you're trading web design services.

Whatever medium you choose as a trading partner, the same rules apply. To trade up, your trading partner has to have local autonomy, excess time or space, and a willingness to offer you a trade multiple when it wants to buy something.

Hotels Trade, Too

Just like a radio station or newspaper, hotels and resort properties sell time and space. If tonight's rooms go unsold, the owner gains nothing. This is the primary reason they are terrific barter partners when your goal is to trade up.

Barter Bits

> The American Hotel & Lodging Association estimates there are 48,062 properties with 15 guest rooms or more, accounting for nearly 4.5 million rooms. With a 37 percent average vacancy rate, this represents 1.66 million unsold rooms each night. If each room night has an average value of $70, that's $116 million worth of unsold rooms each night. Put another way, $4 billion worth of rooms go unsold each year.

The travel industry is also a big barterer because its needs are great. They constantly need advertising and promotion. They also have to take care of their properties, needing everything from roofing to carpet cleaning. If you can show them a way they can barter for some of these needs, hotels may be willing to pay more in the form of room nights than cash.

Not all hotels will trade. As you approach possible trading partners, be guided by the same principles as with the media. You're looking for properties where you can actually talk to the decision maker.

You're wasting your time if the hotel almost never has any vacancies. Also, certain properties are in markets where mega-corporations rule, such as Las Vegas. These, too, are unlikely trading partners.

Put Hotel Trades in Transferable Form

When you trade with a hotel for room nights, make it easy on yourself. Have the hotel give you a transferable "block" of credit, or due bill. That way, the person you trade the hotel credit to will be responsible for making the reservations, not you.

There are exceptions to this rule. If, for example, you find yourself with a due bill at a high-end resort, you might not want to entrust someone else to place the reservation. You value your relationship with the resort too much to risk it being screwed up. Plus, since the value of reservation is of high value, you probably won't mind playing travel agent.

If at all possible, have the hotel issue scrip that includes restrictions and booking procedure right on the certificate. That way, if the scrip is traded and traded again, the end user will know exactly what he or she is getting.

Negotiate Smart, but Fair

Just as a radio station can't be asked to barter advertising during the sold-out week before Christmas, you can't ask a hotel to trade rooms during spring break, or other peak times. If you trade with a hotel, be prepared. They may ask you to abide by their *projected room night availability.*

def•i•ni•tion

Projected room night availability   The practice of a hotel or resort blacking out or excluding from trade times when they think they'll have a "full house." If a property knows that a huge convention will book all the rooms in town a year from now, it may still reserve the right to not want trade during that time, even though rooms might technically be available for cash.

Just as you may allow a property to black out certain dates from trade, don't let them overdo it. You'll want to make sure your credit at the hotel can be redeemed within a reasonable period of time, without a boatload of restrictions. You don't want to encounter a refusal every time a request for a room is made.

Some traders don't transact in an ethical manner. If you're unsure of the character of someone you're trading with, you might want to start off with a small trade, just to make sure reservations can be placed easily and guests are taken care of.

Balance of Trade

Don't issue or receive excessive amounts of scrip for a hotel or resort. A few years ago, a resort in the Florida Keys issued, and traded, so much scrip, the market became flooded with it. Redeeming it became almost impossible. Faced with everyone trying to redeem their scrip at once, the owner repeatedly claimed to not have any vacancies. This alienated virtually all his trading partners.

If a hotel puts an expiration date on its scrip or due bill, be on the lookout. Some hotels or resorts may repeatedly claim to have no availabilities and then tell you the paper it issued has expired.

Don't let a hotel get away with not honoring its promise. If a property tells you its scrip "expired," remind them of certain laws that are found in the books in most states. These are called *escheat laws*.

Be aware that some properties are notorious for publishing rates that no one actually pays. Be wary of bartering for rooms that are priced at *rack rate*. If they are using this standard of pricing, the leverage you think you're getting might not really be there.

def•i•ni•tion

> **Escheat laws** Laws in most states that pertain to property, which, if abandoned, becomes property of the state. If a hotel or restaurant issues gift certificates that are lost or expired, they may owe the face value of the certificate, in cash, to the state.
>
> **Rack rate** The rate printed on a card in all hotel rooms, along with other regulations and conditions. It is often a very high nightly rate that you didn't actually pay. No one pays it, except for maybe on New Year's Eve or other times when every place in town is fully booked.

One option is to base your trade with hotels on a fixed number of room nights, rather than a dollar value. That way, if you own 100 overnight stays, you're protected, even if the hotel doubles its room rate a year from now.

Finally, remind yourself that when you're trading with a hotel, you're essentially dealing with a promise. You're dealing with a promise that it will abide by the conditions of the scrip or gift certificates it issued. When you do the deal, know who you're dealing with.

If a Deal Goes South

If you give hotel scrip to someone else and it turns out to be no good, what then? This can happen if the hotel unexpectedly sells. The new owner, who never enjoyed the benefits of the original trade, might refuse to honor the scrip.

This could place you in an awkward position. Unless the terms of your trade-out stated otherwise, you are morally on the hook for making good on your trade.

If you do enough trades, one or two of them is bound to go sour. Be prepared to make good; your reputation as a trader depends on it.

Location, Location, Location

You can trade for all the hotel credit in the world, but it's no good unless you can sell it or barter it to someone else. If it's in an in-demand destination, and in the middle of sun and fun, or a great ski resort, you probably won't have to think twice. But if it's not, you'll want to make sure your bases are covered. Make sure you have something that's tradable.

You'll also want to make sure the hotel scrip you're receiving is for a nice place. Be sure to check out online reviews; go there yourself, if you can. There is nothing worse than having to apologize to a trading partner for a hotel's poor service, bad food, or dirty rooms.

The easiest scrip to resell or barter is that which is near downtowns of major metropolitan areas. All-inclusive resorts are also easy to move.

Okay, Let's Trade Up!

Let's combine paperclip magic with the leverage offered to you by the media and travel industries. Fittingly, let's start a hypothetical trade with a radio station and trade up from there.

Using the criteria from the first part of this chapter, you have found a radio station that loves to trade, called WTRD ("We-Trade"). You establish WTRD doesn't mind paying more in barter than cash and really needs bumper stickers. In fact, the station needs $5,000 worth of bumper stickers.

You're going to do a three for one. In other words, you're going to be the one to buy the bumper stickers for $5,000 cash, and you are going to trade them to the radio station that's going to give you $15,000 worth of air time. Again, remember the radio station is doing this because it is averse to spending cash, it has unsold advertising time, and it really needs the bumper stickers.

You now own $15,000 worth of advertising that you can barter to anyone, as long as it's not a current cash customer of the radio station. You decide to approach a hotel, called Nationwide Suites.

Nationwide Suites could really use the advertising, but it has no cash in its budget for additional advertising. Plus, it has its share of

> **Barter Bits**
>
> In this example, you spent $5,000 to generate $15,000 worth of product. Doing a three for one is actually pretty easy, but what if you had been able to barter for the bumper stickers? Your leverage would have been even greater!

empty rooms, priced out at about $100 per night. In fact, the hotel has a 20 percent average vacancy rate with 100 rooms.

Are you going to give the hotel $15,000 worth of advertising for 150 room nights? Nope. You're going to ask for 300 room nights.

Is the Hotel Insane to Overpay?

It's not insane; nor is it overpaying. Nationwide Suites is smart enough to realize that it can gain $15,000 worth of advertising for an average of less than one room per night. This won't affect its cash flow whatsoever, plus you allowed them to exclude the few times each year they expect to have a full house.

You're now the proud owner of 300 room nights. Where are you going from here?

No Joke

Your journey now takes you to Looney's Comedy Club. You talk to the owner of Looney's, Lance Looney. Lance tells you that one of his major costs is paying for the hotel rooms of the comedians he brings in from out of town. On average, he sets up three comedians each Friday and Saturday night. Those six rooms currently cost Lance $600 per week.

You've got yourself a live one. You offer Lance the 300 room nights you own. If you weren't trading up, you'd ask for $30,000 worth of gift certificates good at Looney's. But remember, you're trading up.

Instead, you ask for $40,000 worth of certificates. You get it. Not because Lance is stupid, but because Lance has a 30 percent food cost. Because Lance has excess empty seats to fill, issuing those certificates costs him only $12,000 in cash.

Lance used to pay $30,000 cash each year to house his comedians. Now he's paying the equivalent of $12,000. Plus, he'll be attracting new customers who will spread the word about Looney's. Not only that, these new customers, if they like his food and comedians, will be back, to spend cash!

Don't Forget Your Obligations

When trading up, you are bartering products and promises you have received from others. Be prepared to guarantee performance. For example, what happens if you trade TV advertising to someone, but then the TV station refuses to run the spots? That's one of the pitfalls of doing direct trades.

If you find yourself doing more and bigger trades, your upside is greater, but so is your downside. Also, make sure you don't morph into a *trunk trader.*

def•i•ni•tion

> **Trunk trader**   Someone who makes a living doing trades, but usually does it from her living room. She rarely offers any accounting or guarantees to her trading partners. A trunk trader can be responsible for hundreds of transactions, valued at hundreds of thousands of dollars, but seldom sends out 1099s as required by law.

Before you go to bed at night, especially if you want to sleep, you should know that if you do more than 100 trades, you're going to have to start sending out 1099s. Be prepared to spend some time with your bookkeeper or CPA so you can offer legitimate documentation of trades you have conducted.

Your Bottom Line

By the time your barter journey has been completed, you will have turned $5,000 cash into $15,000 worth of radio advertising, that you traded into $30,000 worth of room nights, which you traded into $40,000 worth of gift certificates at the local comedy club.

You've turned your version of the red paperclip into gold. What's your next trade? Or are you going to find a way to sell the comedy club gift certificates? In other words, are you going to cash out?

Before going any further, you've probably noticed that up to this point we haven't used any trade dollars. So how can a deal be made even better, easier, and less risky with a trade exchange at your side? Stay tuned.

Don't Get Caught with Something You Can't Barter

If you trade up by bartering one item for another of greater value, you run a risk. That is, what if you end up with an item you can't barter? For example, in the last example, you traded radio advertising for a large quantity of hotel rooms. Then you traded the rooms to a local comedy club. But what if there had been no comedy club? Who would have been interested in 300 room nights?

It might have taken a year or more for you to wind down your inventory of hotel rooms. It would have been infinitely easier if you had someone else on your side.

A Trade Exchange: Your Selling Partner

If you're a member of a trade exchange, you can sell to hundreds of members who will spend trade dollars more readily than cash. Some of your fellow members are expecting out-of-town guests; others need to accommodate business associates for overnight stays. The point is it's a lot harder to get stuck holding an inventory when you can sell to the captive audience of a trade exchange.

> ### Trade Tales
>
> One member of a trade exchange in Michigan suffered a serious flood in his house. Because his house was inhabitable, he called his broker, who promptly arranged a week-long stay for the member's family at a local hotel. The member was made even happier when his insurance company paid him for his emergency accommodations—in cash.

Trade exchanges specialize in winding down large inventories. For example, an exchange might agree to buy all 300 room nights, credit your account, and then resell them piecemeal.

Depending on what inventory you're trading, if you sell it in total to your trade exchange, it may insist on making a margin. For example, instead of giving you $30,000 for 300 room nights, it might give you $25,000. Since it's dealing with the headaches of reselling the certificates, or booking the rooms, it deserves to make a small margin.

Use Trade Dollars to Buy and Sell

Another way of trading up involves alternately using cash and trade dollars. In doing so, it means leveraging the inherent differences between the two.

Let's revisit the definition of a trade dollar. From Chapter 4, you may recall it's usually based on retail value.

So let's say you buy something on trade, perhaps a lawn tractor for $5,000 trade dollars. Now you sell it for $4,000 cash to your neighbor. At first blush, to someone who doesn't understand barter, you just lost $1,000. But did you?

Lose and Make Money at the Same Time

The answer to the aforementioned question is: yes and no. From an accounting point of view, you did, in fact, lose $1,000. But you actually made money. That's because you haven't yet figured your trade dollar cost into the equation.

In a quick review, how does the actual cost to produce goods compare to retail value? It may cost you 20 cents to make a donut that you sell for $1. So if you bought a lawn tractor for $5,000 trade dollars, your actual cash cost was $1,000. You also incurred a 10 percent commission, or $500 when you bought the tractor. Therefore, your total cost of spending $5,000 trade was $1,500 cash.

But remember, you sold the lawn tractor for $4,000 cash. You had $1,500 into the deal, so you actually made money, $2,500 cash to be precise.

Trade Tales

Back when cordless phones were just being introduced, a creative member of a trade exchange in Connecticut bought a semitrailer full of refurbished, yet perfectly good, phones. The average cost per phone was less than $2. He sold all 4,000 phones to his trade exchange for $30 per phone. He had turned an original $8,000 cash investment into an astounding $120,000 trade. He spent his entire trade amount to buy inventory that he cashed out at 50¢ on the $1.

What if you don't own a donut shop? You own an electronics store instead, and your margin is 10 percent. Obviously, had you bought a $5,000 tractor with trade dollars that cost you $4,500, and you sold it for $4,000. You're going backward.

Trading up with trade dollars means your cost of goods can't be sky high. It has to be less than the cash you're spending in the first place.

Trading Up, Using Multiple Transactions

Having bought a riding lawn mower for $5,000 trade and selling it for $4,000 cash had its advantages. But why stop there? Let's keep the ball rolling.

Let's take that $4,000 cash and turn it into something where you can make a multiple. You find an inventory of distressed vacuum cleaners. You spend the $4,000 to buy 300 vacs that have a retail value of $400 each, or a total of $12,000.

Vacuum cleaners go like hotcakes through a trade exchange, especially if members can pick them up in a trade mart or showroom.

> **Barter Bits**
>
> An exchange in Illinois has a showroom with over $2 million worth of retail-priced inventory in it. Members can use their trade dollars in this store, just like cash, for everything from gift items to clothing.

Wow! You now have $12,000 trade dollars in your account. If you're catching yourself again saying, "Why stop there?" you're starting to get the hang of it.

Something else pops up on trade. It's a travel trailer that's priced at $12,000 trade. You figure you can cash convert it to $8,000. You decide to buy it.

Doing It Again (and Again)

With $8,000 in hand, you have a lot of options. You can certainly put all or some of the money in your pocket. Or you buy even more inventory and repeat the process.

Remember, this all started with you buying a $5,000 lawn tractor with trade dollars, in which you had a $1,500 investment. By trading up, you have now earned $8,000 cash!

When you trade up using trade dollars, make sure the numbers work. Make sure you know precisely what the cost of your trade dollar is. Don't forget to figure in the commission you pay the trade exchange. And don't get involved in time-killing deals, or ones that are too risky. But if you do it right, you can trade up more than you thought possible.

Balance of Trade

Trading up means gaining access to the best stuff a trade exchange can offer. But you won't even hear about juicy offers if you're behind on your cash fees. Your broker will put you on the bottom of his or her pile.

Using Other Players to Create Leverage

Being able to trade up means you have to get a good multiple when investing cash to make trade dollars. If your business already gives you a big gross margin, you don't have to go far. But what if what you sell has a narrow margin? Can you still trade up?

Of course you can. In fact, to trade up, you don't even have to own a business; you only have to have a nose to find good deals.

Some of the biggest traders of exchanges don't sell any one particular product. Rather, they're on the prowl for anything they can buy really cheap. They have a street sense as they discover products other members will buy. And they don't pay much for them.

Where do these traders go to buy really cheap? They find liquidators, businesses, and individuals that are in distress or have nonperforming inventory. In doing so, they depend on various tools, including auctions, Internet sites, other trade members, and simply being in the right place at the right time.

Trade Tales

One member of a trade exchange in Michigan used to go to the landfill and collect huge rolls of off-spec printing paper that had been discarded by major mills. He took it back to his paper converting machine, took off the bad edges, re-rolled it, and sold paper on trade for a dozen years to printers all over the country. Later, he arranged to pick up the paper directly from the mills so they wouldn't have to drive to the dump. The cost of his trade dollar was almost zero.

You might already be a part of an industry where you have inside knowledge of merchandise being sold really cheap. Perhaps it's someone going out of business. Or maybe you know a distributor that got stuck with returned inventory and has to make room in a warehouse. It could even be a manufacturer who has overproduced last year's model and is looking for a way to turn it to cash.

Or it could be a bank. Banks are notorious for liquidating merchandise for pennies on the dollar, often because they don't have the time or expertise to sell at a higher price.

Trade Tales

A member of a trade exchange in New England was in the business of importing winter apparel from China. He became aware of an inventory that had been refused by a national chain—7,000 jackets and snow pants were sitting in a warehouse, with the retail buying season all but over. The member bought the entire inventory from a desperate seller for 10¢ on the $1. He then resold the inventory to a trade exchange for 50¢ on the $1 in barter. With his trade dollar profits, he bought two late-model delivery vans.

Sometimes the best deals are where no one else wants to go. This is especially true of auctions. Auctions beset by inclement weather, or challenged by inconvenient location or timing, can offer the best buys for the knowledgeable buyer.

Be aware that certain inventories will not attract high bids because of shipping or logistical considerations. The buyer who is prepared to physically handle certain items can sometimes steal them at auction.

Virtual Auctions, Internet Deals

Almost everyone has bought merchandise through eBay, Craigslist, and other Internet sites. For the attentive trader, these can represent attractive cash-to-trade conversions.

Anyone can be a liquidator through the Internet. While it offers some terrific deals, there are also pitfalls. Most of these pitfalls are because you might not know the character of the person you're dealing with.

Yet, there are countless closeouts and liquidations that can be accessed from your computer. If you know what you're doing, they can offer some attractive conversions.

Can Your Trade Exchange Sell Our Deal?

In addition to being able to find good deals on inventories, you also have to have a sense of what will, in fact, sell through your trade exchange. When in doubt, contact your broker. Find out if what you're purchasing for cash can easily be traded. If not, stay away from it.

> **Balance of Trade**
>
> Make sure you understand exactly what you're getting. A trader in Minnesota thought he had an unbelievable deal when offered a semi-trailer of dry dog food at a bargain price. He thought he could easily transport and trade it for a huge profit. Then he discovered the three phases of dog food: fresh phase, oil separation phase, and finally, wormy phase. The dog food now occupies part of a landfill outside of Minneapolis.

If you're a member of more than one trade exchange, know their needs may be different. For example, if you offer a large inventory of luggage to one trade exchange, it might not be interested. It already has a source for luggage galore. But the other exchange might not have any member who sells luggage. Stay in the know when it comes to what your trade exchange might need.

Buying Trade Dollars

There's another way you can get trade dollars cheap. But your trade exchange is unlikely to tell you about. It involves buying trade dollars for cash from other members.

Not every member is willing to sell trade dollars. They are, after all, a valuable asset. Some members value their trade dollar as equal to cash; others will wheel and deal.

You want to approach the ones who will wheel and deal. You'll want to approach members who generate lots of trade dollars, yet have a very low cost of goods. You won't be surprised to know that these members are often those that sell advertising.

Full Circle, Back to the Media

The media, especially those that are independently owned, are great candidates to sell their trade dollars. By selling trade dollars, they don't create the perception they're discounting to their advertisers. All they're doing is secretly selling a slug of trade dollars to a third party at a discount.

There are advantages to buying trade dollars. They are typically "no muss, no fuss" transactions. You don't have to buy inventory, ship it, or sell it. You simply make a cash offering to someone who has lots of trade but didn't have much into his or her trade dollar.

> ### Trade Tales
>
> A trade exchange in Missouri hosted a trade fair where members were to sell their products on trade. One member with a low cost of goods brought nothing to sell. Instead he erected a sign that read "Trade dollars on sale for 50 cents!" This incensed the trade exchange, as it denigrated the value of a trade dollar to other members. The enterprising member was asked to leave.

If you're buying trade dollars from a radio station, or other media, try to get a four-to-one ratio. That is, offer $2,500 cash for $10,000 trade. If your exchange has an exceptionally strong trade dollar, this ratio may not be as good.

Find a Motivated Seller

There are plenty of other members who might accept an offer to buy trade dollars. Again, you're looking for someone with a relatively low cost of goods. It also helps if the member is hanging by his or her fingernails, in terms of cash.

As you deal with other traders, keep an ear out for anyone who complains they have "too much trade" and "too little cash." If you catch someone at the right time, at the right stage of desperation, your cash might buy more trade dollars than you think. It's a smart first step in "trading up."

The Least You Need to Know

- Anyone can trade up one item for another of greater value.

- Media and travel industries are key motivated traders.

- A trade exchange can limit risk and expand opportunities.

- Trading up means you have to get trade dollars cheap. Keep your eyes peeled for motivated sellers.

Chapter 14

Real Estate on Barter

In This Chapter

- ◆ Teaching your banker and agent about trade
- ◆ Enticing the seller to take trade
- ◆ Obtaining a trade dollar loan
- ◆ Using trade to upgrade real estate

How can you buy real estate when cash is tight and loans can be even tighter? There is an answer. Bartering through a trade exchange offers powerful leverage.

You can use innovative ways of structuring real estate deals where bankers, real estate agents, sellers, and buyers all walk away from the table with smiles on their faces. If you get into income properties, you could smile even more, if you follow a few simple rules.

Get Your Banker Onboard

A trade exchange will never take the place of your bank. You'll still need cash to buy most real estate. But by using trade dollars whenever possible, you'll need to borrow less of the green stuff. This minimizes the bank's risk, thereby maximizing your chances of getting a favorable loan.

Banks have become understandably gun shy. There was a time, not long ago, when some lenders would hand out cash to almost anyone, especially if they had a pulse. The pendulum has now swung the other way. Banks are becoming increasingly stringent when they evaluate real estate loans. They're not only looking for good credit history, but they also want to see verifiable income and (gasp!) equity.

If you have lousy credit, sorry, a trade exchange can't help. But it can help you prove income to your banker. As you know from Chapter 4, trade dollars are income. Make sure your banker understands this. Show him you pay your taxes on trade dollars (bankers love this), and you received a *1099-B* from your trade exchange. The concept of organized barter might still make his eyes glaze over.

def•i•ni•tion

1099-B A close cousin of the regular 1099. It is an electronic file sent to the IRS and a hard copy sent to the taxpayer that indicates total trade dollars received during the tax year. From an accounting perspective, trade dollars are equal to cash dollars and are accounted for in the same manner.

Banks are averse to creating equity that doesn't exist. This is why appraisers no longer drive by a house, honk, and say something like, "Well, that looks like it's worth about two hundred grand, or maybe three!" (Okay, that's an exaggeration.)

But banks are playing it tight. When equity is created, or a down payment applied, they want to make sure it's real. Look for second mortgages to again become popular. Banks may also accept other real estate, personal property that can be conservatively appraised, and of course, your trade dollars.

Barter Bits

Here's a direct-barter alternative, having nothing to do with trade dollars. If you're buying a home and are short on a down payment, perhaps the seller would allow you to generate "sweat equity," which is another form of barter. You might perform labor for maintenance and repairs, such as painting, drywall, or landscaping. Such services could add value to the house, and represent a down payment. Banks like that.

Throughout the loan process, banks will insist on lending in the first position, and for you and everyone else to be secondary. That's to be expected. First, let's figure out how to spend trade dollars on real estate!

Seek Out a Real Estate Agent on Trade

You probably have a neighbor who is into real estate. Or an uncle. Or a brother-in-law. Or a second cousin twice removed. Disown them, forget them, or ignore them, unless they take trade. Seek out a real estate agent who is on barter.

It's easy to get real estate professionals to accept trade. Their trade dollar cost is low (see Chapter 4 for a full discussion on the cost of trade dollars). They are also fiercely competitive. Most of their investment is in time. To get a listing, or to represent a buyer, they don't have to dip into their pockets to spend cash to replace inventory. They do have some variable cash costs, such as advertising and gas for their cars, but they're pretty nominal. This is why most trade exchanges have almost as many real estate agents as chiropractors.

If none of the real estate representatives in trade is to your liking, find one who is. If necessary, drag her hand-in-hand to the exchange's office. Get her to join. She'll get you as a client, plus others who are members of the exchange. Remember, it's crucial not to let the agent think she's going to get cash from you. It's trade or nothing.

Barter Bits _____

Real estate commission structures vary, depending on the market.
Some markets dictate a 7 percent commission, others 6 percent.
The listing agent, if she finds the buyer herself, doesn't have to share
a commission with another office. However, if the buyer comes from
another agent, she must give half of her office's commission to the other
agent.

To illustrate how real estate agents can accept your barter dollars, let's
say you're buying a house that's listed for $200,000. The seller of the
house has to pay a 7 percent commission to his listing agent, upon com-
pletion of the sale. But she doesn't get to keep all that money. She has
to give half to your agent, who, as we described, is a fellow trader.

Simply by showing up at the doorstep with a real estate agent who's a
member of trade, you are guaranteed of being able to spend half the
listing percent (3 to 3½ percent) in trade dollars. On a $200,000 house,
that's $7,000! If you're lucky and buy a house that's listed by an agent
who also takes trade, you can double that amount, to a cool $14,000 on
trade.

Freddie and Fannie Have Enough on Their Minds

It's always a good idea to simplify real estate transactions, especially
when dealing with entities unlikely to understand the nature of trade
dollars. Take Freddie Mack or Fannie May. How can the deal be struc-
tured so as to not totally confuse them? Simple. Pretend trade doesn't
exist, at least until the last moment.

Buy the house for the $200,000 with no trade component whatsoever.
Recognize the fact that the seller must write a check to his listing agent
for $14,000 who, in turn, writes a check to your agent for $7,000.

Then, by prearrangement, after the dust has settled, make this swap
with your agent: $7,000 trade for $7,000 cash. Go out and buy some
furniture with your windfall.

When you're the seller, you enjoy the same basic advantages. Let's say you're listing a house for that same $200,000. Simply list it with a real estate agent who's on trade. Upon closing, you have to pay him a 7 percent commission, or $14,000. If there was another agent involved, he gets half that. Again, whatever your agent's commission portion turns out to be, pay it in barter.

Don't Forget About the Seller

Just as real estate agents are highly motivated, so are many sellers. Many are desperate to get their asking price, but long ago abandoned that goal. If they plan to move across town, they are candidates to accept trade dollars.

Let's go back to that $200,000 house. Whether the seller was aware of it or not, $7,000 to $14,000 of barter already happened. Let's build from there.

As a part of your offer on the $200,000 house, you ask the seller to accept an additional $50,000 in trade dollars. Whereas the average family, unfamiliar with trade, might initially balk at the idea, you explain the many advantages. You can get the exchange involved. Explain they can get landscaping for their new house. They can go out and eat, have their lawn mowed, buy eyeglasses, take their dog to the vet, or take a vacation.

By the way, remember the people you bought your house from, and they accepted a bunch of trade dollars? They, too, can spend it with real estate agents in the same manner you did. If they're looking for someone to represent them as they buy a new house, they don't have to look far. It can be the agent you approached them with.

Balance of Trade

Before offering trade dollars to nonmembers, such as the seller of a house, be sure to talk to your trade exchange first. There may or may not be an entry fee, but anyone who accepts trade dollars will be expected to pay a commission to the exchange.

Making Offers for Commercial Real Estate

Trading commercial real estate is similar to residential, but with a few wrinkles. Commercial deals can be larger and more lucrative, and their commissions are usually greater. Thus far, you've seen real estate deals from the perspective of the buyer or seller. This time, let's pretend you're the real estate broker, and you've got a car wash for sale. Needless to say, you're also a member of the local trade exchange.

The car wash is large, successful, on the main drag, and it's been around forever. You have it listed for $1 million. You've had some nibbles, but anyone interested doesn't have the money, or if they do, they want to dicker on the price. Last month, you rounded up an offer for $950,000, but your seller nixed the deal. You were so close. You've had the car wash listing for almost a year, and you're afraid of losing it.

Throwing Trade into the Mix

At a loss for ideas, you speak to your trade broker, who comes up with an innovative idea. Why not approach the prospective buyer who had offered the $950,000 and see if she will throw in $50,000 of future car washes? In other words, the new owner would join the exchange and immediately go $50,000 deficit (payable in car washes over the next few years).

Barter Bits

Be aware that there are other players in a real estate transaction who might take trade. Call your broker for the names of attorneys who specialize in real estate. There may also be surveyors or companies that sell title insurance.

The current owner happily accepts the $50,000 trade, which, when added to the $950,000 cash, comes up to her $1 million asking price. If your seller wonders where she can spend that much trade, there's an easy answer. You'll take it as a part of your commission!

If you think about this deal for a moment, you'll see each party was able to claim a good deal. The seller got what she was asking, $1 million. The buyer also thought he got the better of the deal. After all, it cost him only the original $950,000 he was offering. The $50,000 balance was in the form of car washes or soap and water. The trade exchange was also happy because it got a new member and made a nifty commission.

Barter Bits _____

Certain types of real estate barter have been encoded into tax law. One such device is the tax-deferred 1031 real estate exchange. This allows two parties to swap "like kind" real estate. Whenever you sell a property for a gain, you usually have to pay tax on that gain at the time of the sale. The 1031 grants an exception to this, and may allow a party to postpone taxes. This section of tax code is often used by an investor when his property has depreciated to the point of offering little or no tax benefits, and selling it would trigger a sizable capital gain. 1031s can be complicated, so be sure to hire a good tax attorney or accountant—on trade, of course!

Finally, as the broker, you sold the car wash and made your full commission, with $50,000 of it in trade. It was a lot better than having the listing expire.

If you've been involved in commercial real estate deals, you know some go down in flames over an agonizingly small amount of money. The seller digs in and won't go below a certain price. The buyer also refuses to go beyond his or her line in the sand. A trade exchange can create what seems like an oxymoron. The buyer can spend a dollar that costs him or her peanuts. Yet, the seller is able to spend it as if it were a real dollar.

Avoid the Bank of Last Resort

In this chapter, we've had you throwing around tens of thousands of barter dollars, as if it was automatic. It's not. There may be times when you don't have enough trade dollars in your account to complete large real estate transactions. What do you do then?

When a member in good standing needs trade dollars it has not yet earned, a trade exchange can become a secondary bank. Traditional banks issue loans for cash on the basis of boring measurements such as credit history, income verification, assets, and down payment. They also demand collateralization to the point that if you had the collateral, you wouldn't need the loan in the first place.

Balance of Trade

Some exchanges charge interest, in trade, on deficits. When you're in the deficit, you're obligated to sell to your fellow members. If you fail to do so, the exchange will probably pursue you through the courts. By charging interest, a trade exchange partially offsets bad debts when some members are unable to repay their trade dollar loans.

Trade exchanges are different and way easier to work with. When a trade exchange loans trade dollars, or allows a member to spend in the negative, its primary criterion is what that business is bringing to the table, or what it is offering to sell to the other members.

Relationships Matter

If you plan to ask for a loan from your regular bank, what do you do? You engage in advanced schmoozing. You make sure you dress a little spiffier than normal. Then you go to the bank, and wander over to your banker's office. You casually ask him about his kids, and then you ask for a loan. At least that's what you used to do before banks were taken over by giant corporations.

Barter Bits

Always communicate first with your exchange if you expect to go negative. Be prepared for some give and take. If your product has a low mark-up, you may want to ask that your sales be spaced out over a period of time. Be prudent, reasonable, and your trade exchange will treat you in a similar manner.

Relationships still matter to your trade exchange. If you've traded fairly, done them a favor or two by taking care of their other special accounts, paid your fees on time, and maybe bought a beer for the trade exchange owner (I like microbrews), your chances of obtaining the loan improve markedly.

You Have to Be "Good for It"

Even as you develop a relationship with your trade exchange, know your trade exchange still wants to verify you're "good for it." It may do a credit check on you, and it will certainly assess your cash creditworthiness. But at the end of the day, a trade exchange is more inclined to loan trade dollars than banks are to loan cash dollars for a pretty basic reason—money. A trade exchange exists because of cash fees.

Trade for Income Property, If You're Up to It

There's another type of property I haven't mentioned yet: income properties. The very words can send a chill down the spines of even grizzled real estate investors. Barter can make dealing with income properties less arduous. That's because when you spend trade dollars on properties that you either flip for cash or rent out, you can make a killing. But it's not for the faint of heart.

Income Properties at 100 Percent Barter?

Believe it or not, you can sometimes trade for income properties at 100 percent barter. With the housing meltdown, some rental houses have been vacated and landed back into the laps of some unlucky investors. Empty homes are perishable. Taxes and upkeep are certainties, and vandalism is probable.

A current owner might not have the time or money to rehab these distressed properties. If you can identify this desperate owner, even if he's not a member, offer him trade. Whereas he might not get his cash resources to fix up a property and get it back on the market, you have something he didn't. You have barter.

Trading with Contractors

When times are tight, contractors come out of the woodwork to join a trade exchange. This is your chance to use your barter dollars to hire contractors who do drywall, carpet installation, painting, roofing, window and doors, plumbing, and electrical.

By using trade dollars to hire contractors, you can afford to rehab a house you might normally stay away from. After the work is done, you can sell the house and use trade dollars to pay your real estate agent.

Balance of Trade

Sometimes working with contractors on trade can present special challenges. You'll want to work closely with your broker to identify those who have a history of showing up and trading fairly. Contractors rarely have rate cards, and their billing procedures can be inconsistent. Make sure you don't end up with a contractor who overcharges or where finding him is like nailing Jell-O to a wall.

If you're keeping the property to rent out, be sure to pay for ongoing maintenance with barter. If you don't want to get a phone call from a tenant with a leaky pipe at two in the morning, be sure to hire a property manager on trade.

The Least You Need to Know

◆ See to it your banker understands the nature of organized trade. Trade dollars represent verifiable income.

◆ Trade dollars are a legitimate means of making real estate down payments.

◆ Real estate agents compete fiercely for deals and are frequently motivated to accept trade dollars.

◆ Motivated sellers are commonplace and can be enticed into accepting barter.

◆ A trade exchange is a bank of last resort. It may lend you trade dollars when a bank won't lend you cash.

◆ Trade dollars can be used to upgrade real estate that you buy. Big payoffs are possible, with enough work.

Chapter 15

Trade for Nonprofits

In This Chapter

- ◆ Check your attic, warehouse, or calendar
- ◆ Become generous with trade dollars
- ◆ Run a nonprofit? Get trade!
- ◆ Learn tips for nonprofits on how to spend trade

Have you ever fantasized about winning the lottery? We all have. Part of your dream might have included giving a large portion of your windfall to charity. Let's face it. You probably won't win the jackpot. But there are still ways you can be more generous than you ever imagined—through in-kind giving and barter.

In-kind giving is when you make a cashless contribution to a charity, in the form of time, talent, or property. But there's another way you can be generous without spending cash. You can donate trade dollars.

Perhaps you currently play a part in the success of a nonprofit. If so, there are ways you can attract trade dollar donations. There are also useful strategies you can use to spend the trade dollars you get.

Whether you want to give to a nonprofit, or you run one, trading can give you the power to have more impact than you imagined!

Give of Yourself

If you've ever helped out at the church spaghetti dinner, delivered food to shut-ins, worked for the Girl Scouts, rung a red bell outside a mall, worked on behalf of a service club, or performed any of a thousand other tasks, you may have already given more to charity than you thought. When you give of yourself, it's a cashless contribution. In a very real way, you've made a barter, or in-kind donation.

You probably have skills you've never thought of. Some folks can swing a hammer and can help build homes for Habitat for Humanity. If that's you, give Habitat a call. Perhaps you have a sunny disposition and enjoy visiting, but don't have any "marketable" skills. It doesn't matter. There are hospitals and nursing homes seeking volunteers to provide companionship to their residents. If all you can do is read, there are organizations seeking people to read books for the blind. The key is to match your talent with an agency's needs. The easiest way to find a direct match is to contact a local volunteer agency.

There's Gold in Them There Hills!

You've probably heard that "one person's trash is another's treasure." It's true: we all have "stuff" that we have devalued in our minds. It might be just sitting around, and you've forgotten about it. It may nevertheless hold value to a charity.

Take a look around. Perhaps there's a pool table in the basement that the local youth center could use. Maybe you have a used car. Consider donating it to an agency that assists people in getting jobs. What about the slightly used overcoat? Take a trip to the local homeless shelter. You can help others and be green at the same time.

You might want to donate certain personal property, but it's hard to find a nonprofit that will take it. This is where you should think resale shop or thrift store. If you have a used dinette set, for example, you might call Goodwill Industries. They'll sell your furniture for cash, and the proceeds support the mission of the organization. Or you could call the Salvation Army. Many branches now operate resale stores. If you have a used appliance or building material, consider one of the many "Re-Stores" run by Habitat for Humanity. As nonprofits struggle with cash donations, many now welcome merchandise they can resell.

Donate Those Widgets!

If you own a business, corporate giving is not so very different from individual giving. Corporations don't have attics, but they own warehouses. Sometimes these warehouses are filled with excess inventory or other *underperforming assets.*

> **Balance of Trade**
>
> **Underperforming asset** Although it can be many things, typically, an underperforming asset is a distressed item that is last year's model, flawed in some way, or there are simply too many of the item on the market, depressing the price. Corporations with underperforming assets at some point face the prospect of deep discounts, writing them off, donating, or sometimes even discarding them.

Many businesses already donate in-kind to nonprofits. The food industry commonly produces products that are perfectly good, but are either mislabeled, or they made too much. If boxes of corn flakes have the photo of a disgraced sports hero on the front, what's the manufacturer to do? It can't very well sell them to a grocery chain. But it can donate the product to a food bank.

> **Trade Tales**
>
> America's Second Harvest maintains 215 food banks around the country, and distributes $476 million of food annually. Gifts In Kind International distributes $600 million of noncash donations yearly. These are two charities, not as well known as their higher-profile contemporaries, that distribute over a billion dollars' worth of in-kind gifts per year.

A corporate in-kind gift does not have to be merchandise. It can also take the form of unneeded equipment, real estate, or vehicles. Let's say your business has been streamlined, and you now have too many forklifts. You can try to sell them to a wholesaler or on the open market. Guess what? The market is flooded with used forklifts. Prices are depressed. So what can you do?

One option might be donation. The trick is to find a nonprofit that can use your forklifts. Give it some thought. Perhaps that food bank we were talking about could use the lifts to stack pallets. Don't limit your thinking to local charities either. Get online. Chances are, with some work, you'll find a nonprofit that would love to receive what you have.

> **Barter Bits**
>
> Every individual and company tax situation is different. In general, an individual can deduct fair market value, up to $500 without an appraisal. A company can deduct its wholesale cost, or the cost of manufacturing the good, when making a charitable donation to a 501(c)3. If you had donated the forklifts, you could deduct the amount equal to their depreciated value. If your company donates either inventory or equipment, it's a good idea to consult with your tax advisor.

Your business might not actually carry inventory, but instead provides a service. You can still donate in kind. If you're a dentist, the match is easy. You already know about agencies that can match your talents with those in need. Perhaps you're a certified public accountant. That could be a little tougher match, but certainly not impossible. Make a few calls. There's a nonprofit out there in need of your services, not only for daily bookkeeping and quarterly reports, but also a year-end audit.

Giving your time or service becomes a challenge, however, if you're, say, an electrician. Or if you design websites, sell fishing rods, or you're a real estate agent. Who do you call to donate your services? Whereas the local volunteer agency is a nice resource, there are other options. Read on.

Join a Trade Exchange and Get Generous

As you have learned, selling through a trade exchange is an easy way to generate discretionary income. Whereas purchases of a vacation and fine wine are discretionary purchases, so is giving to a charity. Because of the nature of trade dollars, giving is a whole lot less painful. For a review of cost of trade dollars, go to Chapter 4. In the meantime, let's get generous with trade!

You're a member of a trade exchange and would like to increase your charitable giving. Let's start with the basics. What causes are you passionate about? Perhaps it's your church. In addition to its spiritual role, your church is also a business. It must budget and pay for utilities, maintenance, and personnel. At the end of the day, almost all nonprofits struggle with cash. Your church is probably no exception.

Here's how to start. Tell your church leadership that you are prepared to take care of the church's lawn mowing needs, carpet cleaning, and copy machine repair. But first it must become a member of the trade exchange.

There's a good chance they'll react by asking, "What's a trade exchange?" This is not at all uncommon. Many nonprofits are unfamiliar with barter, and joining a trade exchange might seem unconventional. Explain the benefits that you have enjoyed by trading. Show them a copy of your directory. Tell them about the other nonprofits that are members. Above all, let them know as soon as they're ready, you're ready to make a generous contribution of trade dollars.

Your ability to choose from a large number of nonprofits will vary, depending on your trade exchange. Some trade exchanges have been proactive in the nonprofit sector and count 100 or more as members. Other exchanges have just a few. Either way, you'll want to make sure that your favorite nonprofits join. It will be a totally new resource for them.

> **Trade Tales**
>
> In 2006, the trade exchanges that belonged to the National Association of Trade Exchanges (NATE) approached their members and generated $80,000 in trade dollars. This was used to send the son of a U.S. veteran who had served in Iraq to a private college that accepted trade. Room, board, and tuition were all paid with trade dollars.

Run a Nonprofit? Join an Exchange!

When you join a trade exchange, remember that as a nonprofit, you already enjoy a special status. For one thing, the government doesn't charge you taxes. You pay no corporate or sales tax. Merchants may offer you certain discounts. You should parlay these advantages to your trade exchange.

Tell the exchange about the worthiness of your mission and how cash is tight. Chances are good that you'll be able to negotiate away the entry fee and monthly dues. You should also be able to work out a favorable commission structure.

Now that you're a member, there are more ways to get trade dollars than you thought. Just like cash, you ask for it using whatever technique works. Sometimes it's altruism, and sometimes it's not.

Getting Trade Dollar Donations

Many of your fellow citizens share your passion, whether it's saving souls, saving the environment, saving dogs, or promoting the arts. Many profess support, but only a few are willing to write a check.

Most people have to budget their cash donations. As such, giving is usually limited in nature. But members of a trade exchange are different. They can donate a larger amount, because it's not cash. The pain of writing the check is not there. So be prepared. Fundraising for trade dollars can be rewarding, and surprisingly easy. Go for the jugular— I mean, go for a larger amount.

Direct Appeal

Nothing beats a direct appeal for trade dollars. But which members do you ask? How many trade dollars do you ask for? This is where you should sit down with your broker at the trade exchange. Your broker knows who has large trade balances, and who is likely to be the most generous donor. By targeting a predefined "hit list," you won't waste time soliciting members who are either unable or unwilling to give.

Timing Is Everything

It never fails. Some members just don't plan their trade account as well as they should have (see Chapter 8). As the year gets closer to December 31, some members will have an excess of trade. This could mean a pending tax bill, depending on whether the company has offsetting write-offs. This is when you strike.

> ### Trade Tales
>
> One member of a trade exchange in Michigan made too much money during the year. He called his trade broker and arranged for a $50,000 trade donation. He didn't even care which charities he gave to. This large donation brought his trade dollar account negative, but the exchange was comfortable with this because he sold an in-demand product. From an accounting perspective, the donor had gone to the bank, borrowed $50,000, and then given it away, thus entitling him to a deduction that year.

As you ask for trade dollars from those who are in a giving mood, remember that it's not only important who you ask, but how you ask.

Strategies on Asking for a Donation

You will probably want to start out with letters to those on the hit list and then follow with phone calls. You may want to do this yourself, or you might rely on staff or volunteers. When you ask for trade dollars, remember that the potential donor is going to have two questions on his or her mind: why should I give and how much should I give?

Always tie the solicitation request to a specific project or need. "Just because" doesn't tell the donor why he or she should give nearly as well as "because we're adding a new wing to our facility to assist disadvantaged youth." Give the donor a palpable reason to be generous with his or her trade.

> ### Trade Tales
>
> A charity in Indiana made calls to solicit trade dollars. One member unexpectedly donated $10,000 in trade. It turned out that he had been convicted of a nonviolent felony, and he later told the judge that the donation was a part of the contributions he normally rendered to the community. The member stayed out of jail.

When you ask for a trade dollar donation, many members clearly won't know how much they're being asked to give. Are you asking for $50 or $1,000? Give the donor a clue. This can be done by delineating three different levels of giving, each of which offers varying levels of recognition. A Platinum Giver level might be $1,000 or more; a Gold Giver might be between $500 and $999, and so forth.

Other Ways to Get Trade Dollars

Your nonprofit organization has more to offer donor businesses than you might think. It also offers promotional value, or branding. Don't be bashful about offering this as an advantage when you ask for trade dollar donations. Many businesses are eager to have their names associated with a worthy nonprofit such as yours. It proves good corporate citizenship. By giving trade dollars to your organization, they are also tapping into the goodwill, and purchasing power, of your volunteer base.

Don't be afraid to promote this advantage. When a corporation donates trade dollars to your cause, offer it recognition and visibility. Perhaps you can introduce the donor at a volunteer banquet. Or offer the company signage or banners at one of your events. Don't sell yourself, or the brand of your nonprofit, short.

Tickets, Advertising, and More

Does your nonprofit put out a newsletter? Does it sell tickets to events? Taken together, admissions and advertising can generate trade dollars sales. For example, if your nonprofit is associated with the arts, make admission tickets available. If you publish a newsletter, sell display advertising on trade. Or if it conducts a raffle, consider selling tickets on barter.

> **Trade Tales**
>
> Over a four-year period, a chapter of AMBUCS, a service club dedicated to helping disabled children, generated $82,000 in trade, the vast majority of which was through raffle ticket sales. One year, a member who bought a ticket for $150 trade won $10,000 in cash!

Once you've been a member of a trade exchange for any length of time, you soon realize fellow members are almost like family. It's a good idea to get to know the players. Many exchanges conduct mixers or luncheons, where they bring in a speaker, or otherwise promote trade activity. Some trade exchanges conduct holiday gift shows. Be there with a booth, pressing the flesh and describing the attributes of your nonprofit. When the time comes for members to make donations, you'll be top-of-mind.

The Phone Rang, and You Said *What?*

There is one more way to generate a boatload of trade dollars. It's staring you in the face when you sit down at your desk. It's the phone. It rings and a company or individual wants to donate pallet racking, or a sailboat, or a timeshare to Palm Beach. What do you do?

> **Balance of Trade**
>
> If an organization receives charitable deduction property and within three years sells, exchanges, or disposes of the property, the organization must file Form 8282. However, an organization is not required to file this form if the property is valued at $500 or less, or the property is distributed for charitable purposes.

It happens time and again. Nonprofits refuse an in-kind gift because they don't know what to do with it. If you run a nonprofit, never say no, at least until you've checked with your trade exchange. For example, pallet racking might be an in-demand item. Accept the gift, and have your trade exchange sell it for you.

Trade Tales
A church joined a trade exchange in Ohio. It publicized to its parishioners that it could accept in-kind gifts. One member donated a sailboat to the church. The church called its trade broker, who promptly sold the boat for $10,000 trade. The exchange arranged for everything, from title transfer to transportation. The church didn't have to do anything.

Be sure to tell your volunteers and supporters that you can now accept all manner of in-kind gifts. You can get the word out at meetings, in newsletters, or general announcements. You will be amazed at the good stuff people have hanging around. You'll likely attract in-kind gifts from people whose cash budgets were otherwise strapped. Just make it known that you can't accept used pots and pans. Your trade exchange will get turned off in a hurry if you present them with junk.

Spending Trade Dollars as a Nonprofit

Although you run a nonprofit, you still have many of the same needs as your for-profit friends. And if you had the resources, you too, might engage in some discretionary spending. Maybe you wouldn't buy fast cars and fancy vacations, but you might expand your mission or perhaps say thanks to some of your volunteers.

Once you have some trade dollars in your account, don't let them sit there. Call your broker. Set a time to go over some of your ongoing cash purchases. See which ones can be replaced with trade.

You should be able to easily spend your newly found trade dollars on such services as carpet cleaning, office equipment, lawn maintenance, janitorial needs, snowplowing, asphalt maintenance, vehicle repair, and other needs.

> **Trade Tales**
>
> One agency in Michigan whose mission was to help clothe the poor purchased a semi full of socks (which were seconds) from a company in Alabama, all on barter. How many socks fit into a semi? Ten thousand dozen, that's how many.

You may also be able to purchase certain products that relate directly to your mission. Trade exchanges run into all sorts of products, from clothing to used appliances, from switched-over hotel furniture to slightly used computers.

Say Thanks to Your Volunteers, with Barter

You can't just take a volunteer aside, squeeze a $50 bill in her hand and say, "Thanks for all your help." This would be insulting. But if you said, "Please join us for our volunteer recognition dinner next month," that would make a friend for life!

There never seems to be enough money to say thanks to your volunteers. Consider trade dollars to pay for the pizza, take care of the door prizes, or throw a thank-you party. It won't take a penny from your cash budget.

Turn Your Trade Dollars into Cash!

No, you can't go to your trade exchange and swap $10,000 trade for $10,000 cash. But you can still use your trade to generate cash, in a couple of nifty ways.

The first way is to buy certain items or services and offer them for sale. Some charities have purchased restaurant gift certificates and then offered them for sale at cash fund raisers, such as a blind auction. Others have purchased certificates for bowling or going to the miniature golf course, and offered them for sale in the charity's newsletter.

Speaking of Golf ...

Let's assume you have a tidy sum of barter dollars in the account of your nonprofit. Why not put together an event and charge cash for it? Some nonprofits promote golf outings. By trading with the golf course, the nonprofit is able to keep the cash it normally would have had to spend. Some nonprofits have thus converted up to $10,000 trade dollars into cash dollars.

There's one more way for your nonprofit to turn trade dollars into cash. It's to operate a resale store. We've touched on this. Goodwill Industries is probably the most famous purveyor of donated goods.

It's not easy. Running a retail store is a challenging task. It takes planning, an experienced staff, and ongoing dedication. But a number of nonprofits have made it happen.

> **Trade Tales**
>
> A trade exchange in Florida was able to trade for a Pulitzer Prize–winning author to speak at its annual awards banquet. It was able to attract 300 people who paid $75 each to attend. It became a huge money-maker for the charity.

The Least You Need to Know

◆ Donations to your favorite nonprofits don't always have to be in cash. They can be in-kind, or in barter.

◆ As a member of a trade exchange, your ability to give is greater. This is because your trade dollar doesn't cost you a cash dollar. You can afford to be more generous.

◆ If you run a nonprofit, there are strategies to generate more trade dollars. You have more to offer a donor than you think.

◆ Trade dollars can be effectively spent by nonprofits. They can help you on day-to-day expenditures, achieve your mission, and say thanks to your volunteers.

Part 5

Start Your Own Trade Exchange

Maybe you get the ins and outs of a barter economy and the advanced strategies that can be employed by members of a trade exchange. And maybe you're thinking, "You know, I can run a trade exchange."

Maybe you can. But you have to answer some hard questions, first. What's the right market? How big should a trade exchange be? Should I buy into a franchise? This part helps you answer these questions and leads you to answer the ultimate question: "Am I fit to own a trade exchange?"

Chapter 16

Should I Start a Trade Exchange?

In This Chapter

- ◆ Measuring up: Does size matter?
- ◆ Location, location, location
- ◆ Do you have what it takes?
- ◆ Assessing your own unique skills

If you're going to start a trade exchange, do a little digging. You need to know if the market you're interested in is the right size. Large markets have some advantages, but so do some smaller ones. Whichever you choose, your members have to be close enough to one another so trading kicks in.

You also want to give serious consideration to what size business you want to create. There is no right size. What does matter is that you find fulfillment in your business.

A trade exchange can succeed in lots of different locations. It's not where you are, but who you are, and how well you run your business that counts. Avoid the temptation to get too big for your britches with multiple locations. Also, be sure to do your homework. It can be difficult to locate in a market that has lots of competition, or one that has been damaged by an unscrupulous operator.

Before you issue your first dollar, be certain you're a right fit for the unique business of trading. Credibility and trust are critical, but so is creativity. Don't try to be Superman. You can't do it alone. It's important to attract people who compliment your abilities.

If you're going to start a trade exchange, you're bringing your own unique talents to the table. Try to identify these talents and then ask yourself: how will they contribute to running a successful trade exchange? However, the most important talent is really a trait, that of dogged perseverance.

So let's get to it. Let's find out if your market is right for you, and you're right for the market.

What Size Market Do You Need?

Your success in starting a trade exchange is not predicated on the size of the city you're in, as long as it's not too small. There should be at least 250,000 to 300,000 people within a 30-mile radius of your office. That's what it takes to have a large enough reservoir of businesses to get trade off the ground.

If you start an exchange in too small of a market, you've immediately put yourself behind the eight ball. Not only are you limited in the number of sales calls you can make, but you'll never be able to offer your membership a large enough selection of goods and services. For example, if there are only three office-machine companies in town, you might not be able to sign any of them. The result is you have no one bartering copy machines. This might not sound critical, but if you have no members in other key categories, your trade volume and commissions suffer.

Additionally, if your market is too small, there is too great of a chance your members will be put in the position of converting cash business into trade. Let's illustrate. If there are only two well drillers in town, and each gets half of the total business in town, there's exactly a 50 percent chance of swapping cash business for trade. This is not what a trade exchange is supposed to do.

Big Markets, Big Opportunities and Challenges

If you live in a big city, no one has to tell you what it's like to live there. Where there are lots of people, there are lots of opportunities. You never run out of businesses to call on. Nevertheless, selling and servicing your members presents challenges of a different type. Driving 5 miles in a big city can be as difficult as 30 miles in a small one.

Trade Tales

One exchange in a huge metropolitan area, where virtually no one owned a car and everyone took taxis, signed up its members by using the phone, faxes, e-mail, and courier services. In fact, this exchange rarely met its members face to face, an anomaly in the barter world.

Spread Out Means Thinned-Out Profits

If you're in a small- to medium-sized market, it can be tempting to expand your market area by scouring the countryside for new members. But this creates two problems. The first is obvious. Your cost of selling and servicing your members goes up. Just driving to, and servicing, prospective members means the expenditure of valuable time and money.

The other reason you should avoid straying too far outside your area is it's a disservice to your member. If you sign a chiropractor 30 miles away, he might be initially enthusiastic. After all, he enjoys many barter advantages, not the least of which is totally fixed costs.

Balance of Trade

Beware of signing up members over a wide geographical area. One exchange takes pride in its ability to sign up new members over a wide geographical area, counting over 2,000 on its membership rolls. The problem is most of its income is derived from membership fees, not trading. Many of its members are so far from other traders they have become disenchanted with trade. They simply haven't attracted new customers, even on barter.

Yet, if no one is willing to drive the 30 miles to visit the chiropractor, what have you accomplished? Sure, you managed to wrangle an entry fee from the poor guy. But was it worth it? All you did was alienate a member who paid an entry fee, with little prospect of ever getting any business. He's not likely to say good things about your trade exchange, either.

Don't maroon your members. If you enlist a real estate agent on the upper west side, or a veterinarian in Hooterville, but then don't sign other members in the area for them to trade with, you're performing a disservice. Regardless of the size of the city you're in, plan to create "zones" of traders who can spend trade dollars with one another.

Is a Bigger Exchange Better?

Just as you want to look at the size of your market before you start a trade exchange, you also want to ask yourself how big of an exchange you want.

At first blush, you might think this is a stupid question. After all, don't we all want "bigger" businesses? Not necessarily. Bigger is not always better. Some owners are equipped to run large staffs. They want to continuously sell new members, broker more and more accounts, and manage lots of people. But this is not for everyone.

Barter Bits _____

Two leaders of the barter industry took decidedly different paths. Both were located in large Midwestern markets, a few hours from one another. One was intent on hiring lots of sales staff and brokers, and became one of the largest exchanges in the country. At its peak, he had over 75 employees, including telemarketers, sales staff, brokers, and administrative workers. The other entrepreneur purposely decided to maintain a much smaller staff, of only four or five people. Both made exceptional livings.

One dilemma of owning a large trade exchange is it can become increasingly difficult to manage. More membership sales necessitate more brokers and administrative staff to service them. An owner can find herself on a treadmill of increasing costs, with her bottom line getting no better.

Yet, for the owner of a large trade exchange who can avoid these pit-falls, the financial rewards can be substantial. If you go for the big time, be prepared. You not only have to know barter, you have to know how to run a good-sized business.

> **Balance of Trade**
>
> If you run a small trade exchange, you're probably somewhat indis-pensable. This can work against you when it comes time to sell if you're too valuable an asset not to be included in the sale. On the other hand, if you own a large trade exchange and can show a prospective buyer your presence is not required 24/7, the new owner is assured the exchange will continue to run smoothly when you're gone.

When you come right down to it, you're the only one who should determine what size and type of trade exchange you want to create. That's the great thing about the bartering business. There are many ways to achieve success, and there's room for everyone.

Are Some Locations Better Than Others?

When owners of trade exchanges get together, they always seem to compare notes on their markets. Invariably, each contends he has had it the toughest because of his own market's peculiarities.

Most everyone claims their market is more conservative and nonac-cepting of barter than the others. Some might theorize colleagues in another market enjoy an advantage because it's a vacation destination, so they can sign up lots of hotels and resorts. Then you have those who say a boom town is best, or maybe it's the reverse. Then there are a few who claim the West Coast is more conducive to barter, but then some-one points to all the exchanges in Toronto.

Here's what matters: the characteristics of a market don't determine whether an exchange succeeds or not. Rather, it is the attributes of the people running it that counts.

Multiple Locations: The Poison Apple

There is one temptation pertaining to location you should avoid, and that is to have multiples of them. The success of a trade exchange hinges on an owner, or someone with a vested interest, running the operation. Because a trade exchange's currency is based on trust, a local presence is a necessity. This is hard to do if you've succumbed to a common disease in the barter world. It's called Pin-in-the-Map Disease.

Pin-in-the-Map Disease can be diagnosed when the owner of a trade exchange buys a wall-size map of the country, or maybe the world. In later stages of the disease, the trade exchange owner can be seen sticking pins in markets in which he plans to open offices, often while not yet succeeding in his own city.

There are a few exceptions, but if you're starting a trade exchange, stay close to home. Trying to run satellite offices presents daunting challenges. It's almost impossible to adequately motivate and supervise staff, broker from afar, and maintain accurate accounting procedures.

Locating Where an Exchange Already Exists

The landscape is not quite logical when it comes to placement of trade exchanges. Some cities, such as Phoenix, already have five or six. Toronto has more than a dozen. Yet there are cities with over a million people with no trade exchange. Obviously, it's best to start where no one has a foothold.

Trade exchanges in the same market have special challenges. Some maintain good relations and even trade with each other. In other instances, contentious relationships develop. Trade exchanges in the same city sometimes end up raiding each others' directories, or getting into a war of words. Members aren't stupid. Some play one trade exchange against the other, especially when negotiating fees and making product offerings.

Beware of Poisoned Wells

When trade exchanges first started in the late '70s and early '80s, the industry was unfortunately defined by a group of Bonnie and Clyde operators who became high-profile poster children for the pitfalls of barter.

Some of these early trade exchanges failed because of poor management; others because of unethical business practices. A number of markets were "poisoned" for years to come. Imagine calling on a business that had just lost $10,000 trade to an exchange that had disappeared into thin air.

Trade Tales

In the early 1980s a national franchiser sold dozens of territories to eager entrepreneurs. Due to a faulty business model and inability to manage a common trade dollar among its locations, virtually the entire system collapsed. In many markets it was years before the organized barter concept could be sold in markets where numerous businesses had been burned.

Thankfully, those days are, for the most part, over. Today it's tough to find a market where the prevailing attitude is soured against organized barter.

This is because the unscrupulous operators have migrated to the Internet, which, when you think about it, has no location. This is not to say all trade exchanges based on the Internet are unscrupulous. It's just a lot easier to set up a virtual location preying on the unsuspecting than it is to build one from bricks and mortar.

Are You a Fit to Own a Trade Exchange?

This may be the most important question you'll need to ask yourself. You need to determine if you have what it takes when it comes to credibility, creativity, management, and perseverance.

When a business signs up to become a member of your trade exchange, he doesn't have to be convinced you're the smartest or best looking. But he does have to trust you.

Credibility Is the Key

If you cannot establish credibility, you're sunk, simple as that. When you see a new client, he has to be convinced the currency you have established is indeed money. Think about it. This is no small feat. Fast talkers rarely succeed long term in barter. Clients need to know there is substance and competence standing behind their trade dollars.

Your clients also have to know you're going to be around tomorrow. A trade exchange is a different kind of business. If you own a donut shop, run it for a while, and then decide you don't want to sell donuts anymore, you can close your store. No one is hurt.

But closing down a trade exchange is not so easy. This is because as the system matures, there will be no point at which everyone has a zero trade balance. Some members are going to have negative trade balances; others will be positive.

Barter Bits

During the 1980s, several dozen exchanges were about to fail. Some were mismanaged; all were run by owners who wanted to bail. A large national franchiser absorbed most of these locations so the trade dollars issued were protected.

If, after five years, you get tired of the trade business and can't find someone to take it over, what happens to all those holding positive balances? If 100 members all have a $5,000 trade balance, that's $500,000 out there. Before you start a trade exchange, make sure you're in it for the long haul.

Trust Is Earned

You have a leg up starting a trade exchange if you've had a high-profile job, or a name people know. Knowing lots of business owners is a real plus. If you walk into their doors as an unknown entity, you will have to work harder at establishing their trust.

Not surprisingly, many trade exchange owners come from the ranks of the media, especially radio. Not only do they understand the basic tenants of barter, but they know everybody in town.

A Place to Hang Your Hat

A trade exchange can theoretically be operated out of the back of a U-Haul truck. You can run your trade exchange out of the back of your house, too. But does this enhance your credibility?

Barter Bits

For every rule, there's an exception. One of the largest trade exchanges in the country was started by a man who started his trade exchange in the back of his car, and only later in his house. Finally he did rent a real office. The exchange now barters tens of millions of dollars each year.

It's best to not go the home office route. When you start a trade exchange, you're a banker, the keeper of Fort Knox, and the chairman of the Federal Reserve System—all rolled into one! Make an effort to have a real office, even if it's a modest one.

Creativity Is a Double-Edged Sword

Who would dream up a trade exchange? Obviously it was someone who was pretty creative. People who enter the barter business are usually unconventional thinkers. Those who most succeed are able to identify traditional business problems and then solve them—with barter.

Painters and sculptors are creative too, but there's a difference. They don't manage millions of dollars of other peoples' money. Owners of trade exchanges usually have to temper their natural creativity and urge to socialize with quantitative accounting skills that are sometimes foreign to them.

Barter Bits

Not long ago, a trainer was hired to present to a national barter association. He specialized in identifying personality types. He asked attendees to complete a questionnaire. It was designed to force them to choose between traits such as "wanting to be liked," and "fitting in," or conversely, characteristics such as "attaining the bottom line," and "sticking to the rules." As the exercise was completed, the trainer asked each person to join others who had scored similarly. Almost everyone joined the group with traits the trainer identified as belonging to schmoozers.

There are a few people who are both right- and left-brained, but not many. If you've been blessed by being smart on both sides, congratulations. If not, remember from Chapter 4 that trade exchanges have huge obligations. For one thing, they are required by law to send out 1099-Bs to their members, and to report transactions electronically to the IRS.

Operating a trade exchange requires a variety of talents. Don't try to be a president, salesperson, broker, accountant, and business manager. Successful trade exchanges typically have an operations manager who understands barter and makes sure the credits and debits add up to zero.

> **Barter Bits**
>
> A trade exchange must be a "balanced system," in that if you add up all the members' positive balances with all those who are negative, you always come up with one number. That number is zero.

No matter how talented you are as an owner, or how good your salespeople and brokers are, you risk failure if your trade exchange is not run like a business. Someone has to make sure the withholding and sales taxes are paid on time, your rent is paid, you've got the best deal on phones and computers, and many other administrative tasks. That same person will also probably be responsible to supply you with accurate information about the state of your business.

Be sure you have your people in place before you begin calling on your first clients. If you get your act together too late, you may find yourself in an unmanageable mess.

Know Where Your Talents Lie

What skills do you bring to the table? If you're great at getting out in the field and selling an intangible, by all means, that's where you should be. If you're better running the office and supervising people, then do that.

Because operating a trade requires a diverse set of skills, be sure your bases are covered. Hire people who are good at what you're not.

Apply Your Experience

There is no one template to follow when starting a trade exchange. Some owners' goals are to grow it as big as they can; others prefer to run smaller businesses. Yet, in the final analysis, each trade exchange is a unique reflection of the owner who started it.

Trade Tales
One exchange in a city in Michigan had a limited population and little chance at growth. The owner had been involved with numerous charities and sat on a number of boards. The exchange became good at soliciting trade dollars for charities that had become members. It also encouraged them to solicit donated items from their supporters. Nonprofits came to represent over 100 members and a third of this exchange's business.

Every owner of every trade exchange undoubtedly spent many hours naming his business. It probably didn't really matter. In the minds of the members, it comes down to "Mike's Currency," "Jerry's Currency," "Fran's Currency," and so on. Each exchange was started by an individual whose talents and personality led the exchange in a certain direction.

It stands to reason that most exchanges develop a "specialty" based on these early talents. It's been noted that many trade exchange owners have a media background. Others have had experience in the hospitality industry, or have a retail background. Still others have rubbed shoulders with liquidators and have become adept at bartering large inventories. So what are your skills? What type of accounts will you be led to?

Trade Tales
One exchange in the Upper Midwest developed relationships with liquidators early on. Sometimes these liquidators were faced with a market swamped in a certain product. What better way to diversify their inventories than to barter them for other inventories? Today, this exchange trades over $10 million worth of inventories each year.

Needless to say, most successful trade exchanges end up signing a wide variety of businesses that offer lots of goods and services to fellow members. Yet, every trade exchange seems to maintain a base from early on, composed of members of a certain ilk. They still reflect the first sales calls made by the person who started it all.

Ignorance Is Bliss

Starting a trade exchange is hard work and a daunting task. Many of the people who succeeded were too ignorant to know they couldn't do it, so they did! Think about it. Your job is to get hundreds of people to buy into the notion that you're printing money, albeit of an alternate variety. So what's the most important skill you can bring to the table? It's simple. You have to have an abiding belief you cannot fail, no matter what.

Barter Bits

One exchange now has more than 1,000 members. But it started in an inauspicious manner in 1980. The owner actually thought he had invented the concept of organized trade. Armed with a copy machine, typewriter, and spiral notebook to record transactions, he started calling on accounts. He collated statements by crawling around on the floor; he drove a broken-down car. By being oblivious to obstacles, he ended up succeeding. (Okay, yeah, that was me.)

You're enthusiastic about trading. But don't expect everyone you see to share your vision, especially at the beginning. You can't start a successful trade exchange overnight. When you call on your first account, that person will probably say something like, "Sounds great! Who's on the list?" To which your only answer can be, "You."

Be patient. Members will join. Trade activity will start, slowly at first, and then accelerate. After a while, when someone asks who's in your exchange, you'll be able to blow her away with a thick directory and hundreds of names!

The Least You Need to Know

♦ An exchange market can be any size—except very small, such as 250,000 people or less living within a 30-mile radius.

♦ Regardless of size, not every market is right for trade.

♦ A trade exchange can be any size, as long as it fits you.

♦ Identify your skills, and hire people to do what you can't.

♦ Persistence pays off.

Chapter 17

Should You Franchise or Go Independent?

In This Chapter

- ◆ Weighing the pros and cons of joining a franchise vs. going independent
- ◆ Starting an independent exchange: what to expect
- ◆ Selecting the right software is key
- ◆ Training is essential

Now that you've determined whether you've got what it takes to run a trade exchange, it's time to ask yourself some other pretty important questions. Your answers will determine a lot about your future. They will determine whether you get big or remain small, whether you make a lot of money, or just a little.

Before you jump into a trade exchange, know this: you won't make any money for six months to a year. No one wants to join a trade exchange until someone else joins. Plus, experience shows trade won't start happening until a critical mass is reached at about 200 members.

Your first decision will be whether you're going to buy a franchised office, or if you're going to start an independent trade exchange. Then there's software. The right software will pay off dividends in more than numbers.

Finally, don't make the same mistakes everyone in the industry has. It's a good idea to seek out training to help you start your trade exchange. A trainer can help you make more money, sooner.

Should You Go It Alone?

You've made the leap. You've decided to start your very own trade exchange. You've bought this book, so you're ready to start calling on your first accounts, right? Wrong. There are questions you've still got to ask yourself. One of the most important is whether you're going to be an independent exchange or one affiliated with a national franchise.

There is no right or wrong answer to this question. It depends on you, your background, the money you have in the bank, and your ultimate goals. If you choose to start an independent trade exchange, your reward can be greater, but so are your risks. Conversely, some entrepreneurs feel more comfortable if they're a part of a large national franchise or licensed office.

What Are the Pros of Joining a Franchise?

There is a comfort zone created if you go the franchise route. Everything is under one umbrella. The franchiser lets you use its name, performs all accounting functions, offers software and training, and creates all marketing material.

You are also given the assurance someone is there to lend a hand if you run into trouble. Because you're part of a group, you also enjoy the advantage of being able to trade with other offices in cities in North America.

National franchisers offer ways you can improve your skills. They put on conventions where you'll meet and compare notes with colleagues from other offices. Training sessions are also offered, usually concentrating on improving brokering or sales skills.

Trading with Other Cities Lends Credibility

When you open your doors as a part of a national franchise, you can offer your members the advantage of being able to spend their trade dollars with other offices. Most trade is local in nature. Members want goods and services close to home. Yet, it's impressive to offer them something from another city, from another franchised office.

The most commonly traded item is, of course, travel. Trade exchanges that are members of the same franchise frequently trade hotel rooms to one another. Nothing beats taking care of an important member with a nice vacation.

White Hat, Black Hat

A franchiser performs another task. It can wear the black hat and allow you to wear the white one. Let's say you own an independent exchange and you have a client who has fallen behind in cash fees, and she wants to buy something with her trade dollars.

Let's further assume this client owns a fancy restaurant that satisfies lots of your members. Are you really going to bat her upside the head and deny her an authorization if she tries to buy something? Doing so might risk her getting upset and no longer offering her fine restaurant on barter.

When it comes to enforcing rules to your members, it's nice to be able to say something like, "Gee, I'd approve that deal for you, but the home office's computer just won't—not until you pay your old cash fees owed to the exchange." Without this excuse, some of your clients will figure out ways to take advantage of you.

Up and Running Cheaper, Sooner

Franchisers are in the business of supplying turnkey, ready-to-go operations. You put your money down, and you get everything necessary to start a trade exchange. You'll get training, marketing, and advertising material, a professional-looking website, software, procedures, and a billing service.

Barter Bits _____

If you want to become a franchisee of one high-profile barter company, you can expect to pay a start-up cost of around $20,000 in
cash. Your only other expenses would be to acquire office space, a
computer, and replacements for the soles on your shoes, caused by
all the pavement pounding you'll end up doing.

Because a franchise can pool resources, you'll immediately be able to
show your clients a top-notch website. This website not only sells the
barter concept, but it is also a platform where your members will be
able to discover new trade opportunities and market to one another.

Other than the people, software is the heart of any good trade
exchange. A franchise will likely have already spent a lot of money to
develop a top-notch website. You won't have to reinvent the wheel.

No matter how good the software, it's useless if there's no one around
to back it up. Even the best software experiences a glitch from time
to time. Because a national franchise has resources to deal with these
problems, you'll be unlikely to be left in a lurch.

Some entrepreneurs don't want to deal with the minutia of numbers
and accounting responsibilities that are inherently part of operating a
trade exchange. If that sounds like you, consider affiliation with a franchiser.

Because the franchiser performs all accounting functions, including
processing transactions, sending out statements, and reporting all
1099-Bs, you can concentrate on selling new accounts and brokering
transactions.

Barter Bits _____

The largest national franchise of trade exchanges
not only does all the
accounting, it also sends
out all the bills from a central
office. Increasingly, these bills
are being sent out in e-mail
form.

Especially if you like the idea of a
9-to-5 job, affiliating with a franchiser may be the way to go. At the
end of the month, when the independent exchange owner is fretting
about getting his or her statements
out on time, you might be able to
call it quits. But it's not all sugar and
honey.

Disadvantages of Franchises

The biggest disadvantage of signing up with a franchise is not the cost of entry; it's the chunk it takes out of your gross. A national franchise can charge up to 30 percent of all the cash fees you generate.

For a young exchange, that might not amount to much, but if you have a mature exchange that does lots of trading, it can really add up.

If you have a new trade exchange that generates $10,000 in monthly revenue, paying a franchiser 30 percent or $3,000 might not sound like much. But if you're billing $40,000 per month, you could end up paying $12,000 per month, or $144,000 per year, essentially for marketing material and someone else to do your books.

There's another disadvantage. You're not really the boss. A franchise expects you to abide by their rules and procedures. A franchise gives you a proven formula, and you won't be able to deviate too much from it.

This is a doubled-edged sword. Whereas you'll be less likely to try something innovative, you'll also be less likely to do something dumb.

Advantages of Becoming an Independent Trade Exchange

One of the biggest advantages of going it alone is you'll be your own boss. You will be accountable to no one, other than to your members. You're free to change your procedures and rules as you see fit.

If you want to change your logo, you can. If you want to change your entry fees or commission structures to accommodate certain traders, go for it. If you want to send out your own newsletter or design a new brochure, feel free.

When you operate an independent trade exchange, you will be running your own economy. If you feel a certain member is deserving of a line of trade credit, you can extend whatever amount you feel is proper. If you want to open a reciprocal trading relationship with another exchange, you can, without asking for permission.

There Is No Ceiling to Your Earnings

Because a franchiser takes care of so much for you, it's easier to get started this way. But if your goal is to make lots of money, your best bet might be to go the independent route.

This is because once you have paid for your computer, software, and accounting person, it's a fixed cost. You don't have to pay a fee each time you generate a commission.

Barter Bits _____

One entrepreneur started his trade exchange from scratch. Within 10 years, he had created an organization with 50 employees that included 17 brokers. His trade volume exceeded $60 million per year, and his cash in the door was approximately $6 million. Had he been a member of a franchise, he would have had to pay $1.8 million to the franchiser, which would have been untenable. Yet, he employed only three full-time people in his accounting department who earned a fraction of that.

As you grow your independent exchange and show consistent earnings, you'll feel comfortable taking a larger and larger paycheck. Of those making six-figure-and-above incomes, there are probably more from the independent than the franchised sector.

Something to Sell at the End of the Day

If you create a viable independent trade exchange, you will have built a business, not just bought yourself a job. No trade exchange has a lot of *brick and mortar,* but if it has a history of revenue generation and solid fiscal management, it's an exchange you can sell.

When the time comes when you want to retire, or simply move on to something else, your independent trade exchange is something you'll be able to sell to an employee, a member, an interested investor, or perhaps another trade exchange with multiple offices.

Disadvantages of Being an Independent

There are two primary disadvantages of starting as an independent, as opposed to a franchised, office. First, it can be expensive. Second, as you go about the business of building your exchange, unless you've done your homework, there may be limited sources for information or advice.

Because you won't have a franchise behind you, you'll have to buy what you need in somewhat of a piecemeal manner. You'll have to spend money in lots of ways.

Think about it. You'll need to design your logo and sales material. You'll have to print trade slips. Then there will be office machines, computers, and the like.

Finally, you'll have to decide what software to buy, and how to train yourself and your employees.

Don't Start on a Shoestring

A franchiser's fee is going to cost you around $20,000. If that's the direction you decide to take, those numbers are pretty cut and dried. With that, you can pretty much begin calling on accounts right away.

But if you're going to start your own independent trade exchange, you should figure on double that, or at least $40,000. We'll break down some of those numbers later in this chapter. For now, consider another challenge. That is, you won't make any money for six months to a year.

If you have an entrepreneurial spirit, you probably think you can do it faster. It's great to have confidence. But no matter how much you believe in barter, it's doubtful each account you call on will share your enthusiasm. Even if they did, you'll still have to convince them you're going to be around for the long haul, that you won't call it quits.

Think about it. You call on your first account. "Sounds great," the business owner says. "Who's on the list?" To this you can reply with a one-word answer, "You." This is why starting a trade exchange presents the ultimate chicken-and-egg dilemma. No one wants to join until somebody else joins.

The best way to jump-start a trade exchange is to sign up as many members as you can, for free. Give the first 50 members a free membership. The second 50 pay $50; the next 50 pay $100, and so on. No way will you or your sales staff be able to pay for itself in this manner, but that's not the point.

What matters is you sign enough members to make it attractive for others to join. The important thing is not how much a member paid to join, but rather how much trade he or she does later on.

> ### Balance of Trade
>
> At the beginning, it can be tempting to consider a cash entry fee more important than the commission rate. One exchange started by offering clients a choice of a $50 entry fee and 10 percent commission, or a $200 entry fee and a 7 percent commission. A restaurant joined and took the second option. Twenty-five years and $2 million worth of trade later, the discounted commission cost the trade exchange $60,000 in cash commissions.

There's another dilemma: until there are enough members to trade with, trade won't happen. You have to hit a certain critical mass of membership.

Let's say you sign up your first five members. All of them represent high-demand categories. One is a shoe store; another is an auto repair facility; there's a dentist, a dry cleaner, and a restaurant. Although all may potentially be great traders, no one can attract enough customers to make barter worthwhile.

The Barter Tipping Point

When does barter "kick in" among members? For some reason, real trade volume starts to happen at around 200 members, assuming they are within geographic proximity to one another. Here's another oddity. When you reach 300 members, you'll do double the trade; and when you reach 400 members, your trade volume will be triple what 200 members generated.

> **Balance of Trade**
>
> Remember, it takes time to make money. Two partners decided to start a trade exchange. They sought out the most qualified barter trainer and joined both national associations to gain further training. They bought the best software and were off to the races. Their fast start was thwarted because one of the partners became disenchanted and quit because no money was made for three months. The other tried to continue on, but failed, as he couldn't do it all alone.

Trade volume won't continue to grow exponentially forever. Yet it illustrates a key fact. Generating trade volume will quickly become more important than selling new accounts. As time goes on, your attention will increasingly turn away from sales and become focused on brokering.

Software Is an Independent's Most Important Investment

Barter software can get expensive. Don't be tempted to play it cheap. There are a few Internet-based companies that promise to take care of your accounting for a fraction of what you'd expect. But usually these companies offer no training, and no help in brokering, or giving advice.

There are a few other software packages you can pick up inexpensively, but beware. You usually get what you pay for. Be especially attentive to issues of support and service. If you join a national association, you will be able to find out who sells various barter software packages.

When you choose barter software, find a system that offers an in-depth accounting package. It should not only take care of credits and debits, but a host of other functions.

> **Balance of Trade**
>
> Beware of using basic or cheap software packages. An exchange in the western United States started with a cheap software package that offered basic accounting functions only. It took credited and debited accounts, sent out statements, and took care of 1099 reporting requirements. But it offered nothing in the way of brokering. The exchange grew out of the software within two years and made the switch to a more complete system. Transferring data was difficult, as was learning a completely new system. The disruption extended through several months and cost the exchange thousands of dollars.

One of the most important is information retrieval. Your future clients will undoubtedly call and ask if they were credited for a specific sale. Or they want to check an amount. You should be able to quickly retrieve transaction histories, not just last month, but from years ago.

The ability to retrieve information is important as a brokering tool also. In the trade business, you have to know who bought from whom. This is important especially if a member goes out of business or ceases trading. When that happens, you'll want to let your members know they can't expect to spend their trade dollars there anymore.

> **Barter Bits**
>
> One of the first things you'll want to do when you start your trade exchange is to get a sales tax license, assuming it's applicable in your state. Even if you don't maintain a showroom, you will inevitably find yourself buying items, either for cash or trade, and then reselling them. It's critical that the ability to compute and charge sales tax is integrated into your software.

If you don't know where you've been, you won't know where you're going. Effective software should allow you to track trends and determine which categories represent the most trade volume.

Track Members' Wants and Needs

Good software does more than shoot out empirical data. It should also help your broker do his or her job. The typical broker is inundated with information. In trying to keep track of purchasing requests, other trading opportunities sometimes get buried.

As you determine which software to buy, find a system that helps your brokers keep track of a maze of information. A good system should allow all your brokers to share information, right down to members' anniversaries, birthdays, number of children they have, and other information that can reveal purchasing tendencies. If it's done right, your members will think your brokers are telepathic, when in fact they just have good software.

> ### Trade Tales
>
> One enterprising broker was talking to a member and noticed on the computer screen that it was his anniversary. The broker sold the member flowers, dinner out, limousine to the dinner, and to top it off, an all-inclusive vacation to the Caribbean. The broker earned a bonus that very month.

Rate Your Members

By its very nature, a trade exchange will be able to access a limited amount of extreme hard goods. These are products with narrow margins, and are of high demand. Who gets the goodies?

Good software enables you to rate your members. This can be quantified by trade balance (positive or negative) and also cash payment history. It makes no sense to offer a kitchen of new appliances to someone in a low category, just because a broker took a personal liking to that member. Sell to your good members, as it will promote trade volume.

Software Is a Management Tool Also

As your trade exchange grows, there's another reason to have decided on good software. That is, it should also be a contact management tool. Without good software, members sometimes get lost in the shuffle. No one calls them for months at a time. Other members, on the other hand, become "squeaky wheels" and get all the service.

When you talk to a barter software provider, make sure there's a tool provided that forces your brokers to make a notation when they contact a client, what was discussed, and when they should call back.

The larger your organization becomes, the more difficult it will be to determine the effectiveness of each employee. Chances are you'll put together a program that rewards brokers for a job well done. Good software should allow you to do this, and to coordinate it with your commission structure.

How Much Should Software Cost?

This is a trick question. That's because barter software should never be sold as a stand-alone. It's no good without training. Training should not only include the nuts and bolts of understanding the software, but also trading in general.

So what's the bottom line? Figure on spending about $10,000. Combine that with the other expenses mentioned at the beginning of this chapter, and you're probably close to the $40,000 of combined start-up costs.

Learning the Ropes as an Independent

If you start with a franchise, you don't have to worry about training—it's offered to you. But if you decide to go the independent route, where do you turn? There are three ways you can go about it.

1. You can go out and make all the mistakes everybody has already made. (This will cost you a lot of money.)

2. You can join a national association where training is offered.

3. You can hire a trainer or professional who specializes in helping trade exchanges get into business.

If you decide to take the first option, good luck. If you make it, you'll have broken through the norm. The landscape is littered with the carcasses of those who figured they knew it all.

There are lots of ways a trade exchange can fail. The owner can become disenchanted and simply quit. He can mismanage his money supply. He can fail in selling new members. Or he can fall flat on his face in sending out statements and reporting 1099s to the government. A few Lone Rangers have succeeded—but not many.

You may choose to join one of the national associations. Both the National Association of Trade Exchanges and the International Reciprocal Trade Association are economical to join, and both conduct yearly conventions. Attending these events is like joining a gym. You get what you put into it. If you participate, ask questions, and pro-actively search out information, you can obtain the tools you'll need to succeed. At both venues, you'll be able to find people who sell barter software.

Finally, you might decide you want to invest in a personal trainer. If you pick the right one, it will be like having a good trainer at the gym. You'll learn how to strengthen the body of your trade exchange, not injure yourself, and prepare yourself for the future. Combine expert training with quality software, and you've got yourself a great start!

The Least You Need to Know

◆ Franchises launch an exchange quickly, because they offer train-ing, software, and support at a reasonable start-up price.

◆ Going independent allows greater flexibility; however, the draw-backs include higher start-up costs and dealing with basic but essential details before you can start selling memberships.

◆ Choose software carefully for accounting and brokering.

◆ You need solid training for running a trade exchange.

Chapter 18

Finding and Training Your Sales Staff

In This Chapter

- ◆ Know who you're hiring
- ◆ Give them training and tools
- ◆ Determine how to compensate them
- ◆ Know your presentation

One of your first tasks in starting a trade exchange is finding good salespeople. In all likelihood, sales consumes a lot of your own time, especially at first. But you're probably going to need some help. Most businesses face the same vexing challenge: that is, how do you find, motivate, and train good salespeople?

What type of salesperson do you want? You want to avoid order takers. You want order *getters*. Plus, you want to hire someone who shares your excitement about starting a trade exchange. Yet, even the most highly motivated salesperson is doomed to failure unless you give backup, training, and support.

As you grow your trade exchange, you'll quickly address issues of compensation for sales staff. Get it right from the beginning and you'll save yourself a lot of headaches.

Finally, there are the nuts and bolts of the sales call. Libraries have been filled with books about how sell. Each person has a unique style. Yet, a good sales presentation must make certain points and does so in a logical order.

Hire People Who Have the Best Chance of Success

Managers often get wrapped up in trying to define who the best sales candidates will be. Almost everyone has a theory. Some try to get at the meat of the matter by subjecting candidates to tests, a battery of questions, or careful examinations of job histories and resumés. Yet, when push comes to shove, they usually end up following their gut.

Look for Passion

The ideal candidate should share your passion and your vision. There are some people who not only "get" barter, they are energized by it. You want someone who gets up in the morning, eager to spread the barter gospel.

So who is this person? The ideal candidate isn't male or female, young or old, experienced or fresh out of college. There have been successes, and failures, among all types. Yet, there are traits to look for when you hire someone. One is to be fearless, to not be afraid to search out good clients, wherever they are.

Trade Tales

One exchange hired a student, admittedly green, while she was still working on her bachelor's degree. She called on a liquidator who had his office in a warehouse outside of town. Although her presentation was not polished, she ended up getting the new member to trade $40,000 of modular office furniture. The account ended up doing $200,000 of trade that year. Ironically, another salesman, a veteran of barter, had driven by the business on his way to work each morning, but had never stopped.

This underlying ability to sniff out good sales calls is a valuable asset. After all, some of your best traders will be on Main Street, but others could be on a street you've never heard of before, hidden in a warehouse, in the industrial part of town.

Look for a Background

For a salesperson to have the fire in his belly and make lots of sales calls is a huge plus. Yet, some backgrounds are more conducive to selling trade than others. Typically, those who have had experience getting orders are more effective than those who have a history of simply taking orders. Look for a self-starter who has had success in direct sales, personal contact, and especially selling an intangible.

One of the best backgrounds to have is in media. People who have sold advertising already know all about barter, albeit on a direct basis. Once they get the hang of organized trade, look out. They frequently have what it takes to translate their experience into success.

One reason media salespeople make great salespeople for a trade exchange is because they usually know everyone in town. There is no other profession where one gets to meet so many people in so many diverse industries.

Someone who has successfully sold time on TV or radio, or space in a publication, is already familiar with the challenges facing all kinds of businesses. You can't sell advertising to an auto mechanic without knowing he or she makes more money selling brake repair than tires. Or that exhaust systems last so long it doesn't make sense to spend money promoting their replacement. This broad-based knowledge is extremely helpful when calling on barter clients.

> **Trade Tales**
>
> At one time, one of the barter national associations' board of directors consisted of nine trade exchange owners. Six of them had media backgrounds, either in management or in sales. Not surprisingly, each had parlayed their experience with media into success in the barter business.

There are other types of resumés to look at. Whereas it's helpful for an applicant to have sold an intangible, such as insurance, financial planning, or telecommunication, sometimes the best salespeople are "old school." Take the door-to-door vacuum cleaner salesman, or siding salesperson, or guy selling water conditioners. If someone has succeeded at any of these endeavors, you know they're not afraid of hard work. Just be sure they're not too high pressure. But whomever you hire, they're not going to succeed unless you give them the support and backup they need.

Give Them Training

Unless she has had a media background, even the most experienced salesperson is unlikely to know about barter. Selling memberships in a trade exchange is a totally new proposition. Just because the salesperson is enthusiastic is no guarantee she'll be able to get the client to share her enthusiasm, or that she won't confuse the client during the process.

Because most sales calls will be with people who have never even heard of a trade exchange before, it's important your representatives understand the nuances. You might consider visiting the offices of other trade exchanges around the country. Most are generous in sharing information and giving advice. They may even share their sales manuals with you.

Barter Bits

To help you obtain qualified help in training salespeople, you might get on the Internet and search "starting a trade exchange" or "barter training." Each should give you a good list of sources.

But the best thing you can do is consult a professional barter trainer who will teach you the ins and outs of sales. There are several companies that supply this service, and an Internet search will likely give you some nice contacts.

Give Your Salespeople the Tools

You want to make sure your sales staff is supported with the very best in brochures, printed material, and website. Sure, it's possible to sell an account on the back of a cocktail napkin, but it's not very professional.

Don't cheap it out. It might be tempting to save a buck by printing your business cards on an in-house laser printer, but don't. Go to a professional printer instead. Show your clients you have pride in what you're doing, and that you're going to be around to service them.

It's amazing how many companies put up cheesy websites. Be sure to invest in a quality website from the start. Your Internet presence should complement your local sales effort. At the very least, it should allow your members to access your directory. At the most, it should allow interactivity as your members look up balances, trade histories, and make requests.

Advertising Isn't the Answer

You're excited about starting a trade exchange. Everybody gets that. But spending money trying to get people to join is probably a waste of money. A trade exchange, by its very nature, is business to business. If you advertise in the paper, or on the radio, you're likely to get calls from individuals trying to barter pots and pans.

It's hard enough to describe a trade exchange during a qualified appointment. Try doing it in 30 seconds, or in a quarter-page ad.

Leads for your sales staff are best rounded up by your own members. They are the best source because they represent customers for potential new members. Your members also have credibility with their business acquaintances. They can give you qualified leads, with minimal investment.

> **Barter Bits**
>
> Most exchanges offer a referral fee to their members for finding other businesses that end up joining. These fees typically range from $100 to $200 in trade or in cash, depending on the quality and sales potential of the new member.

Supplement Your Efforts the Free Way

Lots of businesses open each month in your community. But do readers of a newspaper really care? Other than the moms and dads, aunts and uncles of all the new business owners, the answer is usually no.

A trade exchange is different. By its very nature, a trade exchange is an interesting proposition. You may be the only one in town. This is the stuff of a great news story. Yes, with a little work and a few connections, you should be able to get yourself free publicity.

> **Barter Bits** _____
>
> Most trade exchanges have, at one time or another, gotten some very favorable press from local papers. Papers are always looking for unique stories, and your exchange is one of them. Not surprisingly, the national media has increasingly run stories about trade exchanges. One large national newspaper ran a front-page story on organized barter, as have several cable networks, and even the network news!

Depending on the size of the local newspaper, it might not be all that difficult to entice them to run an article about your new business. After all, barter is in the news because it represents an alternative way businesses can prosper. You might have one of your members call the paper for you. By getting an article in the paper about your trade exchange, you give your sales staff advertising that money can't buy.

Be Involved in Your Community

There is no better way to gain credibility for your company, and your salespeople, than to be visible in the community. Encourage your salespeople to network by joining service clubs, nonprofit organizations, or the local Chamber of Commerce.

These venues allow your staff to develop relationships and forge friendships while working for a common cause. Sales to these newly found friends will come naturally and not in a confrontational setting that so often accompanies the nonqualified sales lead.

When you or a member of your staff joins a service club, it's possible the club itself may become a member. Nonprofits can earn trade dollars by trading items that had been donated to them, and by selling sponsorships and promotional consideration.

> **Barter Bits**
>
> One salesman became a member of a local service club that sup-
> ported disabled children. The club joined the exchange when it
> found out it could barter for golf outings, social events, and prizes
> for silent auctions. The club ended up spending over $20,000 per
> year. The same salesperson became a board member of a local arbo-
> retum. The organization offered bedding plants on trade and spent its
> trade dollars to buy potting soil.

Similarly, it's a good idea to join the local Chamber of Commerce. And
don't blow off the meetings either. You'll meet tons of business owners
and many of them will be potential clients. With luck, you might even
sign the Chamber itself. By trading memberships that cost basically
nothing, a Chamber of Commerce has nothing to lose.

You might also consider joining a *leads club*. Leads clubs don't exist to
promote public service. They are all about lead generation. You'll find
out which businesses are opening their doors, who is closing them, and
which ones need to buy anything from printing to roofing.

def•i•ni•tion

> **Leads club**   A business networking club composed of noncompeting
> businesses who share leads with one another, as they also attempt to
> do business with one another. You get one insurance agent, one builder,
> one office machine dealer, and so on. Each does word-of-mouth adver-
> tising for the others. Meetings are typically held weekly. The largest fran-
> chiser of leads clubs has thousands of clubs in nearly 50 countries.

If you join a leads club, be sure to limit your participation to getting
leads for businesses that might want to join a trade exchange. If a member shares information that a business in town is looking for a printer, it
would be a conflict of interest to turn that lead over to a printer in your
exchange. The leads, after all, are meant to be for members of the club.

Be Loaded for Bear

When you go bear hunting, you make sure to take a rifle. When you
go hunting for clients, you'll want your salespeople to be specifically

prepared to meet with that client. Especially if you're in a large market, with lots of businesses, you may want to subscribe to one of the online sales lead generation sites. This can get you the name of the business, the decision maker, the size of the business, and other pertinent information.

Even if you don't subscribe to such a service, make sure your sales staff does its homework before calling on an account. At the very least, a salesperson should visit the website of the business he or she is about to call on. A quick web search can also help your salesperson become knowledgeable about the client's industry. A salesperson that is knowledgeable conveys credibility and enjoys an enhanced closing ratio.

Don't Keep Your Salespeople in a Vacuum

Everyone likes variety. Salespeople like to enjoy a day when they don't have to run around like maniacs. Brokers, usually tied to their desks, look forward to "getting out of the office." Both should be accommodated.

> **Barter Bits**
>
> One trade exchange tried an experiment that could have evolved into a reality show. Once a month, its salespeople traded places with brokers. Brokers got to meet clients at their places of business. Conversely, salespeople became "brokers for a day." Each gained an appreciation of the others' jobs.

The best support you can give your salesperson on the street is to, well, take her *off* the street. Do this for only a day a week. Let her help broker the accounts she sold. Give her a feel for what the brokers do, and to see what trades are happening.

By observing and experiencing the other side of the business, the salesperson improves her skills. She will be less likely to fall into recitations about how great barter is. She'll also be able to more accurately represent trading to the people she signs up.

Appointment Setters: Good or Bad?

Some trade exchanges back up their sales department with appointment setters. These are people who are paid to sit behind a phone and make appointments for those in direct sales. There are two schools of thought. One is that an appointment setter saves time and effort because he specializes in cold calls. As such, he is better prepared to get a qualified appointment.

Others feel that someone who pounds the pavement is best qualified to make the appointment. They believe an appointment setter too easily falls into the trap of sounding like a "telemarketer," repeating a canned spiel.

If you're in a small- to medium-sized market, forget the appointment setter. A good salesperson worth his salt is perfectly capable of getting an appointment. If your salesperson is weaker, or you're in a larger market, an appointment setter might be valuable. If you decide you need one, it's a good idea to have that person in-house, where you can keep a tab on things.

Develop a Sales Staff Compensation Strategy

If you want good salespeople, you have to offer them a good salary and decent benefits. This can be hard at the beginning because you have to forego charging entry fees to your very first members. After all, these members are taking a chance, for there are no other members to trade with.

So how do you pay your salespeople? You either don't have any and you do it all yourself, or you dip into your pocket and subsidize your exchange's sales effort, at least until you build your membership base.

But there's one thing you can't forget. You get what you pay for. Pay a livable wage. You should have a sense of what is reasonable. If your market is small and the cost of living is low, you can get by with less. Not so if you live in a large city.

> **Barter Bits**
>
> If you're starting out and having trouble paying a dedicated salesperson, you could offer "sweat equity." That is, if he sticks around and generates profits for the company, he could own stock in your company.

The Case for Giving Away Memberships

There are some exchanges that don't charge an entry fee, ever. The argument for doing this is not invalid. They feel that the assessment of any entry fee discourages clients from joining and spending trade dollars, which is where all the real income is anyway.

But without an entry fee, how do they pay their salespeople? It's simple. They typically hire less qualified salespeople, pay them less, and have them give away memberships all over town. Whereas this brings in new traders, it can also attract nonplayers who are a waste of time. The wheat then has to be separated from the chaff by the brokering department.

Motivate Your Sales Staff with Benefits

As your staff signs members, one great way to keep them motivated is to give them a piece of the pie. In other words, as their accounts generate cash commissions, give them a point or two, or maybe three. That way, if one of the accounts they sign up ends up generating $10,000 of cash fees, they could make a nice additional income, for doing no additional work.

If your salesperson ends up morphing into a broker, which sometimes happens, that percentage can go up, perhaps to 3 or 4 percentage points, depending on the base salary. In short, you'll want to compensate your salespeople especially well when they bring in good traders, rather than names on a list.

There's something else you can offer to keep and motivate a good salesperson. If your exchange is generating positive trade dollars, you can create a sub-account for that salesperson. Over time, a salesperson will undoubtedly earn trade dollars by signing up members who paid trade on their entry fees. You can also incorporate trade dollars into a commission structure or performance bonus. Your salesperson can then use trade just as anyone else would, for restaurant meals, dental work, lawn mowing, or a vacation.

Know the Pitch

No matter how much strategy, money, or training you throw at some-one, it won't matter a twit without a good sales presentation. You and your salespeople have to know the basic ingredients.

How you put these ingredients together is up to you. After all, each person has his or her own style. But the first question to ask a poten-tial client should be, "Would you like new business?" There are indeed instances when someone can legitimately say, no. If some-one is at full capacity, cannot accommodate new customers, or doesn't have any extra hours in the week, it's perfectly legitimate to not want new customers. But for most, the opposite is true. New customers are what they first think about when they get up in the morning.

Barter Bits

Even if a prospect says he can't take on new customers, dig a little deeper. You might dis-cover there are certain times of the year when there is indeed excess capacity. Also, don't overlook the possibil-ity that he could do some account receivable trading.

Once you've established your prospect's desire for new business, you have to describe how a trade exchange works. The tricky part is when you first say the word "barter." Most people, upon hearing the word, immediately think of trading chickens for delivering a baby. Or maybe they think of bartering at a flea market, which is in fact, dickering. You have to get them out of these mind-sets. You have to move them along to what you really do. You run an alternative currency.

Yet, you still have to *start* with the concept of direct barter. Let's say your prospect is a carpet cleaner. Ask him if he has ever traded one-on-one before. Chances are he'll answer in the affirmative. He'll tell you of how he traded carpet cleaning with the owner of a body shop to fix his service van.

When Clients Talk, They Sell Themselves

Your sales presentation should continue with the prospect telling you why barter is good. If the carpet cleaner traded with the body shop, ask him why he did it. Ask him how much he saved. He'll likely tell you it cost him very little out-of-pocket to clean the carpet, and that by bartering, he didn't have to pay cash for his body work.

You now lead the discussion in a slightly different direction. You ask your client if he would like to expand this advantage he just told you about. How would he like to trade with hundreds of businesses? Again, the answer will likely be yes.

This is where you have to make sure your client is able to make a mental leap. Barter is money. And money is barter. You have to guide him to understand this. The best way is to use an illustration. "What if you need eye glasses, but the optical store doesn't need carpet cleaning? What then?" You then describe how trade dollars can be spent with the optical company. The optical company, in turn, can spend its newly found trade dollars anywhere in the system. Perhaps they'll buy some advertising from the local radio station, that, wouldn't you know it, needs carpet cleaning!

Smart People Over-Think Trade

Ironically, smart people can be the dumbest when it comes to figuring out trade. Be prepared for someone who is intelligent and successful to still not get it. Even after you've described the whole process, and maybe even gotten your client to put her name on the dotted line, she reverts back to trading eggs for delivering a baby. "But what if the optical company doesn't want carpet cleaning?" she'll ask with a blank stare.

Be patient. Go over it again, and again, if necessary.

> **Barter Bits**
>
> An effective visual tool is for the barter salesperson to pull cash bills and credit cards out of her wallet. Lay them down on the table and say, "These are all money." Then put out a barter ID card and say, "This is money, too!"

The lesson here is most salespeople are intimately familiar with their product. They think their clients are, too. In their enthusiasm, they jump to the conclusion the client actually gets it. Slow down. Review how trade works. If you get too remedial, your client will let you know.

Kill Certain Words

During your presentation, some prospects assume they understand barter when they don't. You'll know this is happening if they use the "f-word"—"free." When they do, stop them in their tracks. The word free should never be used to describe a barter purchase. Yet, some members persist in thinking that because they're not spending cash, it is somehow free. The best way to counter this logic is to ask them what happens when they accept trade dollars for a sale. Are they giving away their product? Is it free?

As a prospect grapples with the concept of organized barter, he'll use another banned word. You say "trade dollars," and he says "points." Whereas any currency could technically be considered "points," the terminology is more commonly used to describe a parlor game. Even if it's used in passing, don't let your prospect revert to terms that denigrate what you're selling. Gently steer him back to "trade dollars."

Keep Your Client's Attention Focused

It's great to establish rapport, but be careful not to socialize your way out of a sale. There is a point that you have to cut the small talk and direct the conversation to why you're there.

Even with the best of planning, your sales call can sometimes be sabotaged by interruptions. Just as you're closing, someone barges in and asks if they should put decaf or regular into the coffee pot. Stay focused. Don't let it bother you. Get back on message as quickly as you can.

Another huge distraction can be something you bring in. No, it's not an unzipped fly or pimple in the middle of your forehead. It's the directory and sales material you put on the table in front of your client.

Your prospect, who figures she already understands everything you're going to say, is salivating. She wants to see the "list." "Can I see who's on the list?" she clamors. Her eyes focus on the directory you've put in front of her.

> **Barter Bits** _____
>
> Another good reason to not let the prospective client peruse the
> directory before understanding the concept is that she will want to
> "call someone on the list." This could be disastrous if she calls some-
> one who is unhappy. Be prepared. Be ready to give out the names
> and numbers of some satisfied members who don't mind being called
> and who will tell a great barter story.

A sales presentation should never hinge on the magical list of who's in
the exchange. Nor should it depend on just one want or need. Keep the
conversation focused on the advantages of barter. If your client becomes
fixated on who's in the exchange, you may be going in the wrong direction. And you have only yourself to blame.

You're Worth What You Charge

A few prospective clients try to take control of the conversational rud-
der in another way. You're in the middle of your presentation, and what
do they insist on knowing? How much it is going to cost! Whereas this
can be a definite buying signal, be careful to not show your hand too
soon. Whatever number you come up with, someone's going to think
it's too much. From that point on, your client dismisses whatever you're
saying because he figures he can't afford it anyway. Defer your over-
anxious future member. Tell him you're getting to that, but first, "Let's
talk about your capacity to accept new customers."

Other potential members don't understand why you charge so much.
They equate your commission with what the charge card company
charges them. The best way to defend this is to ask how much new
business their charge company brings them. The answer, of course, is,
"They don't." Make the point that a charge company takes money off
the top for business they already had. A trade exchange charges a commission for getting them _new_ customers.

Don't Over-Promise

Some salespeople over-promise when it comes to selling barter.
Whereas this hardly happens in other industries (right!), it can do special harm to an exchange's relationship with its clients.

It's funny, but you can actually make more money by under-promising. Let's say you tell a prospect that new Mercedes are available with trade dollars. They're not only available, but they're growing on trees! What color do you want?

Assume someone falls for it. They sign up. Sure, your salesperson finagled an entry fee. Big whoop! What are the long-term ramifications of breaking such a promise? More than likely, your client will do a sale or two, discover she had been misled, and then quit. Worse, she'll probably spread negativity to everyone she knows, costing you future memberships.

Balance of Trade

Never sell an account based on the availability of just one product or service. If that business goes on standby, your member is ill-equipped to seek out other purchases.

If your salesperson sets realistic expectations, you'll actually make more money, and you could enjoy a profitable relationship for years to come. In fact, if you employ a system that requires your salespeople to make periodic contact with the people they signed up, they'll have to deal with the consequences of an unhappy member. You won't have the problem to begin with.

Know How to Close

There are a hundred ways to close. There's old school, new school, hard sell, soft sell, the assumed close, and all sorts of hitherto undefined closes. Pick your poison. It doesn't matter, as long as your close tactics are effective and ethical.

Barter Bits

The biggest bugaboo is as old as the ages. Many salespeople fail to close because the client wants to "think about it." In actuality, he's got to check with his partner, spouse, or accountant. Make sure you're talking to all the decision makers when you make your presentation.

Whatever your style, you should incorporate barter's key message. That is, "Are you interested in new business?" Everything else is secondary. One good way to drive this point home is to actually have a new customer in your hip pocket.

This is one more reason your sales staff should not exist in a vacuum, and routinely communicate with whomever's doing the brokering. Brokers are intimately familiar with their clients' wants and needs. If your salesperson is calling on the proverbial carpet cleaner, it's powerful to bring him a new customer with dirty carpet. It puts him in the position of saying no to something that's ingrained—that is, the desire for new customers. "I have a new customer for you," says the salesperson. "Let's call him!"

The Least You Need to Know

- A trade exchange depends on a vibrant, growing membership. There are certain key characteristics to look for when hiring salespeople who succeed.

- No matter how good your people, they won't succeed unless you give them training, tools, and support. Yet, some of the best support you can give your salespeople won't cost you a dime.

- Compensation for salespeople definitely costs you more than a dime. Trade can give you ways to compensate or bonus your salespeople when you might otherwise not be able to afford it.

- Knowing the sales pitch is critical. Everyone has his or her own style, but make sure your salespeople know the key ingredients to include when they're selling the concept.

Chapter **19**

Getting and Retaining Great Trade Brokers

In This Chapter

- ◆ How to find a great broker
- ◆ Give your broker the tools and support he or she needs
- ◆ Learn what great brokers know that average ones don't
- ◆ Compensate your brokers generously

A trade broker represents the heart of your trade exchange. Your broker is the person your members look to in order to help them transact with trade dollars, whether buying or selling. Your broker's professionalism goes a long way in establishing the faith and trust that's so critical to the success of a trade exchange.

This begs the question: How do I find a good trade broker? What traits should I look for? Foremost, you want someone who can sell. But there's more. Brokers have to be great at multitasking, and at the same time, be extremely intuitive. They must have a nose for the deal.

Once you find your trade broker, you can't just hand over a phone and membership list and expect him to succeed. You have to be prepared to give him the necessary tools, in the form of training and technology.

There are some things every trade broker should know. Yet, successful brokering is as much art as it is science. You want to really take care of your broker, too, with an enjoyable work environment and a compensation package that rewards productivity.

Get a Broker Who Can Sell!

If a broker can't sell and close a deal, she's done for. A broker is constantly selling. During the average day, she sells everything from restaurant gift certificates to lawn mowing services. But she's also selling when she gets some members to accept trade dollars in the first place. In many respects, an inside broker has a tougher sales job than the employee who sells memberships. The outside rep can focus on one account at a time, whereas the trade broker has to sell unrelated product offerings countless times each day.

It should come as no surprise, therefore, that a good broker should have some sort of outside sales experience. A resumé that includes retail order taking provides little advantage. On the other hand, if a prospective employee has been an order *getter*, that's a different story.

Your new broker will have to work all sorts of accounts, from the buttoned-down CEO to the guy digging ditches. And sometimes she'll be introducing them to each other. Make sure your broker has a diversified background and knows how to relate to all kinds of people.

Find a Circus Performer

There's one performer at the circus who would probably make a great trade broker—the plate spinner. He balances and spins a smooth plate at the top of a long stick. Then he adds a few more. At first, it seems easy. But as he adds more spinning plates, his job becomes more frantic. He must run from stick to stick, stopping to respin those with wobbling plates. He seems to be going crazy.

You have to find someone like the plate spinner, who is unflappable and doesn't panic. But instead of spinning plates, the trade broker is spinning accounts. He's got to keep each going, stopping only briefly to spend out one account, and then sprinting across the room to get a sale for another.

You want someone who thrives in an environment of organized chaos. You want a creative person with a good work ethic, but who may keep a slightly messy desk. You want someone who spends time being empathetic, but is nevertheless able to make many contacts in any given day.

 Balance of Trade

Make sure you don't bury your broker with too many accounts. Unless there are extenuating circumstances, a broker should handle no more than 200 members. If a broker is spread too thin, he doesn't have enough time to develop new relationships. Plus, he becomes so frazzled at the end of the day, you risk losing him.

Look for the Unflappable

A trade exchange, by its very nature, gives rise to some unfulfilled expectations. Top that off with the fact that some members can be difficult to work with. Find a person who can handle the demands of members and not become emotional.

A sense of humor is a valuable asset for a broker. Someone who is self-effacing and doesn't take everything too seriously can do well as a trade broker. This talent can come in handy when a good trade goes bad. It buys forgiveness and defuses stressful situations.

Another trait to look for is someone who can mentally compartmentalize. A broker might make 100 outgoing phone calls in a week, and receive another 100. As the broker tries to match buyers with sellers, keep all the pending deals straight, and smooth all the ruffled feathers, she's got to maintain her sanity. At the end of the day, you'll want to have hired someone who can turn it off at—well, the end of the day.

Good in Person Doesn't Mean Good on the Phone

If someone is impressive in person, that's great. But don't discard the diamond in the rough. Sometimes a person is diminutive or shy in person, but blossoms when on the phone.

> **Balance of Trade**
>
> Beware of the marathon talker. Everyone knows someone like this. The marathon talker can shine during a job interview. You find out only later that their gift of gab is costing you money.

You want to find someone who is not only good on the phone, but who also isn't afraid to make dozens of phone calls each day. A successful trade exchange is built upon relationships. Once your exchange gets bigger, brokers can't spend all their time with just a few accounts. Make sure you hire someone who understands the value of keeping in touch with everyone.

A Broker Has to Fit In

You're not going to lock your broker into a cubicle and not let him out. Your broker will be interacting with your management team, accounting person, sales representatives, and, down the road, other brokers. Look for a team player. If someone is great at brokering, but is disruptive, confrontational, or sabotages the efforts of others, you might as well not have hired that person in the first place.

Because of not being able to get along, some seemingly qualified prospects have an employment history of jumping from job to job. If someone is young, and still looking for that special job, that's understandable. But there comes a point at which a scattered job history becomes a red flag.

Beware of the person who lasts at a job only a year or so. This is not critical if your person is an outside sales representative. But clients value their relationships with your brokers. They want to see stability in your exchange. Each time a broker is replaced by someone new, you lose just a little bit of credibility.

It takes months for a new broker to get up to speed. Training a new broker eats up the time of your staff, too. Your new person will ask a lot of questions as he struggles to learn how barter works, along with procedures and software. To top it off, he's got to get to know all those clients, the nature of their businesses, and become familiar with their wants and needs.

Hire Someone Ethical

Brokers have to be ethical. A broker is akin to an employee at the bank who has access to your financial information. She cannot divulge account balances or transaction histories to other members. She cannot treat trade information in a more cavalier fashion just because it's not cash.

> **Balance of Trade**
>
> Some brokers have been known to "push through" trades that haven't happened yet. They do this because their compensation is based on a certain level of trading activity. Problems occur when the trade falls through later, necessitating a reversal. A few other brokers have fluffed their clients' trade sales by creating totally bogus transactions, knowing full well they'll have to be reversed later. No matter, they figure, they "met their sales goals for the month."

A broker has to act ethically in other ways, too. She cannot make promises she knows she can't keep, just so she can get someone to sell something on barter. She has to be a straight talker when it comes to fees, commissions, and added shipping costs, too. There are literally dozens of ways a broker can act unethically. This is all the more reason for you to dig deep when you hire someone.

Brokers Should Be Evaluated

You took great care to hire the right person. Your new broker showed great promise at first, but then things began to go south. The number of phone calls decreased, while unexplained absences increased. In short, you hired the wrong person.

But six months have slid by. What do you do now? What you should have done six months ago, when you first hired the person: you should have come to an agreement with your new hire so that person understood there would be a *probationary employment period*.

def•i•ni•tion

Probationary employment period A period of time by which both employer and employee agree to abide. It is understood by both parties that after this time, the employment contract can be cancelled by either party. It gives the employee a chance to see if he really likes his new job; and conversely, the employer is able to ascertain if the person is right for the job. Probationary periods can range from 2 weeks to 90 days. They do not, however, totally protect the employer from lawsuits pertaining to an unfair termination.

It's a good idea to periodically offer evaluations of your brokers. They need to know if they're off the track; and by the same token, they need to know if they're doing the job right. Periodic evaluations also give you a chance to offer positive reinforcement, which all employees need.

Provide Necessary Training and Support

Brokers deal with an overwhelming amount of information as they service their clients. If you don't give them the support they need, you risk having them burn out.

There are some pretty basic things you can do to back up your broker. Amazingly, many of them cost very little money. Some do cost more, however, as they involve information technology.

Finally, there are a number of outside sources where broker training can be obtained. Some are effective and others less so.

The Phone: Make It All That It Can Be

Your broker depends on the phone. Yet, it's amazing how many businesses suffer with a clunky phone system. Get a phone system from the get-go that you can grow into. It's better than having to switch later on.

Don't assume your new broker was born knowing every feature of your phone system. Try working with an entirely new system, and see how hard it is. Make sure your broker is comfortable putting people on hold, changing voice-mail greetings, and especially conference calling.

Barter Bits _____

Conference calling is an important tool for a broker. It empowers her to solidify barter deals by putting buyer and seller together. Promises made in the presence of the broker are more likely to be kept. And when the broker checks on the status of a deal a week later, she'll know what was said, and what wasn't.

Do your broker a favor. If you want her to be on the phone six or seven hours a day, make her comfortable. Invest in a quality headset. This will not only alleviate headaches, it will free up your broker's hands so she can look up client information and trade opportunities.

Good Software Is Worthless Without Good Training

When you start your trade exchange, you already know the value of getting good computers and software, particularly for accounting and contact management that can deal with the specifics of barter. They're the key to information management. But what good are they if your broker doesn't know how they work?

Barter software, by its very nature, is custom written. Just because someone knows about Word and Excel doesn't mean he'll know a twit about the specialized software he'll be using each day.

Good training cannot be done on the fly. Initial training should be done on weekends, when there are no phones ringing. This will help in two ways. First, your new person will learn more quickly without all the distractions. Second, your key people won't be spending all their time training someone during the peak of their work day.

Watch Out for Internet Distractions

The Internet is an indispensable part of being a trade broker. Your broker will be able to look up cash prices, promote members who need to sell and those who need to buy, and send out immediate offerings to their clients. It will also allow your broker to conduct online shopping, visit sports sites, find out the latest soap opera news, and even run a cottage eBay business on your dime.

Sure, you can turn yourself into a policeman and covertly monitor all the sites your staff is visiting. But it's better if you simply maintain a visible presence with your brokers. If you see your brokers tapping on the keyboard more, and hear them on the phone less, it's time for a heart-to-heart.

> **Balance of Trade**
>
> Even when used for legitimate purposes, overuse of e-mail can cause problems. It's effective to mass e-mail your members with product offerings, as long as you don't overdo it. Try to limit these e-mail blasts to no more than a couple times per week.

The computer is but one medium or tool the broker uses. Moreover, it is not the most important one. The most important remains the broker's phone and her ability to use it as she develops relationships. Rarely can the Internet take sole credit for selling anything in the barter world. Rather, it takes personal communication.

Outside Training Sources: Are They Worth It?

There are three primary sources for outside training. If you're part of a franchise or large group, it's easy. You simply attend the annual convention. There, experienced brokers conduct training sessions.

If you're an independent trade exchange, you'll want to go the route of one of the two national trade associations (see Appendix B). They put on annual conventions and occasional regional training events where brokers can be trained on topics pertaining to a wide range of issues.

However, these events tend to be generic in nature, because so many exchanges use different software. So too, after a convention or two, redundancy becomes a factor, as the same people tend to deal with the same topics. Yet, for the new broker, it can be a valuable experience. These events also offer an opportunity where the trade broker can become certified.

Another source of broker training can take the form of the company you bought your software from. These companies are familiar with how their software interfaces with broker functions. Ongoing training is something to ask about when you buy your software.

The Makings of a Great Broker

A great broker truly cares about his clients. And they sense it. These brokers take time to know the names of their clients' spouses and kids. They're not beyond sending a get-well card or a gift basket. They know what sports their clients like, and what their interests are. When the broker runs into the occasional bump in the road, or deal gone wrong, he will still pursue the next opportunity.

When there's trust, the client knows the broker is not going to intentionally lead him into a bad deal. The trustworthy broker is going to let his clients make a reasonable margin, and he never strong arms them into selling something on barter they shouldn't.

The great broker never gets rid of his clients by dishing out phone numbers to members he knows are not active sellers. He won't misrepresent inventory either. He will do his best to never get in the way of a client's previously existing cash business. He stays late for his clients, even to consummate a small trade where there's not much commission.

Trade Tales
Incredibly, a trade for a portable toilet probably led to a trade worth $10,000. A broker received a last-minute request for a portable toilet to accommodate wedding guests for a member's daughter. The broker made nearly a dozen calls and successfully chased down the portable toilet for the preoccupied member. The member was so impressed that a few weeks later, he called the broker and asked him if he could trade a dump truck worth $10,000. He could and he did.

Caring about clients manifests itself in enhanced trade volume. Because the broker knows his clients, he gains an intuition into what they want to buy, and what they want to sell.

Brokers Sell Add-Ons

How a broker handles purchase requests makes a big difference. Let's say a client calls and asks for a limousine service. The poor broker, without checking the status of the limo service, simply dishes out a phone number to the inquiring member. The average broker makes sure the limo company is available for trade and then gives out the phone number. The great broker asks, "For what event do you need a limo?"

Trade Tales

A broker in Minnesota received a call from a member who wanted her house painted. Unfortunately, it was the middle of the summer, and all the exchange's painters were already busy. The broker asked why it needed to be painted. "To prepare it to sell," was the answer. The broker called a real estate agent who was willing to take the listing on trade. The house ultimately sold and generated a $15,000 trade for the agent.

If the caller says it's for a wedding, the great broker asks if the bride has arranged for flowers. What about a wedding photographer? And don't forget about groomsmen gifts, tuxedo rental, wedding dress, rehearsal dinner, reception, and honeymoon. By using her noggin, the great broker now has at least a half dozen other trades she can work on. She has turned a $500 trade into a series of trades worth tens of thousands.

It doesn't stop there. The great broker now calls all the wedding-related businesses. In turn, she discovers what they need, and what they want to sell. It is little wonder the great broker is continually immersed in organized chaos.

Great Brokers Find New Golden Nuggets

You can't always rely on your client base. Members come and go. Their circumstances change and their ability to trade changes. That's why it's important to grow your trade exchange. Sure, most of your growth comes from your sales staff. But some of the biggest traders come by way of the broker.

Trade Tales

A broker in Michigan was working with a printer who was in search of two stoves that burned corn pellets. There was no member of the exchange that sold the product. Undeterred, the broker contacted a stove dealer two counties over, presented the trade dollar offer, and consummated the transaction, totaling $16,000.

Trade brokers sometimes receive requests for stuff they don't have. The savvy broker is not limited by the accounts the sales department brings in. He can go outside the system and see if he can get a new player to accept trade. After all, nothing beats being able to call a prospective member with a new customer.

Big Trades Can Be Right Under Your Nose

A great trade broker knows it's important to periodically visit clients in their places of business. Sometimes trading opportunities have become invisible to the business owner. He's too busy running his business. He doesn't see what others see: the windows need washing, the carpet cleaning, and the building painted. Good brokers get out and see their clients. In doing so, they can inevitably dig up new wants and needs.

Great brokers also discover selling opportunities when they visit their clients. It's amazing how many times a client says something like, "I could trade that used forklift. Do you want it?"

Trade Tales
A broker visited a client's location and came across over 3,000 pairs of inexpensive flip-flops. The owner of the inventory had already tried to sell them for 20 percent of their original value, with no success. But the broker saw an opportunity. He bartered with a screen printer to stamp the logo of a large vacation travel agency on each heel. He then bartered the entire inventory for $30,000 of vacation packages, which he sold to other members.

The economy is constantly being choked by all sorts of unsold inventories and underperforming assets. Great trade brokers have a knack for finding where they are, matching them with a buyer, and turning them into gold.

Compensate Great Brokers Generously

Studies show that cash compensation is only part of what employees value most. If they're forced to work in a negative work environment, it doesn't matter what you pay them. They leave.

Be sure to show your brokers you value them. Remember their birthdays. Accommodate reasonable requests for family time. And don't forget to say thanks. But there's something else you can do. You can create and foster a positive work environment. Don't forget the little things either, such as ergonomic office furniture, pleasant acoustics, and fresh coffee.

A positive, sharing work environment enhances brokers' productivity. The best exchanges find a way for brokers to share information with one another. Instead of separate offices, consider the bullpen concept, where brokers have enough privacy to hear their individual conversations, but where they can also hear what's going on with the other brokers.

Barter Bits

One exchange was accustomed to situating its brokers in separate offices. When it moved, it created a "trade floor" where everyone was out in the open. Employee morale improved and trade volume increased nearly 20 percent.

By creating a team approach to brokering, you minimize the temptation of some to hoard special avails for their own clients. When trade opportunities are spread to other brokers, and by extension, all the good traders, overall trade volume is enhanced.

The actual plans for broker compensation are quite varied. Most exchanges pay a base or draw, and commissions are usually in the area of 20 to 30 percent of what the exchange takes in. Add that on top of a base salary, and a broker can make a fine living.

Just don't be chintzy. Your brokers are the heart and soul of your trade exchange.

The Least You Need to Know

- Find a broker who can sell, multitask, and is ethical.

- For a broker to be great, you have to give him the tools he needs—superior information technology, training, and support.

- Great brokers know their clients. They are intuitive and have a nose for the deal. They make deals in unexpected places.

- Be sure to compensate your brokers generously. Also make sure you create a positive and enjoyable workplace.

Chapter 20

Managing Your Barter Economy

In This Chapter

- ◆ Putting trade dollars into circulation
- ◆ Protecting your exchange from bad debt
- ◆ Understanding hard dollar vs. soft dollar
- ◆ Generating trade to cover bad debt
- ◆ Don't eat the poison apple

By now, you've already decided to start a trade exchange of your very own. Before you call on your first account or do your first trade, you'll want to put in place the policies and procedures to make sure your exchange will be economically sound. Running a trade exchange is serious business. Your members have put their faith in you, and your trade dollar.

Not all trade exchanges manage their money the same. Some exchanges have dollars that are "harder" than others. Most agree if lines of credit are too tight, or too liberal, it can diminish trade volume. The best bet is to be somewhere in the middle, where your members have enough trade dollars to buy, but not so many they're discouraged from selling.

Are you ready to become the head of your own Federal Reserve System? Be prepared—running a trade exchange really is like printing money.

Getting Trade Dollars into Circulation

When you sign up your first members, you'll be understandably anxious to get them to start trading. Hold your horses. Your job for now is out in the field, pounding the pavement. If you get clogged up trying to put trades together too early, you'll never expand your membership.

Besides, if you allow your first members to trade too early, they'll be disappointed. There simply isn't enough stuff out there for them to buy.

Wait until you have at least 50 members, preferably more, before you allow any trades to happen. Your members will have a more fulfilling first experience, and you'll not be distracted with brokering. You'll be doing more of that later, as your exchange matures.

A Chicken or an Egg?

When you sign your first members and commence trading, everyone has a zero balance. How do you get things started? Who will make the first purchase? This is the classic chicken-and-egg dilemma. There are several accepted ways of getting trade dollars into your system. You'll want to be prudent in your early decision making. Put dollars in your system the right way, and you'll be fine. Do it the wrong way, and you're asking for problems.

Running a barter economy is filled with paradoxes. You've already discovered no one wants to join until others join. There's another one: members cannot sell unless there are buyers. But if the buyers have not made sales, where does it all start?

You have to somehow get trade dollars into circulation. You have to create a *money supply*. They say if you put 10 economists in the same room and ask them a question, you'll come up with 10 different answers. The same goes if you put 10 trade exchange owners in that same room.

> **Money supply** In the national economy, it's usually defined as the amount of money available for transactions and investment in the economy. Economists may incorporate lots of technical terms, but it's really quite simple. How much money do people have to spend?

But there is one thing all trade exchange owners would agree on. There are two accepted ways of getting trade dollars into circulation. One way is to let members spend in the negative. The other is for the exchange to spend trade dollars, purchasing inventory that can be resold to its members.

You Want Some Members to Be Negative

The first way to get trade dollars into members' hands is to allow some of them to "spend in the negative." These members will have taken out de facto trade dollar loans. They are also promising, by way of the contract they signed, to pay back these loans by making future sales to their fellow members.

To get transactions off the ground, you'll want to encourage your good members to go in the negative. Let's say you sign up a really good restaurant. You know everyone will want to go there. Knowing this, you might encourage the restaurant to buy from the pressure washing company, asphalt seal coater, window washer, and chiropractor. These members now have trade dollars in their hands to buy from even more members. You're off and running.

The Best Categories to Go Negative

The best categories to establish lines of credit are those that are high demand. You don't want to give a line of credit to the proverbial dog psychiatrist because no one wants that service, even on barter. High-demand categories in the barter world include appliances, office-machine companies, printers, quality restaurants, established media, clothing, and a host of other products.

You generally want to be more conservative in establishing lines of barter credit for consultants, graphic designers, and service categories where there's a high rate of business failure.

Barter Bits _____

There is one category most people don't think of when establishing credit lines. That's nonprofits. Nonprofits hardly ever go out of business. If you learn to deal with them, and get trade dollars into their accounts, they are the perfect candidates to go negative.

Beyond categories, you'll be much more likely to give out a line of barter credit to businesses that have been around for a while. Longevity can be a key indicator of continued success. Start-up companies can be especially risky.

The Exchange Can Prime the Pump

If you want to get trade dollars into the hands of certain members, you, as the exchange owner, might decide to purchase inventory for resale. Let's say you've just signed up an office furniture company. You can purchase $5,000 worth of office chairs. This transaction, in essence, puts $5,000 trade dollars into the account of the office furniture company; and it has debited the same amount from your *inventory account*.

def•i•ni•tion _____

Inventory account One of a number of internal accounts a trade exchange maintains. This account allows the exchange to separate its barter purchases from its general-purpose account. As the inventory account records purchases from members, thus debiting its trade balance, it also places product into inventory, for resale later on.

Your inventory account doesn't have to buy stuff you can pick up and hold. It can be a due bill, gift certificates, or other form of IOU. If you sign a pizza parlor, for example, you might consider purchasing one or two thousand dollars worth of gift certificates. This gets trade dollars into the account of the pizza place, so the owners can start to spend. While your inventory account will be temporarily negative, when you sell the certificates, you'll get your trade dollars back.

Protect Your Exchange

Whenever you let a member spend negative, there are a number of factors you'll want to consider. One is the character and reputation of the person you're dealing with. Just like a bank that gives a loan on the basis of a handshake, you will undoubtedly develop these types of relationships.

But you can't know everyone, especially as your exchange grows. That's why it's important for your clients to sign a contract or agreement that makes them personally responsible for any trade (or cash) owed. Sometimes members think they can get out of their obligation to you because they bankrupted their company. Not true. If you did your homework up front, and incorporated a personal obligation clause into your contract, you'll save yourself from getting stuck later.

Trade Tales
An owner of two high-end restaurants in Michigan closed down one of his restaurants while holding $20,000 negative trade. He told the trade exchange he was sorry, but "it was a corporation." Upon being reminded he had signed a personal guarantee on his contract, he relented. He begrudgingly made up the trade by doing sales through his remaining restaurant.

Unfortunately, if a client also declares personal bankruptcy, you're totally out of luck. This is why, when you start your exchange, you want to stop bad-risk accounts before they get started. Letting them spend for the sake of a short-term commission hurts you in the long run.

Don't Go Commission Crazy

You're in business to make a buck. But don't fall into the trap of authorizing transactions just to make a commission. Every exchange has members who don't sell much, but they want to buy everything. Moreover, some of these members are great at paying their fees. The temptation is, especially during a slow month, to allow certain transactions you otherwise would not.

When you establish a line of trade dollar credit for a member, there's a reason you came up with the number you did. It was based primarily on that member's ability to make sales, and thus repay the system. If you constantly expand the line of credit of your "debtor" members, others will get overloaded. You're asking for trouble in the long run.

Perform Credit Checks

As you let some of your first members go negative, you'll want to keep your ear to the ground. It's amazing how quickly a reputation for not paying bills can spread through the business community.

It's also a good idea to perform a credit check when you establish barter credit. There are a number of credit services available, and while it is no guarantee against signing a bad risk company, this information can alert you to clients who might be in trouble.

To Lien or Not to Lien

In most respects, remember that you are a bank, albeit of an to alternate currency. What do banks do if they give out a car loan? They put a lien on the vehicle. You can do the same thing.

Although this can take time out of your day, you can put a *UCC-1 lien* on an account's personal property. This gives you something to hang your hat on, in the event the account you allowed to spend in the negative goes out of business.

def•i•ni•tion

UCC-1 lien When personal property (inventory, equipment, vehicles, and other hard assets of a business) are used as collateral for borrowing, a UCC-1 statement is put together, signed, and filed. This type of loan becomes a secured loan.

A UCC-1 lien protects your exchange, but it does have limitations. For example, if you want to execute a lien on a piece of equipment, you still have to locate it. This can be difficult if it's a vehicle or something easily transported. The equipment might also become beat-up and worthless. But in other cases, a lien can be a lifesaver.

Pursue Trade Debt Vigorously

You won't have bad debt right away with your trade exchange. Don't worry. You will. As your exchange matures, you'll probably find yourself with hundreds of members. At some point, you will encounter an account that spends trade she does not have, and then either goes out of business or simply skips town.

The first thing you want to do is get a good collections attorney. A good attorney can make it so you don't have to show up to each and every hearing. He or she is also familiar with *discovery hearings*.

def•i•ni•tion

Discovery hearing Occurring after favorable judgment for the plaintiff, this hearing requires the defendant to reveal all assets and income. Sometimes bank accounts or even tax refunds can be garnished; other times a payment plan is instituted.

Happy Birthday

When you sign a new member, no matter what, ask her for her birthdate and Social Security number. You might include this on your member contract. If she asks why you need this information, say you might send her a birthday card. The alternative is to tell her if she morphs into a deadbeat and tries to leave you high and dry, having her date of birth and Social Security number will help you track him down.

Trade Tales

A member who was into multilevel marketing of cookware disappeared in the dead of night, leaving his trade exchange on the hook for $4,500 trade. He had a common surname and initial Internet searches proved fruitless. However, the exchange did have his date of birth and Social Security number. Armed with this information, they found him in a resort city 100 miles away. The exchange sued, won a judgment, and even garnished his checking account. It was ultimately repaid in full.

It's a fact that the member you think is a great credit risk today might turn into a bad risk tomorrow. The more information you can have on file, the easier it will be to find him later.

Tight vs. Loose Fiscal Management

As you transition from sales to managing your new barter economy, ask yourself a basic philosophical question. That is, what type of system do you want to run? Some exchanges put more dollars into circulation than others do. Members generally have higher trade balances. Other exchanges are stingier in letting members go negative. As such, as a group, they have lower trade balances.

Extremes should be avoided. Go for a happy medium, which is where trade volume will be maximized. In reviewing Chapter 2, about currencies, you saw how some national economies have printed too much money. These are considered to have been "soft currencies." Yet, the opposite can happen. During the Great Depression, no one had any money. A loaf of bread would cost a quarter. One could have considered this to have been a "hard currency," albeit too hard.

Too Many Dollars, Too Few Goods

If an exchange is going to have problems with money supply, it's usually going to err on the side of having too many dollars in circulation. This is usually the result of too much bad debt accumulating in the system. This can happen because lots of members with negative trade balances go out of business. The same happens when those who are negative represent categories from which no one wants to buy.

Let's think about it for a second. If you have a member go out of business while it had spent $5,000 more than it had sold, what happens to the system? Someone was given trade dollars to spend, but there is no one around to redeem them. If this happens repeatedly, too many members are positive, and too few are negative.

In practicality, this is what happens when bad trade gets out of hand. The member who has made a sale for $5,000 trade attempts to spend it. She searches out a potential seller, but there's a problem. She, too, has a boatload of trade. She might say, "I've already got $20,000 in my trade account." There's nothing wrong with a member having a positive $20,000 trade. But if everyone in the system is in the same situation, spending trade dollars can be difficult. Taken to an extreme, *trade gridlock* can occur.

def•i•ni•tion

> **Trade gridlock**   This occurs when members are unable to buy because everyone has too much trade. Conversely, trade gridlock can also occur when members are unwilling to make purchases because they don't have enough trade dollars in their accounts, in that the money supply is too constricted. Left unchecked, both conditions can lock down a trade exchange's trade volume.

Grow Your Way Out of Trade Debt

If you find yourself with too much trade debt, there is a way out. One way is to grow your trade exchange. Let's say you have 50 members and someone who owes $10,000 trade dollars becomes uncollectable. That's $200 worth of bad debt being covered by each of the 50 members. But let's say you are able to double your membership, to 100 members. Now that becomes only a $100 trade dollar drag on each member.

By adding new members, you not only spread out the trade deficit of the system, you also generate more trade volume. If the bad debt remains constant, or if it doesn't increase as fast as your trade volume, the negative effect of bad debt is, in fact, mitigated.

Who Benefits from a Softer Trade Dollar?

Believe it or not, there are some members who benefit from a softer trade dollar. It is the members with large margins and little cash into what they sell. Consider the case of the massage therapist. In a system that has an extremely hard dollar, this person is not likely to get much business. That's because members save their trade dollars to buy hard goods. They're less likely to use trade dollars in a discretionary manner, because quite frankly, it's not discretionary when they're hard to get.

But if members have more trade dollars in their accounts, that same massage therapist is likely to get a lot more business. The dollars can't be redeemed for as many hard goods, but the massage person probably doesn't care. Because she doesn't have cash dollars invested, and her cost of trade dollar is low, she is more likely to consider her trade money as completely discretionary.

Other businesses that benefit from a softer trade dollar are the media, service industries, consultants, accountants, carpet cleaners, and other industries where fixed cash costs may be high, but variable costs of doing additional sales are low.

Too Few Dollars Can Cause Problems, Too

Some exchanges maintain extremely hard currencies. That's a positive for some, but a negative for others. This occurs when the trade exchange has not put enough trade dollars into circulation. Members are able to buy a lot with their trade—if only they had some.

Take the following example. A member wants to sell a late-model car for $12,000. If no one has $12,000 in their account, or if you, as owner of the exchange, won't let anyone borrow the necessary trade dollars, no one will buy the car. The car sits. Too much of that, and trade gridlock can also occur.

Who Benefits from a Hard Trade Dollar?

Those with narrow margins and high cost of goods benefit most from a hard trade dollar. That's because they're the ones most likely to receive business. They are then able to spend trade dollars on other products that might be scarce in an economy with a softer dollar.

Businesses that benefit most from a harder trade dollar are companies that sell tires, office machines, appliances, computers, and related items. Ironically, these companies are going out of business at an alarming rate, as they face increased competition from big box stores and the Internet.

Goldilocks and the Bell-Shaped Curve

Goldilocks had a tough time figuring which bed was "just right." So too, trade exchanges constantly struggle with how many trade dollars to have in circulation. Too few and no one has dollars to spend. Too many and everyone has too many, and no one wants to sell. Guess what? There is a happy medium. It can be described by a bell-shaped curve.

In any economy, there is a money supply at which gross national product (GNP), or in our case, trade volume, will be maximized. As you develop your trade exchange, you won't be able to call on the chairman of the Federal Reserve System for advice. But you will be able to make intelligent decisions as to whether members are capable of repaying their trade dollar loans.

You will also discover there is nothing wrong with large trades. You just have to make sure the buyers are good for it.

Cover Bad Debt by Earning Trade Dollars

No matter how careful you are, your exchange will ultimately get stuck with bad trade debt. You can try to minimize it, you can try to chase it; but there is another way you can lesson its negative impact on your economy. It's to earn as many trade dollars as you can for your trade exchange.

You've seen how the trade exchange is just like a national currency, but on a smaller scale. Governments can print money; so can a trade exchange. But both can print only so much before fundamental economic problems occur. Strive for a balanced system, where what your trade exchange spends (including covering bad debt) equals the amount it takes in.

Make Trade Wherever You Can

The simplest way to make trade dollars is to charge your members. You'll want to institute this early on, rather than springing it on them later. You might consider taking all or part of your yearly dues in barter. You might also invoke monthly trade charges, or add in a trade fee to maintain sub-accounts or cover mailing costs. All the little trade fees charged to hundreds of members can really add up.

As you start your exchange, consider this. If you attach a mere 1 percent trade charge onto all your commission charges, it could add up to hundreds of thousands of dollars later. Do it now. Members hate surprises.

Trade Tales

One trade exchange, from the beginning, charged its members a cash commission, but also a 1 percent trade fee on all transactions. Years later, when the exchange was generating $10 million dollars of barter each year, that small percentage meant the exchange was taking in an additional $100,000 worth of barter annually.

You might also consider trading entry fees, when necessary. You need cash, that's true. But if you occasionally take an entry fee in trade, it won't kill you. Plus, it creates a sense of equivalency of a cash dollar and a trade dollar.

There's another way to earn trade dollars, and that's to invest cash. You might consider purchasing items for cash at wholesale, or at liquidation. Mark up the product and resell it to your members on trade.

Barter Bits

One exchange discovered that vacuum cleaners were in extremely high demand in trade, something almost every business needed. It decided to become an official dealer. It bought from the same wholesaler the vacuum shops did. It would take $200 cash and buy at wholesale, parlaying it into a $400 retail vacuum on trade. Over 20 years, the exchange sold over 500 vacuum cleaners, generating $200,000 worth of trade and over $20,000 in cash commissions.

There's another way to make a markup, this time without parting with precious cash. But it does mean you'll have to run a showroom or trade mart. Whenever you buy product, or allow someone to place product there on consignment, you should insist on making at least a 10 percent margin. By doing this, you'll make a few dollars to run your retail store and maybe a few extra trade dollars at the same time.

Buy Inventories on Trade

If you don't have a showroom, there are still opportunities to make mark-ups on trade. The world is full of companies who hold excess inventory they can't sell for cash. If you owned a company and had been sitting on such an inventory, which would you rather have, trade dollars or nothing?

Trade Tales

One enterprising trade broker found a company that had a ware-house full of composite decking that was slightly "off-spec." Immersed in a building slowdown and unable to sell to its traditional buyers, the company accepted an extremely low-trade dollar offer from the trade exchange for the entire inventory. The exchange shipped the decking to a warehouse it had traded for. It then marked up the decking to retail, and sold it to members who were ecstatic to trade for a valuable home improvement item.

Buying and selling large inventories requires a knowledgeable and skilled broker. You don't want to end up with inventory that is extremely perishable, totally outdated, or damaged. Another deal killer can be shipping and warehousing costs. Be sure to add these factors into the equation before you buy inventories for the purpose of reselling them to your members.

An Interesting Proposition

Here's something you should build into your system right off Jump Street. Charge your members trade interest on deficit accounts. When a business spends trade dollars it does not have, there is always an element of risk. There is a chance the company might be unwilling or unable to make future barter sales, thereby not paying back its loan.

Your software should be able to compute trade dollar interest. You'll be able to plug in whatever interest rate you want to charge. Be sure to be fair. There's no need to go for the jugular like a credit card company does.

Charging interest is not an automatic proposition. Let's say you have a great member, perhaps a restaurant that has sold liberally and fairly for five straight years. It has always maintained a positive trade balance, but then all of a sudden spends negative trade dollars.

What are you going to do? Tell her she's got to pay interest on her

Trade Tales

One exchange started charging interest on certain accounts when it first began trading. Ten years and 500 members later, it was generating an impressive $120,000 of trade dollar interest for the exchange. This more than covered all the bad trade dollar debt that was incurred.

$2,000 deficit? The first thing she'd say is, "You didn't pay me interest when I carried a positive balance; how can you charge interest when I'm negative?" You'll want to charge interest on deficits only when it makes sense.

A few exchanges make sense of it all by charging interest, but adjust for average monthly positive trade balance. That way, an account that has maintained positive monthly balances and only temporarily goes negative, isn't hit up for interest. The perpetually negative account, on the other hand, will incur interest charges.

Charging interest on trade debt is a proven way to generate trade dollars. When business failure among your members increases, you'll need to generate all the trade dollars you can.

Leverage with media is a great way to make trade dollars. Many broadcasters, for example, are loath to pay any cash commissions on transactions. They would rather pay a time and a half rate, or double, in trade for something, than cough up a 10 percent cash commission.

This fact doesn't make a lot of sense to some outside the media. Yet, when you think about it, it's not all that crazy. If a radio station has excess air time, and it's trading for $10,000 worth of bumper stickers, it might be more than willing to pay $15,000 in advertising. The extra $5,000 of spots cost them nothing, whereas a 10 percent cash commission presents them with an out-of-pocket expense of $1,000.

Beware the Poison Apple

When you stop and think about it, it takes a lot of moxie to start a trade exchange. To succeed, you have to gain the faith and trust of your members. They have to believe the trade dollars they accept can indeed be spent. This is no small matter.

There is no better way to break this trust than to run your economy in an irresponsible fashion. And there is nothing more irresponsible than engaging in wanton personal spending when there are no trade dollars in your account. Some might suggest spending trade you don't have is harmless. It's harmless in the same way shoplifting is harmless. No one person is hurt, but everyone is hurt aggregately.

> **Balance of Trade**
>
> You can't subsist on trade commissions alone. In the early days of organized barter, around 1980, an exchange set up shop in a mid-sized market in the Midwest. The owner was under the illusion he could subsist on trade commissions, instead of cash. He quickly found out he needed cash to pay his mortgage and feed his kids. Faced with a cash shortfall, he spent trade dollars for everything in sight. He bought jewelry, toys, cars, and restaurant gift certificates. He promptly sold these items for cash out his back door at a huge discount. He did this over and over until the exchange collapsed upon itself, leaving dozens of members with unredeemable trade dollars.

What are the results of reckless personal spending? Well, you can act rich, at least for a little while. In the early days of the trade industry, it really was the Wild West. Trade exchanges popped up all over the place. No one really had an idea of how an exchange should work. Left to their own devices, some operators bought the equivalent of fast cars and expensive liquor. They were all rich, or so they thought.

There's a problem with this. Each time an owner sucked something out of the system, a seller ended up with trade dollars. Then the unscrupulous owner would buy something else. Again, someone had a bunch of trade dollars. Repeated purchases loaded up everyone with positive balances. So who carried the negative balance? It was the shyster owner of the trade exchange, that's who!

More than likely, the aforementioned shyster didn't start out with the intention of being a shyster. Rather, he just fell into it. Faced with no cash, he figured no one would mind if he "primed the pump" himself. The first members he bought from were probably pretty happy. After all, they had received trade dollars which were, at first, spendable. Only later, when it was discovered that everyone had large positive balances, did everything hit the fan.

The results of this destructive behavior not only degrade your business, but harm your fellow business owners. As members have higher and higher trade balances, the dollar becomes less valuable. This can cause inflation, just as printing too many cash dollars can affect a national currency. At some point, total gridlock can occur, when everyone has lost the faith and trust that was promised by the owner.

There is nothing wrong with an owner of a trade exchange spending trade dollars. In fact, you'll want to spend trade, instead of cash, for your rent, office machines, accountant, lawyer, garbage removal, and lots of other services. But do this much: earn your trade dollars first.

The Least You Need to Know

- ◆ In the beginning, you need members to spend into the negative, so long as they can repay the trade dollar "loan."

- ◆ Once you get going, you'll need to protect your currency from bad trade dollar debt.

- ◆ Trade volume is maximized when you get the right amount of trade dollars into circulation.

- ◆ One of the best ways to protect your currency is to earn trade dollars through fees and markups.

- ◆ Overloading members of your exchange with trade dollars because you became a shopaholic is just plain wrong.

Chapter 21

Planning for a Good Economy or a Bad One

In This Chapter

- ◆ Love it, don't leave it
- ◆ Diversify your membership
- ◆ Trade is good when times are good
- ◆ Trade is just as good when times are tough

Congratulations! You've decided to take the plunge and open your very own trade exchange. But know what you're signing up for. Owning a trade exchange is not a passive investment. Your members are depending on you for the long term. Make sure no one at your exchange is indispensable.

As you build your exchange, you're going to find yourself signing up certain categories more than others. Try to diversify as much as you can. Go for the big accounts, but don't forget, little trades make the big ones happen.

Will your trade exchange do better during a good or a bad economy? If you build your exchange right, it won't really matter. There are opportunities whichever direction the economy turns.

You're Taking on a Unique Responsibility

Your reasons for starting a trade exchange are probably two-fold: (1) you want to own a business from which you can draw a nice paycheck and ultimately make a profit, and (2) you love trade.

Which is more important? Love of money, or love of trade? The answer is: you have to love trade first. The money will follow.

You have to love trade because, if you start a trade exchange, you can't just abandon it if something more lucrative pops up. It's not like you opened a coffee shop and decide two years later to close it. Think about the awesome responsibility you're taking on. You've sold your clients, many of them who are friends, on the fact that your exchange's trade dollars are, in fact, money.

> **Balance of Trade**
>
> There have been a number of incidences when trade exchanges have, in fact, simply packed their bags and disappeared into the night. Most of these failures were caused by either greed or incompetence. Be sure you have what it takes to be an owner.

At any given time, some of your members are going to have positive trade balances. Others will be negative. Those who are positive have faith and trust in you and their fellow members that they'll be able to spend their dollars.

The longer you're in business, the more members and trade volume you'll have. When you have 100 members, perhaps 50 will have positive balances, and 50 will be in the negative. But when you have 1,000 members, it all gets multiplied by 10. And the trades get bigger, too. This means some members might have positive trade balances of 20,000 trade dollars or more.

Your responsibility to these members has grown exponentially. You need to plan for the future. You want to create an organization that runs without you. In doing so, your business also becomes more valuable.

Barter Bits

There have been many other instances where a failing trade exchange has been saved or absorbed by another trade exchange. In one case, in the late 1980s, over 1,000 members were absorbed into another exchange, which is still in business today.

Cross-Train Your Employees

Many business owners inadvertently create an environment where employees become territorial. They learn a critical task, but don't share their knowledge with anyone else.

Let's say your I.T. person is the only one who knows how to close a month and send out statements. What if that person leaves or gets sick? By the time you find a replacement or are able to figure it out, your billings might not go out for another month. This doesn't exactly instill confidence in your exchange among your members.

As you grow your exchange, it's important that you occasionally take time out. Set aside time to train your staff in multiple tasks, so no one person becomes indispensable, including you.

Own a Business, Not Just a Job

In training your employees in multiple tasks, you're doing more than protecting your members. You are also building your business. You love trade, and want to keep your hands in it, but there will come a day when you'll wish you had developed an exit strategy.

Because it's really hard to just "close" a trade exchange, there are two main exit strategies you can choose from. You can (1) sell to someone else, or (2) stay in it forever and then die.

Let's not figure on dying. So the question becomes: how can you create an exit plan that takes care of your members, and at the same time, takes care of you?

Partnerships Can Work

In spite of the potential problems of partnerships, they have been known to work nicely in the barter business. This is especially true if each partner specializes in a different area of the business. For example, if one is a natural salesperson and marketer, and the other is great at numbers, you've got most of the bases covered.

> **Trade Tales**
>
> Some spouses can never work together. But if they can, they can form an ideal sort of partnership. A number of very successful trade exchanges started this way. The main advantage is all the profit stays under one roof.

If you do form a partnership, be sure to take care of the basics. Buy life insurance on each partner, so if one of you dies, the death benefit goes to buy out the deceased partner's spouse.

Similarly, one partner might be younger and plans on staying in the business longer. It's a good idea to discuss such potentialities with your partner.

Groom a Successor

Nothing beats being backed up by someone else with a vested interest in your business. Consider putting together a plan where one or more employees are able to purchase stock in the business. They'll work harder now and be less likely to go job hunting later.

> **Trade Tales**
>
> A very large exchange was owned by two partners. One was the consummate marketer and the other took care of the business side. Years ago, it invited its employees into a stock ownership plan. Productivity improved, raising the value of the company. When the exchange sold for millions of dollars, the employees shared in the proceeds.

Giving an employee the opportunity to earn sweat equity, or to purchase stock incrementally, can be good for both parties. You'll have a better, more dedicated employee, and they'll have something they can call their own. At the same time, you'll be able to retire without leaving your members high and dry.

Consider Brick and Mortar as You Grow

The value of a trade exchange can be difficult to ascertain. Like anything, its value lies with what someone is willing to pay for it.

Banks are unlikely to finance someone who wants to buy a business that has no brick and mortar. To them, a trade exchange is really nothing more than a list of clients that generates a certain revenue stream.

Once your trade exchange reaches a certain size, you might want to purchase a building. The building could include another tenant or two, thus creating an additional source of revenue. Not a bad idea for the future.

Protect Your Future with a Diversified Membership

You can protect yourself from ups and downs of the economy by diversifying your client base. Develop as many "calling cards" as you can. Some exchanges do lots of trade with the media or nonprofits. Others are heavy into accommodations and travel. Still others get into large inventories.

It's natural that your trade exchange becomes especially proficient in one area. Compare a trade exchange to a magnet school. Magnet schools specialize in a specific course of study, say, writing. But that doesn't mean it doesn't teach arithmetic. So, too, a trade exchange shouldn't put all its eggs in one basket. Diversify your membership as much as possible.

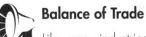

Balance of Trade

Like many industries, trade exchanges can't get away from the 80–20 rule. In other words, 20 percent of your clients will invariably do 80 percent of your trade volume, while 80 percent will do the remaining 20 percent.

Little Deals Can Make the Big Ones

There can be a temptation to just call on the big accounts. There's nothing wrong with that. But remember, the little traders often satisfy the needs of the bigger ones.

These purchases can really add up. A diversified membership means your big traders will be able to spend trade dollars to grab a pizza for a staff meeting, or to get their windows washed. Aggregately, these trades can be extremely important. They help insure your big clients' continued willingness to trade.

Make the Big Calls; Grow Your Trade Volume

Just as some exchanges are always "going for the homerun" by calling on large accounts, some exchanges are gun shy when it comes to making a presentation to the larger client.

It's true that, by and large, big box stores are not going to trade. They simply cannot give that kind of autonomy to a local manager. Yet, it's surprising how many franchisees can, in fact, trade. For example, a hotel might have a national-sounding name, but you can still call on them. The results just might surprise you.

> **Trade Tales**
>
> For years, I placed too much emphasis on restaurants and printers. Then a bunch of them went out of business, diminishing our trade volume. Later, we decided to sign up nonprofits, which more than made up for our losses.

Create a diversified membership base. Doing so will help protect your company's future by creating more trade opportunities. Plus, you won't be overly dependent on one group of traders.

Good Time Trading

Many people assume trade prospers only in a down economy, but this isn't quite true. Even when the economy is booming, most businesses are still seeking additional customers, same as when the economy is bad.

There are some businesses that are indeed less likely to trade when the economy is running smoothly. Media, in particular, can become fat and happy with cash. If they have no unsold space or time, they're unlikely to barter it.

Contractors are also less likely to trade during good times. If there's a building boom and an electrical contractor is already working his staff overtime, he simply doesn't have man-hours to trade. The same would go for an individual contractor, carpenter, or handyman.

Businesses That Make Money Can Afford to Trade

But a good economy does offer advantages to a trade exchange. For one thing, when businesses have cash in hand, they can more easily pay their entry fee. And they're less likely to fall behind on their commissions. Not having to spend time to collect your money helps you build your business.

There's another advantage to a good economy—your members are able to afford to trade. Remember, most businesses incur an out-of-pocket cash cost when they sell something on barter. A restaurant, for example, might have a good cost of 30 percent, meaning a $10 meal cost them $3 to put on the plate.

If that restaurant is making money, that cost is no big deal. But if the restaurant is struggling to make payroll or pay its utility bill, it's a different story. The owner might decide he or she can't afford to barter.

If your clients aren't worried where their next dollar is coming from, they're more likely to trade for discretionary items. That same restaurant owner, instead of sweating over a stove and agonizing about accepting trade, is now calling his broker to arrange for a vacation.

Barter Bits

Because my trade exchange is in Michigan, we've seen good and bad times in extremes. When times are good, we probably do double the amount of vacations as compared to when the economy is tanking. This is in spite of more availability of properties during bad times.

Your Trade Exchange When the Economy Is Bad

Just as there are pluses and minuses to trading when the economy is good, so it goes when the economy is bad. Some of your members won't be able to afford to trade. But others come out of the woodwork.

New traders will include all sorts of businesses that are desperately searching for ways to fill unsold capacity. Remember the media? All of a sudden they can become your best pals. Contractors who previously were too busy to give you the time of day are now clamoring to join your trade exchange.

Barter Bits

A bad economy really stirs up media interest from the perspective of news coverage, too. If you can't get free publicity for your exchange during a bad economy, you never will.

A less than great economy can also spur trade of certain inventories. Some of these inventories would never be traded during boom times. For example, when retail chains cancel orders, certain products can become backed up. Ultimately they might be purchased by liquidators. And liquidators can become members of your exchange!

Economic Doldrums Spur Creative Trading

When businesses don't have cash options, they seek out alternatives. This is good for a trade exchange.

Some of your members might practice account receivable trading. That is, they might accept and trade products from their cash debtors. Or they might do the reverse with some account payable trading, paying off cash debt with trade dollars. You can dramatically increase your trade volume through trading of real estate, too (see Chapter 14). Through it all, your membership will grow impressively.

The Downside of a Down Economy

There are lots of trades that happen because of a sour economy. But there are pitfalls to watch out for. Not only will some of your members not be able to trade, others will go out of business. Moreover, they can go out of business owing trade to the system, or cash to you.

Just as you'll want to plan for good times, you'll want to do the same when it's bad. Make sure your collections don't get out of hand. Keep a close watch on negative accounts. And don't hesitate to shut down a client's spending if you feel they're in survival mode. You are, after all, caretaker of your own economy.

Balance of Trade

Whereas most exchanges see trade volume increase during a bad economy, collecting their money becomes much harder. In my exchange, accounts receivable doubled in four years.

The Least You Need to Know

- ◆ Operating a trade exchange is unlike any other business. Have a plan that insures continued vitality and long life of your trade exchange.

- ◆ Sign up as varied a membership as you can. Remember the little accounts. They take care of the big ones.

- ◆ A good cash economy works positively for a trade exchange. Members can afford to make trade sales, engage in more discretionary spending, and pay their bills.

- ◆ When the cash economy suffers, a trade exchange can prosper, but in different ways. New members and trading opportunities abound, but don't get saddled with bad debt.

Appendix A

Glossary

1099 form   Similar to a W-2 but meant to report various types of income other than wages, salaries, and tips. If your company issues you a W-2, it cannot also issue a 1099. A 1099 is tendered for an independent contractor, nonemployee, or other types of vendors.

1099-B   A close cousin of the regular 1099, the 1099-B is an electronic file sent to the IRS (and a hard copy sent to the taxpayer) that indicates total trade dollars received during the tax year. From an accounting perspective, trade dollars are equal to cash dollars and are accounted for in the same manner.

brick-and-mortar business   One that has physical assets, including real estate and inventory, which ostensibly can be appraised. Everything being equal, it is generally easier to sell this type of business. Although trade exchanges are traditionally not of this variety, it is generally easier to sell an independent, rather than a franchised, office.

broker   In a trade exchange, the broker helps to arrange trade deals between members of the exchange, particularly large deals. Compare to a sales representative, who sells memberships to the exchange.

Chapter 7   Filing bankruptcy under this chapter does not involve filing a plan of repayment to debtors. Instead, nonexempt assets, if any, are sold off with proceeds split among the company's creditors. Usually Chapter 7 businesses have little if anything to offer creditors.

coincidence of need   The basic requirement in a direct trade, where one party possesses what a second party needs, while coincidently the second party possesses what the first party needs.

countertrade   A transaction that links imports and exports of goods or services in addition to, or instead of, financial payments.

discovery hearing   Occurring after favorable judgment for the plaintiff, this hearing requires the defendant to reveal all assets and income. Sometimes bank accounts or even tax refunds can be garnished; other times a payment plan is instituted.

escheat laws   Laws in most states that pertain to property which, if abandoned, becomes property of the state. If a hotel or restaurant issues gift certificates that are lost or expired, they may owe the face value of the certificate, in cash, to the state.

Fiat money   Currency declared by an authority as legal tender, even though the currency itself has no intrinsic value, as does commodity-backed currency. In a barter system, trade dollars such as Ithaca Hours are authorized by the system's governing body—or for a commercial trade exchange, the company owner—to be accepted as tender for transactions between members of the system.

found business   A new customer for your business. Generally, you want to use barter to expand your business and not have existing customers switch from paying cash to paying on trade.

hard goods   Products or services that are of high demand and low margin. Hard goods are, as a rule, harder to find in a trade exchange.

inventory account   One of a number of internal accounts a trade exchange maintains. This account allows the exchange to separate its barter purchases from its general-purpose account. As the inventory account records purchases from members, thus debiting its trade balance, it also places product into inventory, for resale later on.

leads club   A business networking club composed of noncompeting businesses who share leads with one another as they also attempt to do business with one another. You get one insurance agent, one builder, one office machine dealer, and so on. Each does word-of-mouth advertising for the others. Meetings are typically held weekly. The largest franchiser of leads clubs has thousands of clubs in nearly 50 countries.

leverage   As used in barter, the advantage gained when a seller of a soft good willingly pays more in trade than a prevailing cash price. This process allows the buyer to "trade up" into items of greater and greater value.

money supply   In the national economy, it is usually defined as the amount of money available for transactions and investment in the economy. Economists may incorporate lots of technical terms, but it's really quite simple. How much money do people have to spend?

part cash   When a seller splits what he or she charges in a barter transaction to part trade dollars, part real cash. The practice is frowned upon by trade exchanges.

probationary employment period   A period of time by which both employer and employee agree to abide. It is understood by both parties that after this time, the employment contract can be cancelled by either party. It gives the employee a chance to see if he or she really likes his or her new job; conversely, the employer is able to ascertain if the person is right for the job. Probationary periods can range from two weeks to 90 days. They do not, however, totally protect the employer from lawsuits pertaining to an unfair termination.

projected room night availability   The practice of a hotel or resort to black out or exclude from trade times when they think they'll have a "full house." If a property knows that a huge convention will book all the rooms in town a year from now, it may still reserve the right to not want trade during that time, even though rooms might technically be available for cash.

rack rate   The rate printed on a card in all hotel rooms, along with other regulations and conditions. It is often a very high nightly rate that you didn't actually pay. No one pays it, except for maybe on New Year's Eve or other times when every place in town is fully booked.

sales rep   In a trade exchange, a sales representative sells memberships to the exchange. Compare to the broker, who helps to arrange trade deals between members of the exchange, particularly large deals.

scrip   Substitute money, usually issued by someone other than the government. Most common when regular money is unavailable, scrip represents an IOU, redeemable at one or more participants or businesses.

Section 179   This section of the U. S. Internal Revenue Code lets a taxpayer deduct the cost of certain types of property as an expense, rather than requiring that the property become capitalized and depreciated. Section 179 limits this to tangible property having to do with conducting business, not real estate.

soft goods   Products or services of minimal costs to the seller, but are sold with a high markup. Such products are generally easy to offer for barter and easy to find in a trade exchange.

space-available basis   Newspapers and magazines sometimes barter ads on a space available basis, or when it has space that otherwise would have to be taken up with free promos or filler copy.

standby   When a business decides it has too many trade dollars in its account, it chooses not to accept any more trade sales until it spends some.

sub-account   An account created from a main trade exchange account specifically for individuals, not other businesses. Trade dollars are periodically transferred into sub-accounts from a business's main account.

tax credit   A one-for-one dollar reduction in your total tax bill. A tax deduction, on the other hand, simply reduces your taxable income.

time dollars   Credit paid for hours of service in a time-based currency. Everyone's contributions are valued equally. A person who volunteers to work for another member within the system for one hour receives a one-hour credit. That credit, paid in time dollars and accounted for in time banks, can be redeemed for an hour of service from some other member of the system.

trade gridlock   This situation occurs when members are unable to buy because everyone has too much trade. Conversely, trade gridlock can also occur when members are unwilling to make purchases because they don't have enough trade dollars in their accounts, in that the money supply is too constricted. Left unchecked, both conditions can lock down a trade exchange's trade volume.

trunk trader   Someone who makes a living doing trades, but usually does it from his living room. He or she rarely offers any accounting or guarantees to his or her trading partners. A trunk trader can be responsible for hundreds of transactions, valued at hundreds of thousands of dollars, but seldom sends out 1099s as required by law.

UCC-1   When personal property (inventory, equipment, vehicles, and other hard assets of a business) is used as collateral for borrowing, a UCC-1 statement is put together, signed, and filed. This type of loan becomes a secured loan.

underground economy   Transactions, both legal and illegal, that are either cashless or unreported. This includes all commerce where taxes and/or regulations are being avoided. It can include a vast array of activities, from painting houses to running drugs. The underground economy is generally smallest in countries where taxes and regulation are the lowest.

W-2 tax form   The form prepared by an employer and given to an employee listing wages earned during the year, along with federal and state taxes that are withheld, along with social security tax information. This information is also submitted to the Internal Revenue Service.

Appendix B

Resources

Media and Association Websites

BarterNews Magazine
www.barternews.com

An online news and advertising source covering the barter industry.

Complementary Currency Resource Center
www.complementarycurrency.org

Website dedicated to community dollars and alternate currencies. Includes numerous downloadable articles and a worldwide directory of community-based alternate currency systems.

International Reciprocal Trade Association
www.irta.com

Website for an international association that provides resources for member trade exchanges and information for prospective members.

National Association of Trade Exchanges
www.nate.org

As with the IRTA site, the website for NATE provides resources, a calendar of events, and information about business-to-business barter for members and nonmembers.

Further Reading

Derkas, Tom G. *The Barter Bible: A Guide to Increase Your Cash Flow Using Barter.* Blue Ribbon Publishing, 2000.

Langrick, Roger. *Barter Systems: A Business Guide for Trade Exchanges.* Longmeadow Press, 1994.

Suhr, D. *How to Profit from the Next Great Depression.* New American Library, 1989.

Index

E

N

O